CW00546963

MY DARLING BELLE

A sist

Susar

First published 2017
by the Lasse Press
2 St Giles Terrace, Norwich
www.lassepress.com
lassepress@gmail.com

ISBN-13: 978-1-9997752-0

Typeset in Garamond by
Curran Publishing Services

Manufactured in the UK by

Contents

Illustrations

Maps

Photographs and drawings

African Steamship Company.

UNCORPORATED BY ROYAL CHARTER.

Managers:
ELDER, DEMPSTER & CO.,
LIVERPOOL.

S.S. _____

Sep 26 th. 190 8

My own darling belle.

Here I am really

at sea. It's two hr chopper
but I don't think that. Charlie
is very fond of really, fed
full of luck. In glass we
have really started, when
the Pilot goes off at Bull
Bay, all means of escape
will have gone.
The Governor is on board but

w† his wife she went ashore,
she was the image of Mrs
Taylor Morgan took away,
plump. Charlie has just
introduced me to say. Torres
his wife she is going out too.
has been not a year now before,
she is my like Lucy Knox,
shall I think. Shall
Stork at 6. Mrs †...
like her. we are going to sit
a Table up together. She has
just told C. to go stir my
box of chocolates, all ladies,
to b. africa get them, chings
for us.
Sarah, now Stella Campbell
came here no off then

Introduction

In 1908 Mary Adelaide (Maida) Hunter set off for Sierra Leone with her husband, Dr Charles Hunter, a physician in the Colonial Service who was to take up a year's posting there. Maida was relatively well travelled, but she had never before been to West Africa. She wrote letters frequently, both during the journey and after her arrival, especially to her sisters and father back in Wales.

The letters of hers that survive were mostly written to her younger sister Beatrice Annie Roberts, whom she addresses as Belle (and by a variety of nicknames),[1] although there are a few to her sister Elsie and her father. The collection, which is now in the Rhodes House Library division of the Bodleian Library, Oxford, also includes some letters from Dr Hunter (not all of which are included here). Maida wrote to her sisters and her family both of her impressions and on practical matters: the Hunters' destination, the small town of Bonthe on Sherbro Island in the southwest of Sierra Leone, was quite isolated and primitive, and she and her husband were dependent on the family back in Wales to provide them with various necessities that they could not obtain locally as well as with news.

The Roberts family was a comfortably off middle-class one, and like many others in Wales, strictly Methodist. Robert Roberts, J.P. (1828–1916), Maida's father, was the sixth son of a family living mostly in north Wales and Manchester, and for much of his life an agent to woollen manufacturers. The family had lived when Maida was young in a pretty old house called Crûg (pronounced Creeg) behind the small coastal village of Port Dinorwic (now known by its Welsh name of Y Felinheli), between Bangor and Caernarvon. Behind its expansive grounds the open farmland and moor ran up to the slopes of Snowdon. Maida's daughter, also known as Maida, recalled in 1991:

> It must have been a most charming place, and certainly seemed like an earthly paradise, if not to all of them, certainly to my mother, who could never bear to go back to see it as long as she lived, which is why I know it only by photographs and the memory of her voice speaking of it, with longing. It had been the home of my great-grandfather, Ebenezer Roberts, of the family of the Roberts of Castell, Llanddeiniolen, and after his death of my grandmother, Ellen Roberts. Unfortunately it did not belong to them but to a family called Wynn Griffith, with whom there was evidently an unfriendly relationship, as so often between landlord and tenant.

Ellen died on 23 December 1900, leaving her husband and a family of nine children, of which the four daughters figure most in this book: Kate (known to

---

1 Maida junior knew her as Aunt Trixie; presumably Trixie expanded into TrixieBelle and elided again into Belle – which led in turn to (bell)Rope and an assortment of other names.

A family photo
presumably of Robert
Roberts and his wife
Ellen, date unknown

her niece as Nonin) born in 1871; Elizabeth (known as Elsie); Maida, born in 1875, and Beatrice Annie (Belle, also known as Trixie or Tricka), born in 1878. Of the four, only Elsie was to marry young: she married Dr Richard Williams, a distinguished eye surgeon in Liverpool, nearly twenty years older than herself, and had two sons, Roderic (killed in the Royal Flying Corps in 1917) and Robert (Rob or Robin), who lived until 1977. The remaining three daughters continued to live with their father.

Like her sisters, Maida received very little formal education, but she was clearly an intelligent woman with a wide range of interests. Her daughter adds:

Crûg, photograph from a family album

Crûg today. Photo by Andrew Bulman.

Left, Maida and her father (and a family dog) at Crûg, family photo, date unknown; below, the same doorway today (photo by Andrew Bulman)

She had attended a course on botany at Bangor College (now Bangor University) and had also learned much from Miss Gulielma (Julie) Lister, a niece of Lord Lister, who was a great friend of [her cousin] May Bradford and a distinguished botanist. She used to tell me of botanical expeditions led by a Professor Phillips on which in her long skirts she would scramble up the Idwal Slabs, known to initiates as the home of various rare plants which may now have been scraped off by the boots of generations of modern climbers with their ropes and ironmongery.

Possibly because of Ellen's death the lease on Crûg was terminated in 1905 and the family moved to Bronceris, a sizeable detached house on the outskirts of Caernarvon.[2] Here they maintained a small staff, including a cook and a house-

---

2 Bronceris is a Grade II listed building: the listings record (http://www.britishlistedbuildings. co.uk/300003904-bronceris-caernarfon#.WVTf2OmQyM9) describes it as: A late Georgian house of 2 storeys with attic and basement. A symmetrical 3-bay front to the main house has

Charlie's parents Wilhelmina and William Hunter, family photos, date unknown

parlourmaid and a coachman/gardener, who lived over the coach house at the back.

Maida junior wrote:

It must have been potentially a pleasant house. I drove past it a few years ago without stopping, but could not see much of it as it is surrounded now as it was then by a high brick wall; but it cannot have been happy. My mother seems to have been prejudiced against Bronceris from the start. She always loved the country, and hated exchanging the free life of Crûg for the small

---

2 further bays set back to the L, probably housing the original service rooms, and with only a single tier of windows set at an intermediate level. The entire front is scribed stucco. A hipped slate roof has wide eaves with replaced boarding and slender corner brackets, a rendered stack to the R and altered ridge stack L of centre, and small inserted skylights on the L side. Windows are 12-pane hornless sashes. The main entrance has a fielded-panel door with 4-pane overlight, while a second doorway set back to the L has a panelled door and plain overlight. The R end wall is pebble-dashed and has an 8-pane sash window in the upper storey, and a 6-pane sash window offset to the R in the lower storey.

The rear is also pebble-dashed and has mainly 12-pane horned sashes similar to the front. The 3-bay main house has a central replaced half-lit basement door with inserted window to its R and 9-pane sash window to the L. Further R, the service end has a small-pane sash window on the R side with side light and panel beneath the sill, possibly converted from an earlier doorway.

A family photo, perhaps from Charlie's first stay with the Roberts family at Bronceris in 1904: left to right, Dr Charlie Hunter, Maida Roberts, Robert Roberts, unknown (perhaps a family friend)

provincial town that Caernarvon then was, in spite of its castle and romantic history.

The girls' life was enlivened, however, by regular winter holidays. Their father chose to avoid spending the anniversary of his wife's death in Britain, and took his unmarried daughters with him to destinations including the Riviera, Algiers, Florence and the Canary Islands. Maida junior commented:

> I accepted [this] as quite normal when I was young, but now realise that they were really enterprising for the time, especially as Bamps [her grandfather, Mr Roberts] was not a rich man, and they used to stay in quiet inexpensive hotels where my mother and aunts were, I fear, very often bored. I seem to recall hearing that he always returned about Easter to supervise the planting of the new potatoes.

The 1904 holiday was certainly not boring for Maida, since during her return

Bronceris today. Photo by Andrew Bulman.

with Belle and her father from a winter holiday in the Calary Islands, she met Dr Hunter on board ship. (He was returning to Britain on leave from a Colonial posting in upcountry Sierra Leone.) As her daughter recalled, it 'seems to have provided a case of love at first sight. While on leave my father stayed at Crûg, and an engagement ring for which I still have the receipt was bought in Glasgow on 6 June 1904 for £40.'

Maida junior barely knew her father, but she pieced together his history with the help of other family members, and the account below is primarily hers.

Charles Buchanan Hunter (known mostly to his wife as Charlie) was born on 22 December 1859 at Laphroaig, Isle of Islay, the youngest of the nine children of William Hunter (then working as an accountant in the famous distillery) and his wife Wilhelmina, née Buchanan. With such a large family the sons would have had to make their own way in the world. He was educated at Rothesay Academy and Glasgow University, and qualified as a doctor, M.B., M.S., in 1881. There is a strong medical tradition in the family owing to the connection with the two famous eighteenth-century brothers, William, an anatomist, physician and obstetrician whose substantial and varied collections now form the core of Glasgow University's Hunterian Museum and Art Gallery, and John, his even more celebrated younger brother, an anatomist and surgeon. He also made an anatomical collection now in the Royal College of Surgeons museum in Lincoln's Inn Fields, London. Neither had direct descendants, and Charlie's branch of the family was descended from their uncle Archibald.

Maida senior told her daughter that Charlie had been a brilliant student. She

Dr Charles Hunter as
Surgeon-in-Charge of the
Colonial troops at Edward
VII's coronation, 1901

may have learned this from two doctor friends, Dr Quinton McLennan and Dr
Norman Maclehose, whom she met later. He does not seem to have had a hospital
appointment, and perhaps went into general practice at Cornwath near Glasgow.
At that time he got to know Mr Hozier, Parliamentary Private Secretary to Lord
Salisbury, whose daughter Lady Mary Cecil he married. Mr Hozier, elevated to
the peerage as Lord Newlands, became a very kind friend to Dr Hunter, who
apparently helped him with Conservative Party work. Maida junior recalled,
'I remember my mother once described him as "Charlie's patron" in the old-
fashioned sense of the word, and it was probably due to his influence that my
father got the post of Medical Officer to the HHNGS Railway, India,[3] and was
stationed at Secunderabad in the early 1890s.'

At the age of 32, in 1891, Dr Hunter married Mary Ethel, daughter of Mr
William Pendlebury, agent of this railway, and they had a son, William Charles,
born in 1893, who only lived seven weeks, and a daughter, Wilhelmina Ethel,
known as Ena, born in 1895.

---

3 (His Highness) Nizam's Guaranteed State Railway, according to Kerry Edwards on http://
   archiver.rootsweb.ancestry.com/th/read/INDIA/2000-01/0947664488 (accessed 29 May
   2017).

Maida junior writes:

It must have been not long after Ena's birth that her mother transferred her affections to William Cumberland Nicholson, an army officer whom she married in 1901. My father told my mother that his first wife, who was, I believe, very beautiful, persuaded him not to divorce her for adultery, as this would have meant in those days that Nicholson would have been cashiered from the army for being cited as co-respondent in a divorce case, but to leave India so that she could divorce him for desertion. I have no documentary evidence of the divorce, but remember Mamma telling me that a relative of her family had been working in that part of India at the time, knew the circumstances of the affair and reported that great sympathy had been felt for my father. ...

Certainly my father left India for South Africa, where I think he served, presumably as a Medical Officer, in the Second Boer War of 1899–1902. He was in England for the Coronation of King Edward VII in 1901, at which he was Surgeon-in-Charge of the Colonial troops. The Coronation was postponed for two months because the King had appendicitis (one of the earliest patients to be operated on for that condition), so the troops were in England much longer than intended, and my mother used to wish she had known my father at that time so that she could have seen the procession. He must have joined the Colonial Service shortly before this, as he is mentioned in a letter to *The Times* on 15 August 1902, thanking [him] for kindness and hospitality shown to the Colonial contingents on Coronation duty as Dr Hunter, Colonial Medical Service.

As Maida junior comments, Mr Roberts must have 'felt some apprehension about the engagement of his favourite daughter to this stranger, very understandably at that period and with the family's strict Methodist background'. These events had clearly disrupted Dr Hunter's career, and had a long-term effect on his finances, since he evidently retained responsibility for his daughter, whom he had brought back to England and entrusted to the care of his sister Jess (Jessie Wilhelmina, known to Maida junior as Aunt Billy). Hunter himself stayed with his sister during his periods of leave in Britain, and did not have a house of his own. He was 12 years older than Maida – 43 when they met, to her 31 – and his career in the Colonial Service meant that his wife would need to spend long periods separated from either her husband or the rest of her family. Dr Hunter was also by no means rich. So this could not have been regarded as a brilliant match for Maida, which perhaps explains why the couple had a relatively long engagement, but it was one that she was clearly determined to make. Her daughter comments:

My father must have been a very attractive man, tall (6 ft) and handsome with very dark hair and moustache and blue eyes, and always very well dressed.

Mamma often told me how proud she was to introduce him to family and friends. He was good at all sport, tennis, golf, the Scottish sport of curling, and was an excellent shot. More importantly, he was a devoted husband 'in sickness and in health' and a dedicated doctor to the patients of all races whom he treated in Africa. I only remember one fault that Mamma found in him, that he had little small talk. She once threatened when in West Africa to buy a parrot as 'at least it would talk'. But this was a very small complaint. She was obviously deeply in love with him and remained so all her life.

They were married on 15 January 1907 at the Presbyterian Church, Regent Square, St Pancras, London. He was then 47, she 35. The witnesses were her sister Belle (Trixie) and his nephew Cecil Hunter, then aged 23.[4] After the wedding Mr Roberts was the host at a reception at 8 Manchester Square, the home of Maida's cousin May Bradford.

Their daughter continues:

They went to the South of France for their honeymoon, and planned to come home by way of Switzerland for a reason which makes a curious story. As my father was travelling home on leave in 1906, the ship's doctor came to him to ask for his help in treating a patient who was lying dangerously ill in his cabin. This proved to be the Count de Bielandt,[5] a young Dutchman who had boarded the ship in West Africa having *walked* across from the East coast. Fortunately my father was able to cure the high fever, and as the patient recovered they became friends. As well as exploring, the count's great interest was in winter sports, and he was a champion tobogganer. He was intending to go to Switzerland on his return to Europe, and hearing of my parents' approaching marriage he invited them to join him at St Moritz. They were much looking forward to this when one morning my father read in the *Continental Daily Mail* that his friend had been killed on the Cresta Run the day before. He had been the first man to go down on his luge in the morning; one of the big logs which were put across

---

4   Cecil Hunter had travelled out to Sierra Leone to meet up with Dr Hunter in 1905, as he related in a letter to Maida:

'Batkanu, Sierra Leone, Tuesday 11 April 1905 … Fancy that dear boy Cecil turned up on Sunday night about 8.30 pitch dark, he had been walking from about 10 o'clock. Just like the youngster he is to do a mad thing like that. It is five years since I've seen him. He was at Woolwich then. Enormous he is, 6 ft 2 in, and well set up too, a nice cheery chap. I think he is enjoying himself here …. Do you remember my niece who was at the theatre with us that afternoon? I think I told you all the family had gone out to Cape Colony. Well, on the voyage out her elder sister got engaged to a man. Wicked I call it, she is only 16, I think, isn't it?

   Cecil brought a dozen bottles of beer with him. I had been longing for one, I don't know why, as you know I hardly ever drink beer, it's a year since I had any, and how I did enjoy a bottle last night, it would have done you good to see me drinking it! Fine it was.'

5   His name was actually Bylandt.

the track at night had accidentally been left in place; he struck it at high speed and it penetrated his chest, killing him instantly. My parents returned sadly to England where they found a very large parcel waiting for them. It contained a beautiful old Frisian clock which Count de Bielandt had sent them for a wedding present. It is now in Claire's[6] possession and still going well after 200 years.

It seems as if my father must have gone back to West Africa for one more tour on his own in mid-1907 and returned in 1908. Certainly in September 1908 they travelled out together on the SS *Karina* for him to take up the post of Medical Officer at Sherbro Island, Sierra Leone. Previously he had worked in the interior. They arrived in October, going via Freetown to Bonthe, Sherbro, to start what Mamma always described as 'the happiest year of my life'.

Maida's intention was both to support her husband in his work and to pursue her own interests. She planned to make a collection of pressed plants for the British Museum (Natural History), something that proved more difficult than she had perhaps anticipated in the hot damp climate, and two letters acknowledging receipt of her collection and the Museum's list of identifications are preserved with her letters at Rhodes House Library. She also collected butterflies and birds (both she and Charlie evidently practised taxidermy). As Maida junior recalled:

There is no doubt that Mamma was an 'elitist', horrid modern word, in the sense that she enjoyed the society of well-mannered and intelligent people in all walks of life; with her intellect, charm and sense of humour she never lacked friends who invited her to their homes, and were happy to visit her in the very small houses which were all she could afford as a widow. Having many interests, ornithology, gardening, dressmaking and embroidery, she preferred her own company to that of people she found dull, and I can truthfully say that I was always proud to introduce my own friends to her as I grew up, especially when she moved to Cambridge when I was an undergraduate.

In these letters Maida was writing privately to her family, and it would be pointless to expect from her a modern degree of political correctness. But her open-mindedness and broad interest in the people and events that she encountered come across very strongly. Inevitably her social circle was confined mostly to other expatriates in the Colonial Service or attached to the different trading companies that operated in the region, but she also interacted with a wide range of local people. Food was evidently of great interest to her, and one of the most enjoyable aspects of her letters is the descriptions of meals good and less good, of her attempts to have her servants reproduce Welsh cooking without anything resembling an oven,

6   Claire is Maida Bulman's daughter.

and not least, the gushing gratitude when the boats brought not just mail but renewed supplies of cakes from home.

Life in Bonthe was clearly not easy, and the contrast between the life she was living there and the life of her sisters in Wales, with their tennis parties and horse riding, must at times have been sobering. But Maida was no whiner: she dedicated herself to making a success of her time as a colonial wife, and her absorbing letters prove to what a remarkable extent she succeeded.

A note on Sierra Leone

Sierra Leone (the name derives from the Portuguese and Spanish for 'lioness mountains') is situated on the north-west African coast, and bordered by what are today Guinea and Liberia. A relatively small country by African standards, it has a total area of 71,740 km² (27,699 sq. m.) and a population today of 7,075,641 (based on the 2015 national census).[7] Its climate is tropical, and its vegetation ranges from savannah to rainforests.

Sierra Leone has a long history as a trading nation, with European traders first establishing themselves there in the 15th century. For many years it was a centre for the slave trade. After abolition, it saw a reverse move, with several major attempts to resettle freed slaves in the country. These resettlements added further complexity to an ethnic make-up which includes a wide variety of local peoples, and Krio, the language derived from the Creole of the former slaves, is still very widely spoken. The main ethnic grouping around Bonthe was and is the Sherbro, fishing and farming people who are virtually all Christians (unlike the country's Muslim majority), with a history of intermarriage between their chiefs and the European colonists and traders.

In Maida's time Sierra Leone was a British colony (the area in which the colonists generally lived, with an area of only 256 square miles) and protectorate (the remainder of the country). It was administered from Freetown (as its name suggests, the capital was founded by traders), partly through the native chiefs who retained an important liaison role. The 1911 census gave the population of the colony as 75,000, of whom about 600 were Europeans, and of the protectorate as 1,400,000.[8]

K. J. Beatty, who wrote about Sierra Leone in the early 20th century, claimed:

Sierra Leone was and is still known, though now quite undeservedly, as the White Man's Grave. Mrs Falconbridge, the wife of one of the early agents of the Sierra Leone Company, records that during her residence in the Colony (1793-4) it

---

7   https://en.wikipedia.org/wiki/Sierra_Leone, accessed 16 June 2017.

8   This and other information derives from K. J. Beatty, *Human leopards: an account of the trials of human leopards before the Special Commission Court; with a note on Sierra Leone, past and present* (London: Hugh Rees, 1915).

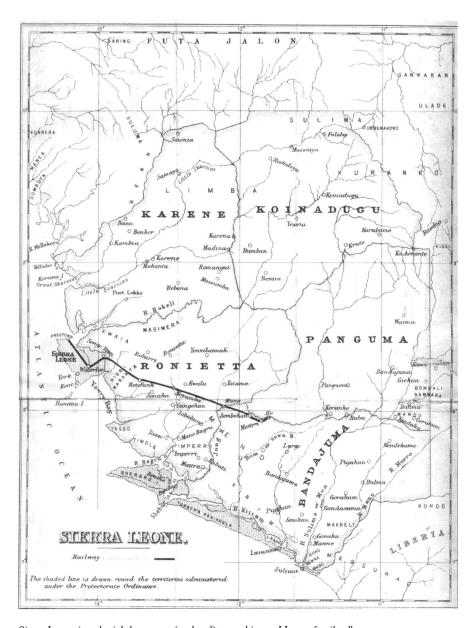

Sierra Leone in colonial days: map (undated) posted into a Hunter family album

was usual to ask in the morning 'how many died last night'. This can still be heard in Freetown as a form of morning greeting, but it now helps to start the day with a laugh, and that in West Africa is about the best tonic known.

Bonthe, where the Hunters lived, is the main town on Sherbro Island, an area which remains underdeveloped even today, without a reliable road system, mains water or electricity. It lies on the eastern shore of the island, with its port not on the open Atlantic but on the Sherbro River estuary. The island continues the oil palm cultivation and mining that were important activities a century ago. However in the late 19th and early 20th century the island and Bonthe town were relatively more important than they are today:[9] it was Sierra Leone's first administrative capital and municipality, and one of two crown colonies (the other being Freetown). York Island (not to be confused with the town of York near Freetown) is a small island in the river, which Dr Hunter visited regularly as part of his duties.

With extensive mangrove swamps, the area enjoys an intense rainy season: from May to November an average 168 days have rain, with annual rainfall of 366 cm (approx. 12 ft).[10]

A note on the editing

Maida Bulman (Maida junior, 1910–1993) undertook the laborious job of transcribing her mother's letters before passing the originals to the Rhodes Library. They have been further edited by Susan Curran, who worked from these transcripts. For the convenience of modern readers, Maida's fondnesses for multiple exclamation marks and for semicolons punctuating long sentences have been toned down, and the punctuation modernized. Maida abbreviated extensively, particularly in the periods when she was short of paper, and again in the interests of readability her abbreviations have mostly been written out (except where it is not clear what the full version might have been). She wrote of her husband as 'C', 'Charlie' and 'Charles'; the 'Cs' here have routinely been expanded into Charlie. Dates have been regularized and expanded. Notes have been provided by Maida Bulman (appended M.B.M.B.), by Susan (mostly not identified, occasionally appended S.G.C.) and by Maida and Charlie's grandson Andrew Bulman (appended A.B.). Andrew also reviewed and corrected the text. For other acknowledgements and sources, please see page 205.

There is a long and at times perhaps confusing cast of dramatis personae; where possible a reminder of each person's (or animal's) identity is provided in the index.

---

9   See http://slconcordtimes.com/bonthe-sherbro-island-is-abandoned-and-forgotten/ (accessed 16 June 2017).

10 http://reliefweb.int/report/sierra-leone/sierra-leone-bonthe-district-profile-04-december-2015 (accessed 16 June 2017).

The letters

The life she left behind: Maida riding 'The Doctor' at Bronceris, c. 1904

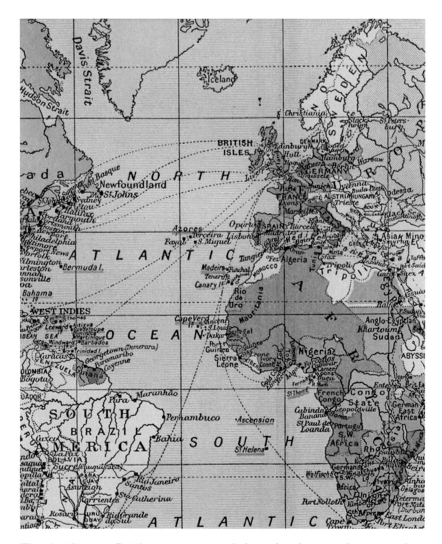

The colonial journey: British possessions are marked in pink in this extract from a map of
'The world: colonial possessions and commercial highways, 1910', originally published by
Cambridge University Press

[Unless stated otherwise, the letters are written from Maida to Belle.]

S.S. *Karina*
26 September 1908

My own darling Belle,

Here I am really off at last. It's fine but choppy but I don't mind that. Charles is very kind and I really feel full of buck. I'm glad we have really started, when the Pilot goes off at Bull Bay all means of escape will have gone.

The Governor is on board but not his wife, she went ashore; she was the image of Miss Taylor Morgan to look at only plump. Charlie has just introduced me to Major Ponce and his wife, she is going out too, has been out a year once before. She is very like Lucy Knox to look at and I think I shall like her. We are going to fix up a table together. She has just told Charlie to go and find my box of chocolates, all ladies for West Africa get them, a huge box it is.

Sally Owen and Ella Dempster came to see me off, they are so kind and jolly. Sally said she would send you a postcard. She brought me Mrs Humphrey Ward's new book *Diana Mallory*, and Ella a lovely box of Pullers sweets, kind wasn't it? Willie Dempster came too. His Pa old Mr Dempster was on board. I fancy they are hoping he will get a rise up now that Mr Davey is dead, they were flying after Sir A. Jones!

It's very fine and sunny, and I feel much better now that I have started; I felt awfully bad last night and this morning. It's very nice that Mrs Ponce is on board, she will put me up to things. The Governor is very like the great Hugh Leslie to look at. We stop at Las Palmas going out so you'll get a letter from there. Mr Hudson, the Circuit Judge, is also on board.

That poor woman had committed suicide at the hotel, horrible wasn't it? She had just come off the Irish boat.

Ever, my own darling, with our best love to you, to darling father, to Kate and the black kitten,
your own Twisty

P.S. The boat is very full, I wish you could see the cabin opposite, three men in it and luggage crammed in, I don't know how they can ever get in. Two are young officers of the West African Frontier Force. One came down when I was coming out of my cabin, and all he said was 'Well *this is awful!*' Ours is a jolly one looking on to the sea, but the sunset side of the ship which will make it hot in the tropics.

Now all of you keep well and cheery, what's the use of moping? I dare say I shall have many a fit of longing, if I thought of it now I could howl, but I'm not going to.

Bestest love to darling Auntie Kate and Mona.
Ever your own Twisty

A postcard of Las Palmas, 1910, sourced from https://s-media-cache-ak0.pinimg.com/originals/4b/86/16/4b8616b6bce4edd3fa400dd7824bfb43.jpg

I hope you will enjoy your coffee.

At sea
2 October 1908

My own darling Belle,
We left Las Palmas today at 12 o'clock, we reached there at 6 o'clock this morning, and as I wanted mosquito boots and a chair on shore we got up at 6.30 and just had a cup of tea and went ashore, took a carriage and drove into Las Palmas. It looked just the same, muddy and dusty, and the Metropole awful, as the middle block has all been burned out; and the overflow has to go to the Catalina. We got a chair, but the boots I got on board. They are top-boots made of untanned leather, or rather a thick-looking suede, and as soon as you get out of bed you are supposed to pull them on. They cost 8/-. At Las Palmas we drove into the fruit market and bought some peaches, 2 lbs for 1/- and three lbs of large pears for 9d, but the peaches are of course not nearly as nice as what are grown in hothouses in England. There were men on board selling drawn thread work of the most appalling kind; they say the best people don't bring their wares on the outgoing boats.

There was a grand concert on board last night. No persuasions under the sun would ever make me sing a note on board. They were mostly professionals of sorts who were going to the Canary Islands.

Three new passengers came on board today, Colonel and Mrs Bryan, and a Mr Smythe of the West African Regiment. Colonel and Mrs Bryan met at the Islands, at least he came there to meet her for his two months' leave and she is coming on with him. He is Cecil's Colonel, so Charlie says.[1] Mr Smythe is quite young but his wife also came to the Islands for his two months' leave, but she goes home tomorrow. And now the next thing will be Freetown, where we are due to arrive at 5 o'clock on Wednesday morning. I shall be very thankful to be settled down at Sherbro if we go there, and I hope we shall not have long to wait at Freetown. There are five missionary women on board, and two nurses, and one doctor's wife who, they say, is going out to her husband on the Gold Coast, and that he does not know she is coming. She is very fair, quite like a Norwegian, and very stout. I have not spoken to her. Only one of the missionaries gets off at Freetown. One of the black firemen has disappeared, they think he must have gone overboard, horrid, isn't it?

Monday 5 October

Since I wrote last it's been gradually getting hotter and hotter; but before I go any further, please forgive these awful blots, it's that horrid stylo pen I gave Father to try, and the only one I have with me.

They say last night, today and tomorrow will be hotter than I shall ever feel on the coast; and the cabin at night is stifling, beyond giving me a headache. I feel very fit but it's next thing to impossible to do one's hair. Saturday passed by just reading and in the afternoon they play quoits. While they were playing I heard a noise on the lower deck and I thought the second-class passengers were also playing, but instead my dear it was a black man being carried by six others out of the engine room. It was the lost one; he was found lying between two plates of iron under the water tanks only nine inches high, and he had been there since Tuesday. They think he must have been fed part of the time but for two days at least he had had nothing.

Yesterday the missionaries took service on board at 10.30. Mr Webster, the Wesleyan, read the service (Church of England, only that prayer for bishops and curates he changed to ministers). He is a very good sort and plays a good game of cricket. Then the Baptist took the sermon, not bad but rather like Mr Hind-Smith's style. Mrs Ponce and I made a great mistake by going without hats; then in the afternoon I regret to say my poor Charles joined in a quoit tournament, he and the Governor against two second-class passengers. Six couples played, second against first class. The second class lost hopelessly. Then there was a tug of war, also first against second, with the same result. Today and tomorrow the sports are being held. Charlie is on the committee and one of the judges. He is going in for the quoits and potato race. There are only two ladies' races, needle race, you and

---

1   Cecil was Charlie's nephew: see page 10n4.

a man, which consists of your running round a certain place giving a needle to the man to thread and running back; and also the egg race, picking up a potato instead of an egg on a spoon, and running with it all round the deck. I'm going to try but I doubt if I shall be any good as I have no tennis shoes for one thing and that helps you so much.

I heard one of the missionaries say today that her cabin registered 82°, and ours must be much hotter at night as it gets the evening sun.

The fruit we got at the Islands is now ripening beautifully, but some of the juice has trickled out of the basket down on to one of my nice cushions. Please will you tell Kate[2] that my face was never so green as to clash with the green cushion cover. In fact my face is like a rising sun, like one of those Indian Chiefs over her mantelpiece!

It's just 9.30 a.m. Charlie is at a committee of the sports, and I have come into the saloon to write to my Belle. I've had some pretty bad longing fits, awful just at times, but I'm trying just not to think of it, as it would worry dear old Charlie and really I've been quite happy, only I sometimes feel strange among all these officers, you know, but Mr Murray and Mr Smythe and Major Ponce are all very nice. I must say I don't think I've ever had such good laughs as at meals, simply could hardly stop, Mr Murray has been so awfully funny. His father, Mrs Ponce tells me, is a doctor at Kingston-on-Thames.

Now I must stop, the heat is awful. This will be a most uninteresting letter. I'm sure I shall get to feel less strange as time goes on. I shall he truly glad when we land and we get our orders. I think Mrs Ponce feels the same, she does not know where they are going to. I spoke to Mrs Bryan yesterday, she is a most distinguished-looking woman, very tall and thin, and dark. She has brought none of her silver with her, but she is only staying six months; that's rather jolly for her.

Sierra Leone

At last we are here. I must honestly say I rather dreaded the arrival, and getting off the ship with all our baggage and all that, but instead of that I enjoyed it hugely. But before I tell you about the landing I must finish off with the *Karina*. The last two days were devoted to the sports, and there was no time for anything, not to speak of the heat. Monday was terrifically hot, the cabin in the evening was too terrible, and that was the day the two races for ladies took place. One was the egg and spoon race; we had oranges instead of potatoes, and mine rolled anywhere but on the spoon so that I came in next to the last, Mrs Ponce last! Captain Boyle was my partner for the needle and thread race, I had to run down the ship with a needle in one hand and thread in the other, up to the men who stood in a line, give it to him to thread it and fly back the other side of the ship. Half ran first and

2 Belle and Maida's elder sister.

Freetown, east end of the wharf, photo from the family album

then the other half, so the winners had to run twice. I got first prize, Captain Boyle was simply splendid; and I got a silver fruit knife, very ugly but a nice memento.

My poor Charles just lost the single quoit race, he got third prize which he gave to the one behind him. They were finishing the quoits by electric light at 9.30 p.m. and after that the prizes were given by Mrs Bryant. And then we went downstairs and finished our packing, and went to [bed].

A slight tornado came on, thunder and lightning, nothing very much, and when Charles woke me next morning at 5.30 a.m. we were slowly steaming into the harbour. I got up and stood at my porthole, and could see the shore. It looked very lovely, low red earth cliffs, the tops covered with low brushwood, in lovely shades of 'Liberty' greens, and then behind high hills covered with trees too; and palm trees arising out of the brush everywhere. We could hear the anchor go down, so got up and dressed and very soon people began to come on board.

First of all a letter came from Mr Brooks, the Head of the Police, saying he was so sorry he had to go away on patrol for a week, but that he was sending his boat, and that Dr Forde was going to offer us lodgement, but Dr Keenan had already asked us.[3] Then came such a kind letter from the Head of the Customs for Charlie

---

3   Maida uses Mr/Dr Forde/Ford, to refer it seems to the same person, the Principal Medical Officer. I have standardized on Dr Forde. Dr Keenan (also spelled Kennan) was evidently a physician stationed at Freetown. A Dr Cleaver Keenan had much the same posting in the 1950s and was perhaps his son: see http://yourlifemoments.ca/sitepages/obituary.asp?oid=653812.

saying that he was sending a paper to pass all our luggage through, such a very great help.

When we got on board we could see the Government boat coming off with a canopy at one end rowed by about eight men in blue trousers and white jumpers, and Mr Haddon-Smith, the Acting Governor, under the canopy.[4] He is a very fine-looking man, rather of the Izzard Davies type. Charlie introduced me to him and he was very nice. He went down and had breakfast with the Governor, and then they landed at 9.30 a.m.

We could see crowds of people coming down to the quay and some bunting up. It was rather funny, they had expected us on Tuesday, the *Karina* always gets in that day, and all the officers and soldiers had been down all day waiting broiling in their uniforms. How it was that they had not wired from the Islands I don't know, they had wired but simply said the day they were leaving.

Then we got ready to go off, Dr Keenan, Charlie and me. The police boat had sailors in dark blue with black sou'westers, they looked rather sinister. We got our cabin luggage all into the boat and then got in ourselves, but the tide was running with such frightful force that we very nearly got jammed in between the big barge that brings water and our ship. The shouting and shrieking, you never heard such a thing, and in the middle one of our wicker chairs fell overboard, but was fortunately rescued. Charlie got hold of a boathook and I think really saved the situation, and we finally got off. I simply shook with laughter, Mr Murray and the Ponces all looking on, it really was killing.

Well, when we got near the slip (very much the size of the slip we get off the Anglesey boat) Charlie detected Sam and Mormoh,[5] Sam in dark blue trousers and a white surplice over it and a large black umbrella with a huge shepherd's crook handle, Mormoh in a red gown and emerald green plush fez cap, also a huge umbrella, and Dr Keenan's boy Ali. They all grinned and looked very pleased, and I was introduced and immediately relieved of all my packages.

There were two ladies there who had been down to see the Governor arrive, a doctor's wife, Mrs Burrows, and Mrs Beddington, wife of the under-officer of Police, her third husband, and 17 years younger than herself. They were all very jolly, and I was put on to Charlie's hammock to ride up to Dr Keenan's house. Never shall I forget that ride! I had not got on properly, and consequently was nearly cut in half. You don't lie in them, you sit as if you were on a swing with your legs dangling down. As I passed up all the black mammies laughed and clapped and wished me luck; how I laughed, but I was thankful to get off. A little more and I should have come in two, I really think.

(accessed 20 June 2017), S,G,C.

4   George Basil Haddon-Smith, CMG (1861–1931) had been Colonial Secretary in Sierra Leone since 1901. See http://prabook.com/web/person-view.html?profileId=749435 (accessed 20 June 2017).

5   Evidently Sam and Mormoh (also spelled Mormo) had been servants to Dr Hunter on his previous posting to Sierra Leone, and they now resumed their positions as the leading servants to the family..

Police station and lawcourts, Freetown, an early 20th-century postcard. Souced from http://www.sierra-leone.org/Postcards/SL729769.jpg

From the ship the town and harbour reminded me very much of Algiers, only of course no fine buildings. The Cathedral stands out well, but the Government offices are very poor-looking. Otherwise it's all very like Mustapha at Algiers and the railway runs right up on the road. This house stands on a corner, and an avenue of cotton trees goes up straight in front leading to Government House, a big rambling old building. This house is just like the little farms and villas round St Maxime, no carpets and bare painted walls, and I dare say might look rather comfortless to anyone who had not been out of England, but being abroad has cured me of all that, and I like it all very much. No doubt the climate will be very trying, and at Sherbro where we go today or tomorrow it will be very lonely. I don't think I shall feel it but time will show.

Sam and Mormoh and the four hammock boys hang round the house waiting for any orders, and Sam 'maids' us. Our bedroom is upstairs with sloping roofs like attics and of course bare floors, and just a bed and dressing table, and Sam [is] in charge of those and keeps them tidy while we are here. Dr Forde, the Principal Medical Officer, came in to lunch, a very good-looking man.

Charlie went out before lunch and came back with an invitation for us to go to tea with Mrs Haddon-Smith at Hill Station. He is the Colonial Secretary. Dr Keenan's table was so nicely set with four vases with variegated croton leaves and little ones spread about the table, it looked so nice. For lunch, first savoury eggs were handed round (cold); then fish salad decorated with sliced tomato and cucumber, then a piece of roast meat which we none of us took, and I forgot before that chicken cutlets and green peas, then fruit.

Just before lunch a tornado came on. I must tell you it had been cloudy all morning, but isn't it funny, you have to be almost more careful those days not to get touched by the sun. I was standing at one of the windows watching the people. Four roads meet so it's awfully interesting, all laughing and joking, you never heard such a thing. At the bottom of one big cotton tree a woman was selling nuts and they were all dressed extra well, I fancy, to receive the Governor, when suddenly a downpour of rain came down, and in a second a squall of wind. All the windows banged too. Charlie's panama was blown through the window and he would have lost it only Dr Keenan saw it go! I thought all the china and glass was blown over, and the shrieks outside and the crowds tearing in all directions accompanied by a flock of goats who had been grazing in a waste place opposite. It was really killing. Where they all scuttled to I can't think.

The rain continued and I was awfully afraid we should have been prevented [from] going up to Hill Station by the 3.30 train. However at 2.30 it began to clear, and I went up and got out my Teneriffe dress which I had fortunately kept clean. I proceeded to undress and do my hair, and Sam walked in and out! – emptying water. He looked at me and I looked at him but we neither of us said a word, so I concluded it must be all right, and I thought it a pity for him to have nothing to do, so he pinned up my placket hole, and tidied up the room. I twisted that Liberty scarf round the hat I bought the morning I left, and was ready to start. (As usual my hats are weak.)

The train stopped under huge cotton trees just outside, and as 3.30 approached a crowd of men, government officials, gathered round to whom I was introduced. As I stepped into the train my suspender came off! Wasn't it too awful! I managed to get into Mrs Haddon-Smith's house all right, and before I left she let me put it up.

In the train one of the men had a box of chocolates which he handed round. We walked up with a Mr Evelyn, Assistant Colonial Secretary. Hill Station is charming, little bungalows dotted about and gardens all round; long covered steps lead up into covered-in verandahs which are practically drawing rooms. As we rang, a little black Pom came barking along and slipped and caught his nail and wrenched it and began to cry – very much so. Mrs Haddon-Smith and a Mr Denton, who had been their aide de camp, rushed out. She is a tall edition of May[6] and was very nice. She rang for tea and then Mr Haddon-Smith came in. She had a Queen Anne tea-pot and a nice little aluminium (I think it was) hot water kettle and lamp, and white fluted china. We just had sandwiches and a plain cake.

She had one nice grey parrot and Mr Denton had one. She took me round her

---

6 Lady May Bradford, Maida's cousin (see also p. 207 for details of her book).

garden and while we were there Sir Philip and Lady Smyly came in.[7] She is rather pretty, but dressed, my dear, in a dark blue coat and skirt. She had a little stick like mine, they are considered good, so will you look after mine? We left then and went to the tennis court, and from there we walked with Mr and Mrs Evelyn to their bungalow and had vermouth. She was very nice too and played a very good game of tennis. Her drawing-room was very pretty. She told me she washed and ironed all her own blouses. They go for leave in two months. We travelled home in the train with Mr Murray. Wasn't it funny? He and the Ponces are leaving today for Lokko.

As I am writing, Ali has brought me a glass of milk and soda, and a plate of mixed biscuits. I don't object to the milk at all. We had dinner last night, but as you can imagine we were both dead tired, and who came in after dinner but Mr Murray! However Charlie and I went to bed at 9.30 and slept till 7.00, when Sam brought in a lovely cup of tea and a pile of little snippets of buttered toast, and two bananas, 'It was good, wee auntie.' Then breakfast at 8.30, poached eggs handed round, and tea, then chicken rissoles and fruit. I do hope Mormoh is as good a cook as Dr Keenan's. I like Sam, he looks a very good staid old sort. After breakfast Charlie and Dr Keenan went off to the Hospital and to the Customs, both in their hammocks, they looked so nice, and I sat down at once and wrote all this. I wonder if I've half told you all you want to know. Be sure to make no bones about telling me. I could watch these niggers all day. They are so full of airs and graces, little girls with short frocks go along holding up their skirts! And another little tiny boy passed with his slate on the top of his head (they carry everything on their heads). The boat we go on ought to have been in last night, but they are so irregular it may not come for a day or two.

My darling Belle, I'm so distressed to find I came away with your comb. My hair is coming out in handfuls, you never saw anything like it. Charlie is getting a hairwash made up today, and it's so greasy I can do nothing with it. Will you let dear Elsie[8] see this letter if she cares to? I'm afraid I shall not be able to write any more till I'm settled at Bonthe. A note came on board from Cecil:[9] in hospital, broken a rib! We are going up to Tower Hill to his place to tea today. There are three military stations here, 'Oriel' the West Indies Regiment, Tower Hill (Gunners) and 'Wilberforce', the West African Regiment. The West African Frontier Force is moved up country, that is the only regiment under Colonial Government.

My best and dearest love to Father and Kate and your own dear self from us both.

Ever your own Twisty

7   Sir Philip Crampton Smyly (1866–1953) was Attorney General of Sierra Leone from 1901–11.
8   Belle and Maida's sister, to whom she also wrote.
9   Charlie's nephew.

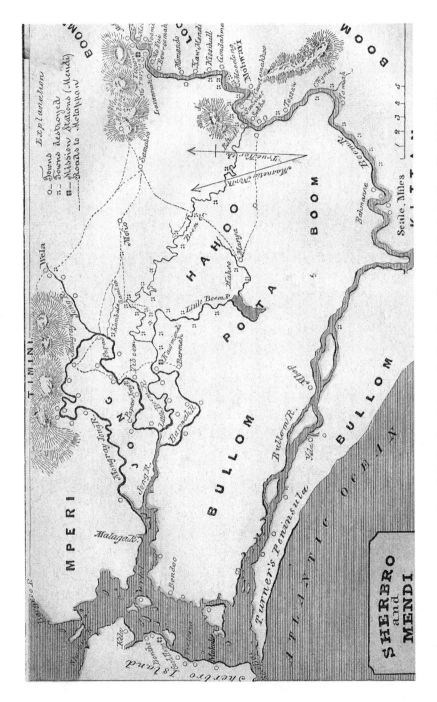

Antique map of 'Sherbro and Mendi' from *A Cyclopedia of Missions* by Rev. Harvey Newcomb, Charles Scribner, New York, 1856.
Sourced from http://www.sierra-leone.org/Postcards/SHERBRO163.jpg

Freetown, 9 October 1908

My darling Belle,
Just a wee line. We are off tonight by the steamer *Axim*, quite a decent boat. We all three went and had tea with Dr and Mrs Burrows yesterday, and then up to Tower Hill to have tea with Cecil; he has broken a rib but looked well. He has given me a very rude! looking young cat, all white with black spots. He sent it down last night, but I had to send it back in case it ran away. Sarah is going for it today. Its mother's name is Mary, a great pet with the officers.

When Charlie went down to the Office yesterday Mr Haddon-Smith came in and said 'I'm sorry, Hunter, you can't go to Sherbro', and then burst out laughing and said Mrs Haddon-Smith thought I ought to stay at Hill Station. Charlie said, 'The Government don't recognise wives, Sir.' We are lunching with the Burrows today, Dr Forde and Dr Keenan, and I've asked Lionel Rees down to tea.
Ever your own Twisty.

Bonthe, Sherbro
Sierra Leone
Sunday 11 October 1908

My darling Trixie,
We left Freetown on Friday evening. We had been to lunch with Dr and Mrs Burrows, and Dr Forde and Dr Keenan were there, then I went down in the hammock to buy a solar topi which cost 9/- but they say I need one, and when I got back I packed, and then Mr Rees came. Dr Keenan had such a nice dainty tea for us, tomato sandwiches, cake and biscuits, and he came in himself before we had finished. Mr Rees only stayed a short time as he had to go back to work, he seems a nice boy but very shy! Then Mr. and Mrs Beddington[10] came and they walked down with us to the boat. It was just sunset and nice and cool. We found Sam and Mormoh surrounded by carriers and our baggage, and Charlie stood in the middle bargaining with them, and Mormoh pointed out with his umbrella to the deserving ones!

Wednesday 14 October

We got on board and then the boat went back for Sam and Mormoh, and their baggage. It was dark when they arrived on board, each with a small tin box with their bedding strapped on, and Sam was struggling up the ladder with a black bottle under his arm. Charlie asked in severe tones what it was and Mormoh said 'His water for drink.' He is a Mohammedan and never touches wine. We had the usual sort of dinner on board; the Captain arrived as we were finishing. We had ours just with the ship's officers. It was one of the best boats that comes here, the

---

10 Spelled Bettington here but presumably the Beddingtons mentioned earlier.

Assim. She left today and is going back to Freetown to take troops. However, to go back, we had a very comfortable night. The cat wailed from a basket in the next cabin! And early next morning we got up and could see the trees of Sherbro.

We dressed and I went on deck after having breakfast. It was a dull cloudy morning and we had to crawl along in case of sticking on a sandbank. The whole place is a series of low islands covered with mangrove trees only about 30 ft high. We wound in and out, and then anchored off York Island. The steamers can go no further. That is a pity as we don't get the excitement of seeing them come in. We can just see their masts over the island opposite us. York Island had just the two trading firms' buildings, and clustered round little mud huts with thatched roofs. The sea was covered in one part with little canoes (dugouts) with one or two men in each fishing, and after we had anchored they rowed up. Wild-looking individuals they were too, with hardly, if any, clothes on. Charlie bought a fish weighing about 4 lbs called 'Spanish', and it's well he did so, because Dr Jackson Moore had not provided much for us. He knew we were coming. To look at he is the image of Mr Ernest Jones! The first thing he said after saying 'How do you do?' was that he had had no breakfast, and he went down and had some and kept us waiting no end of a time. At last we got off, into the boat which had an awning on, and rowed off for this place, an hour it takes. We reached here, just a little black landing stage, no one on it, and got off, to find to my horror my skirt soaked through, my new pique! by Puss! and the red of the rug had come off on to it. I only hope it will come off, but have my doubts.

We walked to the house. It was in an awful state of dirt, I never saw such a filthy, untidy place; it did give me such a turn, and I could do nothing until Dr Moore left. He said he was going up to the District Commissioner on Monday and to my delight he left. If you could have seen the state of the dispensary, really words fail to describe it. Our bedroom was upstairs, not even swept. Sam swept it, just the bare boards, and one bed in it, no table, no chair! Eventually we got a small table for the washing table and two enamel basins on it; and then a tiny camp table of Charlie's I put my brush on. The bedroom opposite ours upstairs had a lot of rice on the floor which had brought no end of cockroaches into the house. When I came down on Sunday morning (I had to dress under the greatest difficulties) I came into the part of the room screened off for the drawing room and sat down on my own chair. I felt as thought a pin pricked me high up on my leg. I got up and felt another, and I suppose I shook myself because down dropped a huge horny centipede 3½ inches long, with spikes all down it and two big claws like pincers in front. I nearly had a fit. Charlie and Dr Moore caught it and killed it; fortunately it hadn't bitten me, as they have nasty poisonous bites. I fancy all the dirt brought it because they killed another upstairs next day.

The other bedroom, no. 3, opens out of the drawing room downstairs, quite a small room. Dr Moore was sleeping in it. I couldn't have believed anyone could have slept in such a place; a big iron bed, *filthy*, covered with rust and dirt. Well, he cleared out on Monday and then we began! Upstairs first. With a long broom they brushed the rafters (which are painted white) of all cobwebs, then the walls, and then the floors of the two bedrooms, and the passage between, which is very wide, almost a room to itself with a window at each end, and then they (Sam and the four hammock boys) washed the floors, but you never saw such clumsy fellows. Charlie shouted and yelled at them and eventually we got them done and felt it was a comfort we had clean floors. We have no carpets on them of course, it's better not in this country. Then they roughly swept the stairs down, the bannister of which is nearly off. We moved all our boxes into the other room, but I have not unpacked yet, as I have no drawers or shelves and only about three nails to hang things on! All this I don't mind now the place is cleaner.

Yesterday we cleaned all the downstairs rooms, namely the dining room, hall, dispensary and bedroom (they all open out of one another), swept the ceiling, walls and floor, cobwebs everywhere, and they just washed the floor of the bedroom and dispensary or medicine room as they call it, had all the bottles out, cleaned and put back. The disgraceful state it was all in, I think he feels rather ashamed of it now he sees what we have done. But just fancy, we sent to all the firms for scouring brushes, not one to be had! But by today Sam unearthed a hard blacking brush, and we found another small brush, and two hammock boys scoured and the others mopped and dried. Of course, it was all very rough and ready, but when I think we poured about five bathfuls of dirty water through the window I know it's cleaner. I am not going to describe the house this week, I have not had a minute to write in nor any place to write on, and I was in such despair and depressions I knew my letter would be horrid, but now I'm beginning to feel my feet under me, things begin to look more cheerful.

I have felt so sorry for my poor Charles, I could not disguise my feelings as you will know, and I felt too awful for anything, but I believe once I settle down and get things straightened out a bit I shall feel quite different.

I have had two walks with Charlie after tea. These native huts are so weird, I'll try later on to sketch you one roughly. The District Commissioner has not been near us, just fancy, he will get a cool reception when he does come! So different from the people at Freetown.

There seem to be hardly any flowers at all, and we hear that the big stretch of ground on one side of the house does not go with the house, so we do not feel inclined to pay extra rent, but the landlord is away up the river until Saturday. When he comes we can ask him to paint the floors of the dining room, drawing room and hall, and bedroom for us and a few odd jobs. I will describe the house next week, but I will tell you now that the only furniture in it is two tables and two broken chairs in the dining room, neither of the tables painted! a huge table covered with green baize in the hall, and a big thing of pigeonholes enamelled pale blue on it. This, let me tell you, was littered to the very top with all kinds of litter, but has now been emptied and scoured. This is in the hall, which really is all in one

'A big thing of pigeonholes' – Maida's photo from a family album

with the dining and drawing rooms, the doors all take out; the drawing room runs along the top and the bedroom beyond. It has one deal table and a few native chairs like those stools we have in the drawing room at home, only with backs to them, not bad at all. The walls of the hall and drawing room are panelled and painted white and dark green, and on the floor are two large strips of dark green oilcloth, which when polished will look nice, and at the top end a Kensington square of rose colour, so there is a good basis for making things look nicer. My cushions go beautifully with the dark green paper and red carpet, so that's a great blessing.

Now, I'm going to end for tonight, my wee Belle,
Your Twisty

P.S. I have to write to Dr Keenan to thank him for all his kindness to us; what a different man he is to Dr Moore.

Thursday

This has to be posted at 2 o'clock today. Don't be alarmed if letters do not come regularly from here, the steamer may stick on the sandbanks, or goodness knows what might happen to them. We heard to our disgust that only the letters come regularly now overland, not the papers and parcels. Isn't it too bad? Our papers will have to come by steamer and they are not very regular.

It was raining all day yesterday and most part of the night, which is unusual at this time of the year, but I was glad as we had used so much water for scouring. Today they are doing the pantry. It's just 10 past 9 a.m., Charlie has just started off to York Island in a boat rowed by six men, and an awning over his head. He took a little cold the first day he was here in his head, otherwise we are both quite well. I feel the heat rather, they say it will take a month or so to get used to it, but it's really not very great, in the afternoon a lovely breeze comes up. This is a very nice airy cheerful house. I am writing now in the drawing room, it has four windows down one side of it and I can see the sea and the low island in front, and away behind that the mainland. Could you, my wean, order me enough of the green stuff from Liberty's at Chester to make curtains for five windows, of pink for two windows: that is, ten green curtains and four pink ones, I will give the measurements at the end of this letter, and get Miss Parry to put hems at both ends. I can get nothing here, and the green curtains could be drawn as blinds, and be such a blessing, with little bands to tie them back with; if I could have them by return of post I should be so grateful. The narrow width will do, I think; also, could you get me a dozen little cheap dessert mats, and another afternoon tea-cloth. I think I will have the one you made me, I could wash it myself and it would be such a pleasure out here. You must put the value on the outside of the parcel.

Will you also order me two butterfly boxes and a killing bottle, and one fixing board, medium size, the 2/6 boxes will do, and tell them to put camphor balls inside and send them to me here and the bill inside; I would order them myself, only I haven't their book. I am awfully hoping that we shall get our letters on Friday by the *Batanga*. If not they will be here on Sunday overland.

One of the traders has his wife here, a Mrs Pidgeon. He sent for Charlie at 9 o'clock the other night to see her. She came overland three months ago and arrived here in the rainy season and got remittent fever but it's some other thing now. I did not want to be left in the house, so I went with him, a man in front carrying a lantern. I stayed outside, but they called me in. She is a nice little thing but common. All these firms have watchmen round them at nights, and they ring a bell every hour which if you are awake is very cheerful. Fortunately I haven't heard their bells! We have had no thunderstorm yet, only lightning after sunset.

I don't feel that this letter is a bit interesting; when I settle down more I shall write nicer letters I hope. I won't give you our meals yet either, as we are living just now as best we can till things are straight. The bread is awful, we have no baking pot yet, but when we get it Mormoh will bake bread. Charlie says it is much nicer.

Will you give my very best love to dearest Father and ask him if he will be such a dear as to share this letter with you this week; and give dear Kate my love too and dear Elsie, and plenty plenty to you my darling from us both,
Your loving Twisty

The curtains have to be 2½ yards long, not including hems, so that would be 25 yards, not allowing for hems, and 10 of the red not including hems. I can't make these niggers work when Charlie is not here, and Sam has disappeared for his breakfast!

12.00 p.m.

I turned to and made them work. I got two and made them scrub the stairs. It took them two hours to do 14 steps only! But it looks cleaner.

Kindest remembrances to Williams[11] and the servants. I have thought so much of Walters[12] when we got first to Bronceris, and wished she was here. I can see her looking at the place, then pushing back her glasses firmly on her nose and settling to work!

Bonthe, Sherbro, Sierra Leone
17 October 1908

My darling Trixie, I was upstairs at about 11 o'clock yesterday morning when I heard a steamer 'tooting' and I looked through the window to see the *Batanga* pass up to her moorings behind the island in front of us. I knew she had the mails on her, I was so excited. In about an hour a boat came round the corner and came up to the landing stage here, and I saw the mail bags thrown out and ours arrived just as we were finishing lunch about 12.30. You can't imagine how lovely it was to see them, two bundles of *The Times* and *The Lancet*, and the letters on top all tied with string. I came to the drawing room, tried all the chairs, and seated myself in the most comfortable, and started on yours, then Elsie's, and then the others. I was most thankful to find they all contained good news and that dear Father's back was better. I hope in your next he will be quite all right again.

Before I forget, be sure to keep an exact account of all stamps you put on letters to send to me. Have you enquired whether it's necessary to re-stamp them? And I also think I forgot to ask you in my last to send the bill for the green and pink linen, and for the making and postage, so that I may send [a] cheque for them.

We have got very nicely cleaned up.

11 The coachman/gardener to the Roberts family at Bronceris.
12 The Roberts family's parlourmaid.

The servants (probably Sam and Greenlegs, a later servant) from a family album

Sunday 18th

I only got this far yesterday, it was so terribly hot the perspiration was rolling off my hands, and Charlie came back from Hospital with a little cold. He took it one of the first few days we were here, when he was looking after the hammock boys cleaning up, and got very hot, went upstairs, got into his gown and took cold, so he lay down yesterday afternoon and I did too, and then sat with him and mended an old pillow-slip of his.

I really must go back and give you my day's history; when I get more settled down and used to things I will write a little every day, just what I have done. Well, I must tell you that I found at Sherbro that Charlie had very little crockery, and what he had was in a wooden box with a cord round it. In getting it on to the steamer they pulled it up by the cord which of course broke, so, we were reduced to one vegetable dish and one soup plate, and two small pheasant pattern pudding plates and two other wee plates. I used to ladle out my soup and Charlie had his out of the tureen!

So we went on Friday a.m. to see what we could get at the French Company. They had only one kind of china in any quantity, but as that was pure white it did nicely. We got a nice little soup tureen, half a dozen soup plates, a dozen meat and pudding plates. They had no vegetable dishes, so we use two soup plates and they look all right. We also got a little round wicker table with a place below, 10/-, very nice; also he (the manager) let me have a dressing table of his, with a good-size mirror, all in one; it's such a boon to be able to see myself, and it has four drawers. They will want washing tomorrow; and Charlie has brought me some nice white paper from the Hospital which I will put in. We also bought three dining room chairs, brown wood and wicker seats; we had one. We also bought bedroom crockery, but the funny part is we got two fine basins, imitation Crown Derby, two nice soap dishes and two toothbrush holders, *but* no jugs, they hadn't any to match. Evidently they are never asked for. The way they do is the basins are emptied two or three times a day and filled with clean water. I shall just have to get an enamel slop pail, and jug for carrying the water up.

We got groceries too, and a baking pot for making bread. Mormoh made some bread yesterday, but baked it in the French Company's oven, and we had it for tea. Three rolls he made, rather the shape of those we used to make in the long tins, and it was nice; I quite enjoyed my tea. With bread and oily butter. Up to now we have just had dry toast of that awful bread with jam, and the mixed biscuits. What should I have done without the mixed biscuits? I really don't know. I have never opened that little tin of biscuits you gave me for the ship from Freetown, I didn't want them and the food wasn't bad, and now I'm keeping them till we get quite settled.

We may have Mr and Mrs. Beddington here too and I should like to have them then. We bought two white fruit dishes too, one low for biscuits and one high for fruit, so we are getting on.

On Friday evening the agent of this house came. Charlie had met him once before and sent him scooting, as Dr Moore had said he was no good. However Charlie thought he would try him, and said he was upset when he had called the other day, and soft-soaped him, with the result that he says the whole of the garden is ours! And he is going to put the fence right. At present it's barbed wire that has all come untied. It's rather too big a plot, that's the only thing. He says he is going to paint the floors of all the downstairs rooms, and paint the dining room walls green and white like the hall. It will look so much nicer, as it all shows. You

The house in
Bonthe, from a
family album

see, one wall of the dining room is composed of doors, there are four, which you
can lift out. We only have two in, so you see it's all open to the hall. You see the
drawing room has five windows.

The downstairs bedroom has four windows, two looking into the garden. You
see, you come up four steps from the garden, then up eight stone steps covered
over with a roof and trellis sides, and find yourself at the front door. On the
left there is a door, open it and you find a passage leading to the stairs, which
start from the end window. Upstairs, the broad passage extends right through,
a window at each end, and we sleep in the bedroom over the chop room, which
has three windows in it. We have our boxes in the other room, and the washing
stand, and use it as our dressing room. We shall have shelves there too, where we
keep our stores. In the medicine room are shelves with the drugs, now all most
beautifully tidy, but before in too filthy a state to think of. There is a table where
he mixes his medicines (this is all for his private practice). I love messing about in
there with him, and we have got it all quite tidy. The house is very light and airy,
but we have asked the landlord to give us grass mats outside the windows. I don't

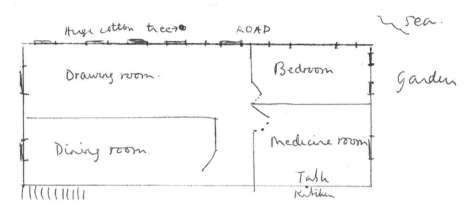

Maida Bulman's redrawing of the plan in Maida's letter

know whether he will; but the green curtains when they come will be a great relief in the drawing room, to draw when the sun is too strong. I'm going to try to get some young palms for the drawing room at least to stand in the corners near the hall. The difficulty is to get pots to grow them in.

On Friday night, Charlie got all the hammock boys working in the garden. He got 50 empty tins smashed flat and thrown away into the sea. If left outside empty, the rain fills them with water and that breeds mosquitoes. He makes the boys work, and is dead set on getting the place tidy. To think of a week today, the filth I was sitting in and that awful centipede.

I had two visitors on Friday just after tea, the two Sisters of Mercy, one Irish and one Breton girl, quite nice but uninteresting, like Miss Worsley, you know. If I asked any questions about the birds and butterflies, they looked stolid, and all I could get from them was that two parrots passed over their house each day. 'I've remarked that,' said the Irish one!

It was terribly hot yesterday and very black all round. We thought there was a tornado coming but it never came, but we have had a slight shower today.

There has been a case of the Leopard Society today,[13] but I will write about it to Father.

From the windows in the drawing room we see the sea about 50 yards away. The big garden runs down to the road along the beach. There is not a thing in it. There is a narrow strip of garden up from the gate, with a small cocoa shrub, an orange (Seville) tree, a Pawpaw tree, and one or two other small trees in it, and a few miserable flowers below, a pink periwinkle etc.

Now to go back to your letter – thank you darling, so, so much for putting all our things away. We have given you a lot of trouble, I'm afraid, and thank you for the instructions about the camera. I'm going to take one set of photos and send

---

13 See the box opposite. Unfortunately Maida's letter to her father has not been preserved.

The leopard murders

Perhaps the only reason that Maida and the other Westerners in Sierra Leone were not more frightened by the 'leopard murders' was that they did not generally target foreigners; they appear to have been a form of inter-tribal violence. The Leopard Society, also called Anyoto Aniota, was a West African secret society active in the early to mid-20th century. Secret societies and tribal conflict were both rife in West Africa, largely owing to the complex ethnic make-up (see page 12). The members of these societies dressed up in leopard skins, and were thought to become possessed by the spirits of leopards. (Similar societies channelled crocodiles and other dangerous indigenous animals.) They would then attack their victims with sharp claw-like weapons which were based on leopards' claws and teeth. The bodies were frequently mutilated and some at least of the murderers appear to have practised cannibalism.

These murders were frequent at the time the Hunters were in Sierra Leone. Colonial doctors (including Charlie Hunter) were typically called in to examine the corpses, and colonial adminstrators to preside when suspects were brought to trial.

A law was introduced in Sierra Leone in 1895 which banned the possession of leopard skins shaped and designed for wearing by men, three-pronged knives and a native medicine known as 'Borfima' which was reputed to be used in the societies' rituals. During 1903 a special circuit court, presided over by a judge who sat with assessors, was set up to try relevant cases. From 1903 to the middle of 1912 it tried 17 cases involving 186 people accused of murder. Of these 87 were convicted, sentenced to death, and in many cases executed in public. Other perpetrators were not identified.

There is a full account in K. J. Beatty's *Human leopards: an account of the trial of human leopards before the Special Commission Court; with a note on Sierra Leone, past and present* (available online at https://archive.org/stream/humanleopardsacc00beatuoft/humanleopardsacc00beatuoft_djvu.txt). Beatty was of the opinion, from his experience of leopard murder trials, that the main perpetrators were older men, and that one of their objectives in devouring parts of the victims was to increase their virility.

'Poro devils', from Beatty, *Human leopards*, p. 14.

them to Dr Keenan. He will get them done at Freetown and then tell me what I'm doing wrong, and then send the remainder to you.

We had breakfast at 8 o'clock today, porridge for Charlie and ham and eggs, tea and bananas, very good. I'm now beginning to enjoy my food. It's now lunch time, so I will stop.

I don't think I've told you about our cat. Mr Rees told me his name is Ermine, because I suppose he is black and white. He is all white except his nose which is black, also the whole of his tail, which is fairly thick, all his fur is very thick and soft like a rabbit, and he has very ugly ears, big and pink, which make look him like a rabbit. I'm not devoted to him yet, I think because we got him when he was nearly full grown. He is very funny though. I heard a great barking the other day, and there at the bottom of a palm tree was a white fox-terrier and a pup belonging to the Swiss Company, barking furiously, and Puss half-way up the tree, which had a very slippery trunk. We rushed out and sent the dogs flying, and he came down round and round, and when he reached the bottom and I carried him in he was panting with his mouth wide open, such a killing sight.

I went to the window of the drawing room just now, and down below was walking a young girl in a skirt of brilliant green plush, and a sort of mantle of brilliant Reckitt's blue plush. When she saw me she stopped and laughed, and there she is standing bolt upright. I've just been to see, and she is still there with some boys and laughing, but I stood for quite two minutes and she never moved, just stood staring straight at me. Her skirt is just a piece of stuff which is pulled round her and has white braid round the bottom. She has a dark blue cotton handkerchief tied on her head, like housemaids put to keep off the dust. I can hear her laughing now, they have a most infectious laugh. The ones who have learnt English when you pass them on the road say 'Good-evening, Missis' but those from the country say 'Boa', which is Mendi for 'How do you do?' I go for a walk generally with Charles after tea, and it's so funny to see their dusky faces over the window sill and then a broad smile with lovely teeth. Mormoh has lovely teeth, but Sam's are not good.

Monday

I have spent such a lazy day, the fact is I could not sleep till after 12.00 last night, as the cat had got into the place under the roof and was chasing lizards and frightening me out of my senses; so I felt a great rag this morning.

Mormoh had some nice fish for breakfast, which we had with coffee, which is very good, and the 'Ideal' milk I like very much. Charlie went off after breakfast to see Mrs Pigeon, who is now all right, also the priest with blackwater fever is getting up today for a little. He then went on to the Hospital, and I washed my best nightdress and best bodice in my bath water and put them through the window to dry, came down and mended two towels, and that's all I did. I find I have been such a young goose and brought no white hooks and eyes with me!

For lunch, we had fish and curried beef done with some tomatoes a woman brought to the door, they were the size of marbles. The curry would have been very good only too hot, but he really is a good cook, and two big tumblers of limeade made by Sam, he knows to a twist how to make them.

After lunch I went and lay down on the camp bed in the corridor. Upstairs there was a lovely breeze blowing, and I slept soundly and enjoyed it. We are going to have tea quite soon. I'm going to teach Mormoh tomorrow how to make 'crampog'.[14] Wouldn't you like to come and have tea with us?

Charlie is in the medicine room, making a list of drugs he wants, and I must go and help him! He says I've no trust in him when I'm frightened at night, but he sleeps so soundly that bogeys and all sorts of things could do anything they liked!

Wednesday 21st

Tomorrow is posting day, so I shall end this up today, it's already got too fat! Just when we got down to breakfast today two men came to begin the painting; so they have been at the dining room this morning, green and white. We have asked Mr Boddy the District Commissioner and Mr Reaney to dinner tonight if Mr Reaney arrives.

This morning directly after breakfast I washed my head, it had got too dreadful, then I came down and had an orange, and then tried to make a cake which is a ghastly failure. I had only eggs, flour and sugar as our butter was finished, so I tried a small sponge cake, but I had to use icing sugar which is no use. Next time I'll try a cake with butter in it, but it's so difficult to know with a cooking pot whether it's hot enough.

Oh, before I forget, my wee Belle, I tried to get the pineapple fibre dress at Freetown and they had not one left, they hoped to have one in six weeks or so, so I hope to get it some time before next summer.

We had a slight tornado last night, lovely really! Lightning and the thunder far away, but it has left the air beautifully cool.

I've not done a stroke of botany. Until the house is straight I really cannot, and even then I don't suppose I shall be able to do much. The flowers are disappointing, but I'm getting to like this place very much, and am quite well I'm very thankful to say. I don't think the mails will be here till Sunday this week.

We both think that walk round by Cefn y Coed too far for you, now don't be stupid, Belle.
Ever your very own Twisty.

P.S.   22nd October

Mr Boddy, the Assistant District Commissioner, and Mr Reaney, ditto at Victoria,[15]

14 Anglesey-style drop scones (A.B.)
15 This was transcribed as Victoris, but Victoria seems more likely. Victoria is on the main road,

came to dinner last night, and a very good dinner we had, in the hall as the dining room is being painted. Pumpkin soup, boiled fish (a new kind called mango pay or some name like that with a very nice sauce over it), roast shoulder of mutton (rather tough) and boiled pawpaw (very like vegetable marrow) and potatoes, boiled bread and butter pudding, and a savoury (scrambled egg with tomato in it), all handed round but the meat, and really very well cooked. It's wonderful how they do it. They were both very jolly. Mr Reaney announced at dinner something about his two daughters! I had forgotten for the minute that Charlie had told me he was married! I pretended not to know. They are 16 and 17 but he won't let them call him Father, they call him by his Christian name!
Ever, my own, your Twisty

24 October 1908

My own darling Trixie,
We have just had tea at 3.30 p.m. and I have seen Charlie go off in the Government boat with six oars, sitting under the awning. He was going with the dispenser to the smallpox hospital about ten minutes row down the river.

Did I tell you, we both went there the other evening, and there were a lot of young palms about, so Charlie has taken a small barrel I espied at the Hospital and is going to get me one to put in for the drawing room.

Before I go on with any more of my own news, let me tell you how interested I was in your account of your dark blue coat and skirt. It sounds exceedingly nice, also the 'Jambo' hat, and with your spectacles on! You and Bessie had a nice day at Chester. I wonder how Kate's coat and skirt has turned out, I must write to her next week, only I know that this will do duty for Bronceris for this week, as Charlie and I are starting on Monday morning for Victoria, and shall not in all probability be back till late Wednesday and the mail leaves on Thursday. So in case some unforeseen event turns up to keep us at Victoria, I'm going to leave your letter stamped here with Sam, and he can post it on Thursday.

We are taking Mormoh with us, also a piece of cold ham, which is to be carried in the saucepan it was boiled in, some plates and knives, my little kettle and condenser, the box of biscuits you gave me for the boat (I opened them today, they are *delicious*!), a pot of jam and butter; two camp beds, one of them is borrowed from the French Company, and mosquito net, bath, and one small steel box with our clothes.

The coxswain came this afternoon to say we are to start at 12 o'clock, that being the time the tide will suit us best, and Charlie says I'm to be ready in the quay at 11.30! It only takes one minute from the house. Mormoh and he can go with

---

about 50 miles north of Bonthe, half-way to Freetown. I have assumed that Mr Rainey, the original spelling here, is the Mr Reaney, Assistant District Commissioner, who occurs frequently later in the letters. S.G.C.

A native Mandingo family, old postcard sourced from http://www.sierra-leone.org/Postcards/SL195224.jpg

A Mandingo Family, Sierra Leone

the luggage and I shall go down when I see it all on board. I'm looking forward to going most awfully, I hope nothing will come and interfere. Sam is to be left here in charge. I have just been showing him how to make beeswax, so that the hammock boys can polish the dark green oilcloth on the hall and in the drawing room under the carpet while we are away. The painting is finished, but Sam and the pantry boy and the cat walked backwards and forwards over it while it was wet, so that their red footmarks are all over the green oilcloth and the stairs.

The big white wardrobe or rather cupboard (it's all shelves inside) arrived the other day before we had got up. Any furniture or big thing arriving you can always tell by shrieking and shouting as if someone is being killed! They got it no further than the bottom of the stairs, so there it has to remain. It had been painted white, but they carried it here with the paint still wet, so you can imagine what it looks like, but it's most convenient. Charlie carried all the linen into it for me, I thought it so good of him, he began while I was resting after lunch. I begged him to wait till I could help him. I found he had taken the most convenient shelf for his own shirts! when I came to examine his handiwork

We went for a very nice walk last night, and I found so many new tiny little plants. I do so wish I could identify them. I also found a lovely white honeysuckle and brought home a huge spray, which is now in a big black port bottle, my only flower vase! on the top of the case of pigeonholes, and has looked lovely, it's beginning to wither now.

It is so funny to see these big fat mammies pass. They generally look up as they pass and I say 'Good-morning', and they say 'Good-morning, Missis, ye-e-es.' Sam and Mormoh always say 'Yes, Mar' or 'No, Mar'. We woke up this morning to see Sam, Mormoh and the cat walk in at 6 a.m., Sam bringing Charlie's shaving water and the two glasses of coconut water, and Mormoh saying 'They kill beef, Sah', and the cat came to see whether we were getting up. He walked on our bed all round trying to get in under the mosquito net. He is a great nuisance at meals, he cries and although I whip him with my napkin he goes on wailing till he gets what he wants. His two favourite dishes are soup and curry and rice. How he can eat the curry I don't know, as it is so hot I have to sit with my mouth open after it. I do not like curry and it does not like me. The food here suits me very well, and I do so enjoy my meals now. Fancy, my wee Belle, I only have tea once a day and I've spoilt this half pound by putting the remains of those spoonfuls you gave me in my dressing bag into it, it has scented the whole tin, so I don 't even really enjoy my two cups at tea-time. Charlie rejoices over it and won't let me throw it away.

I must tell you it's the more genteel mammies who say good morning. The native women or Mendis, who go about with their shoulders all bare and just a country cloth put round them, right up under their armpit, when they pass and look nice, and I bow, they say 'Boa, isha.' 'Boa' means 'How d'ye do?' and 'Isha' is 'Thank you'. Sometimes they go into fits of laughter after it.

Charlie and I are going to dine with the District Commissioner Mr Boddy, tonight. I'm going in my haik skirt and lace blouse; the other night I wore my white that Miss Parry made, it is very pretty and very nice. My poor Charles had difficulty in fastening it, as the hooks and eyes were that disobliging sort that open as soon as you do the next. All I heard him mutter was 'Law', bless him!

He came back from the Hospital yesterday with the joyful news that the cucumbers were up, and today he says the French beans are well up. It was dull and rainy all yesterday, and poured all night, but yesterday was quite a cool day, and this morning it is nice and cool, and the temperature down to 75 degrees. It is now 4.30 p.m., 86½ in the hall. I have a box of seeds planted here too. Those blue convolvulus Mrs Bodvel Roberts gave me came up in 36 hours! The tomatoes have not come up yet.

All morning I sat and tried to paint the honeysuckle and one or two other tiny plants. The honeysuckle is too big a job and looks horrid. I find white flowers so difficult to paint. There are no end of sedges here and grasses. The walk we took last night was straight up through the village and then on to a little path through the bush; it was rather wet on each side of the path, hut heaps of flowers I had never seen before. They wither so quickly though. Do you remember that lovely red flower at Algiers, poinsettia? It was really floral leaves that are red. Well, there is a big white one here. Charlie says you see it in India too.

I'm expecting the mail tomorrow.

Sunday 25 October 1908

My darling, Charles and I were sitting at the open window of the downstairs bedroom yesterday evening, when we could see boats arriving full of people and their friends meeting them on the pier, and soon we saw people pass with open letters. Charlie says 'The mail must be in!' and there over the island we could see a thin line of smoke go up and we knew they had been brought by the steamer. They arrived in about ten minutes, the Post Office is just round the corner, lovely it is getting them, the 'home mail', they seem such tame little words of just four letters each, but what volumes they mean.

I got my long chair out, turned it with its back to the light and waited in it till Charles handed me mine, dear Father's, yours, one from Mrs Haddon-Smith for me, two for Charlie, one from Jess,[16] and my bill from Lees, which I told them to address to him, and which he handed over to me as if it contained an infectious disease! I read them, then had a look at the *Throne* and Charlie had a look at *Punch*, just a glance, then we had to go and have our bath and dress, and started off at 7.10, the pantry boy carrying the lantern in front.

I went in my grey and my mosquito boots. Mr Boddy was so very kind, he is due for leave on the 9th or 16th and you should have seen the red XX on his calendar! We had a very good dinner, stuffed olives, tomato soup, tinned salmon rissoles (no fresh fish came in yesterday), grilled chicken on mashed potatoes, then roast beef, boiled peas and tomatoes and potatoes, sago pudding and stewed tinned fruit and cheese savoury! Wasn't that a great dinner for a bachelor? First of all we had madeira, then champagne! and we drank the health of wives and sweethearts! That toast was done twice over by his request, which Charlie pointed out was strange! We came home at 10.00 after a very pleasant evening.

He has given me such a quaint old stone image, it is a little chimpanzee, very old, made of soapstone. He made a collection some years ago and sold them to the British Museum for £100.[17] They don't seem to know what they are but think

16 Probably Charlie's sister Jessie Wilhelmina (Aunt Billy).
17 I still have one. My brother Charles has another. Our mother Maida jr. enquired at the British Museum, which was unable to locate the remainder (100 or so). A.B.

One of Maida's flower paintings, probably done shortly before her departure for Sierra Leone. From a sketchbook in the family collection.

they must have been brought by a tribe from the interior, who got exterminated. I hope mine will bring me luck. It's a most weird-looking thing; it has a hole in its head in which a candle might have been put. He also gave me a green gauze net for butterfly-catching. He was so generous. His father is a canon of Toronto, Canada. He came out as captain in the WAF Force, and is now Assistant District Commissioner, doing Mr Page's work, who is due back on the 9th or 16th. He was due to sail yesterday, 12 o'clock, Prince's Landing Stage. Mr Boddy was repeating it over and over again, it seems to be a grim joke out here.

You ask me if it seems strange to see Charlie at his work. It did at first, he sent people spinning. It's awfully nice though, and I look forward to seeing him come back from the Hospital or wherever he has been on his rounds. If I don't hear him arrive, Sam comes in and says, 'He come.' He seems to think it my duty to be on the steps to meet him. When he is going out, he goes to the steps and calls 'Hammock' and out fly the four boys from under the house. They sit there and it's awfully nice and cool. Sam has hung a hammock there, and is off duty every afternoon from lunch till 3 o'clock. Yesterday I went out to look at my seeds and he was fast asleep in it.

Charlie got back from Hospital yesterday at 12 o'clock and at 1.00 one of the French men came to see him, and at 2.00 he was sent for to the Hospital. Such a hot time of the day. A girl had been brought in very ill; the hammock boys had not come back, so he had to walk. Sam was furious with them, said if they did it again 'Master drive them!' We had tea at 3.30 then he went by boat to the smallpox hospital and brought two very jolly palms. We had heard by wires which get sent on to York Island that you were having 'Gold Coast weather'. You can imagine what it's like here. I am today in my brown holland dress and I feel like we used to when we put on our winter flannels, but I can't say I dislike the heat at all, nor do I feel it too much, but it's early days to talk yet!

I fancy you will have got my first letter from Freetown yesterday or today, so now you will be beginning to count the time. I could have done without the white piqué coat and skirt from Hamley's; two more white drill skirts and three or four more blouses would have been far more useful. I shall go tomorrow in my holland and take a white drill skirt and blouse with me, and a complete change of under-linen.

Poor Edith, I am so sorry she feels so lonely, it's very nice your having her and Bessie. There was no news in this letter of the dear Aunties. Sambo[18] seems a great pet, I'm very glad I didn't bring him out here.

Before I forget, I should think the chest quite worth buying if you could get it for 7/- or 8/-. Would it be better as a bottom for that cupboard in the hall?

We start tomorrow all being well at 6 a.m., so I am leaving this letter addressed. Good night, my darling.

18　This refers to a cat at Bronceris, not the servant of the same name.

29 October

Here we are back again after a most wonderful trip. I really felt I was in the wilds of Africa. I have given dear Father an account of the trip, so I will not go over it again to you. I enjoyed it all thoroughly, and nothing more than coming back to our own comfy house. There is such a queer smell in the mud huts and Charlie tells me the mud is mixed with cow dung to make it stick. In our hut one night there was one of those horny black caterpillars we used to see at Crûg, do you remember, but it was as thick as my middle finger and a quarter of a yard long! There was one there when I left too. I'm most thankful we are at Bonthe and not at Victoria for many reasons. They get no fish and have to live so much on tinned stuff which I can't bear. I think though that's perhaps a habit bachelors get into of just taking a tin of something, instead of troubling to get native stuff. Mr Reaney had no oranges or bananas, said he could not get them, but Mormoh went out and very soon returned with them. We had boiled Indian corn green one day, I did not very much care for it, my piece was very hard.

Mr Reaney was so generous giving me all sorts of things, pen nibs, stamp holders and no end of things. Charlie says I'm getting spoilt! I am writing with the nib now, it's heavenly, do try and get one, Creswick's Oblique, London.

All you tell me of Sambo is very rude. I wonder if George ever got our wedding present, I've not heard from him. There was no letter from Elsie this week, I was so disappointed. Give my love to Kate and loads to you, my ownest of Belles, from Your loving M

To her father

27 October 1908[19]
Victoria

My darling father, I am going to write my letter to you from here and give you an account of our journey here.

We got up yesterday morning at 5 o'clock hut did not get away till 7 a.m., as the water was too low. We got all our luggage on board, but found in the hurry and bustle that we had come without our mosquito net, so we stopped on our way at York Island, and Mr Cortie[20] very kindly lent us one. Both our camp beds fit under it. It was a delightfully cool morning, and we were most comfortable.

We had six oars and a coxswain. Charlie and I sat under the canopy with Mormoh, plenty of cushions and our chop box at our feet. We went rowing along in and out of these low-lying mangrove islands, but did not see a crocodile or life at all, except a curlew now and again.

---

19 This letter was clearly begun before the long letter to Belle was completed.
20 The spelling of this man is variously given as Cortie and Cortes, and it has not proved possible to identify him and check which is correct.

'Life on the river', old postcard sourced from http://www.sierra-leone.org/GSpostcards-3.html

At 10 o'clock we pulled up on an island with a tiny little *fakai* (small village) on it. The men got out to stretch their legs and bought oranges for themselves. I had brought my spirit lamp with me and I boiled a cup of tea, and had it with bananas, and Charlie had the remains of a rice pudding which we had brought with us and a little bread. We rowed on and on. At one place we passed through a narrow canal. The stroke oar makes the most curious noises to encourage the others through his nose, and one sentence sounded like 'dipian d'oars'. In the boat were three instruments that looked like birch rods. The coxswain had one, but they are for lashing at mango flies and tsetse flies that come round the boat, and two were for the boatmen.

At about 12 o'clock we began to come up this river, and every now and again we would pass these little *fakais*, clusters of three or four little round mud huts, with thatched roofs and a pretty little winding sandy path leading down to the water. Nearby in the water are generally a few fish traps and lovely palm trees about them. The vegetation in patches now began to get tremendously tropical and lovely butterflies fluttered over us. One was green like the green of verdigris.

As we came up the river we passed a big coffee farm, where nearly all the coffee of the neighbourhood is grown. We landed and the chief was there dressed in blue plush; they seemed to regard me with great interest! As far as I can gather only one missionary lady had been here before. Charlie and I walked up and soon Mr Reaney came along to meet us. On each side of the road are these square or round mud huts, all detached, and perhaps a few banana trees in each garden. Mr Reaney very kindly gave us his office for our quarters, a square mud hut with five windows (no glass, only wooden doors which are open all day and shut at night if there is a tornado expected), a door, thatched roof and native matting between us and the roof proper; mud floor, and two native mats on it, but all so tidy and clean; a little rough washing stand and two little tables and a writing table at which I am now writing with every thing you could wish inside. There is a tiny little verandah just outside the door with just a thatched roof, and he has very kindly given me a photo of our quarters which I will keep to show you.

We enter through a little gate in a fence to his sandy yard, and his house is also a mud hut with an open verandah all round, a big sitting room, bedroom and pantry inside. His sitting room is a long room, and really last night after dinner it was so very romantic and picturesque. At the far end he had a gramophone and two lamps, one on the table and one on a little side table, and at the dark end of the room we three sat. I had the seat of honour, a long deck chair, and I lay back in a sea of cushions, he on one side sitting on a box and Charlie on the other, and we had songs and pieces on the gramophone and through all the open windows and doors lightnings were flashing preparatory to a tornado which came on in the night. But I wish I could give you an idea of the room: the walls covered first of all with mats here and there and on them postcards, then walking sticks hanging round, handcuffs, scales, Elder Dempster's sailing lists and all sorts of things. Outside in the distance we could hear the native tom-toms going.

I had sat on the verandah in the afternoon listening to Mr Reaney take evidence from the father and mother of the murdered girl. The mother had just a cloth from under her armpits pulled tightly round her waist and her baby on her back inside the cloth. Apparently the father is suspected of the murder, and he is now coming with us to Bonthe tomorrow to await trial. It was all very weird and Mr Reaney had an interpreter who translated as he went on. In a wild place [like] this, this is the fifth murder in five weeks, so you can imagine how thrilling it is to be here.

We retired to our hut at 9.30 last night and had a pretty bad tornado. This morning after breakfast Charlie gave his evidence and afterwards sent messengers to get children to vaccinate; he did about 30. He gets 6d a head! After lunch a man came with a present for 'Missis': a country hat, a different shape to the one in the hall at Bronceris. Charlie had operated on him in Freetown and he heard he was here. Later the interpreter came to say that he had been requested to ask if the villagers might come and dance for the doctor's wife. I was delighted and Mr Reaney told them to come after tea. Charlie had gone off with Mormoh to shoot bush fowl.

Such a crowd came. I sat in state on the verandah with Mr Reaney. I should think 100 or more men and women and a few children came. They all passed single file first just doing 'stymia' to use a Welsh word that I have no idea how to spell, but which exactly conveys my meaning. Just like children they were. Then there were six women with calabashes in a network of string with the seeds of a plant netted in. They came and shook them in my face and made a most frantic row. I bought one afterwards for 2/6. I gave a little money to the principal woman musician, and she took off her turban and wrapped it in a corner and knotted it up.

It was a weird scene and I shall never forget it. They did stare unmercifully. Mr Reaney got up and made a little speech, and said it was a great pleasure to the white woman to see them dance and she had not been prepared to see so many. The white woman had just come out from England for the first time, and it was very interesting to her to see them dance, etc. etc. I got up and made some bows to them and they grinned and rattled their shake-shakes and the two drums set to also. I shook hands with what appeared to be the two principal women and they dispersed.

Charlie came back without any bush fowl. The bush was so thick and so high, he shot one but could not find the corpse! Next morning he was up at cockcrow after them again and came back with a plump bird. It's bigger than a partridge, about the size of a hen pheasant. He missed another to his great disgust; it's a new gun he has got and one trigger goes off with hardly a touch, and the other is stiff. He had not taken aim when the wretched thing went off.

We left at 11 o'clock. As we proceeded down the village, the women and the 'shake-shakes' came up and rattled them in my face, and then the crowd went down in front of us, music all the way! It was too killing. I never had such a send-off. I was only wishing I could understand what they said to me, but they wished me no harm I fancy by the shrieks of laughter. I am very glad I got one of their shake-shakes. It will be a nice memento of a very novel experience.

We had a pretty hot journey down. The prisoner was in the bow of the boat with a warder, who fell asleep for half the way. We had two more prisoners in the boat coming to the jail here to do three months for stealing palm kernels. We got out at York Island to give Mr Cortie his net back, and he came down and made us come in. He had seen us coming ever so far away with a very powerful telescope of his, and he had got tea ready on his verandah. It was just 4 o'clock and I had had nothing since 10 except a banana, so you can imagine what that tea meant to us both. He has such a nice house and verandah, and a billiard room, all fitted up by the firm of course.

Charlie saw two patients there. One of them had put his finger in the cog wheel of the crane. As we got near Bonthe (we came at a fine pace, as we were racing another big boat with natives in it) we could see the faithful Sam at the window. I was delighted to get back, it really felt quite homelike, and Sam had got everything so beautifully clean, I really think my dear Aunt Kate would have been satisfied.

Fancy, we did not arrive back till 6 o'clock, and they had to boil a big kettle full of boiling water for the baths, and Mormoh had to feather the bush-fowl, and at 7.30 we had dinner, a very good soup, roast bush fowl, potatoes and boiled onion with an excellent sauce over it, and a savoury omelette and coffee. Pretty expeditious, wasn't it?

I was awfully amused at the way the sailors pulled when they found we were being raced; and the stroke simply shrieked out 'Dipian d'oars, *send* the watter, pull, Matsu, my friend, do,' and they stood on the seats when they were pulling the oars. Under the canopy of the other boat I could see two native damsels craning their black faces out to see how we were getting on. However we beat them as far as we went together. They were going to the French Company landing stage.

Now this is a long selfish letter, I've hardly alluded to yours which I was so delighted to get, and I shall also be looking forward to another nice walk together birds nesting, but you mustn't find a robin's nest first next time!
With best love from us both,
Your loving Maida

Bonthe, Sherbro
2 November 1908

My darling Belle,
Fancy, your letter did not come till this morning. We were expecting the overland mail all yesterday afternoon and it never came, most unusual, but there were the letters when we got down to breakfast. But no papers, they are not sent by the overland mail now, some economy of the Government, it would mean an extra carrier or something, so they have to wait for a boat. In a way it's not a bad thing, we have something to look forward to. I had only a letter from you, and one from Dr Keenan. I thought for a moment that Father had not written till I saw Charles reading one from him, and I got Kate's for me. Thank her so much for it. I shall hope to answer it by the next mail.

To begin with, I must answer your questions about the climate and my health. It's much too soon to speak yet of how it will suit me, but I've been on the West Coast now a month on Wednesday, and I can honestly say I've never felt so well; it's been quite wonderful. I'm sure I shall get to feel washed out and all that, but for all the time I've been here I've never felt better and full of buck. It's all so interesting, I don't seem to be able to convey to you in my letters how interesting it all is, and I've been so happy. Charlie has been so very good to me; and the food here is so good, and it seems to suit me; I feel so very thankful and I do hope that we shall both keep well for our tour. The days simply fly along, too short they seem, but I'm very lazy. I waste a lot of time lying down after lunch each day, but I think it's better to do so.

I've started pressing plants! Chiefly grasses so far; every one I see is new to me, so it's rather bewildering but by pressing a few every day I shall get to know them, and recognise the ones I've got. There seem to be a great variety of grasses and sedges, and also a great number of the pea-flower family. There is one dear little vetch that twines itself round grasses, with lovely green leaves and the most lovely light blue flowers, very tiny and dainty it is.

I was so amused the other night when we were going to the smallpox hospital. Charlie had gone to the District Commissioner's office, and I began collecting some grasses that were growing on the quay. A man came up. 'Them good for chop, Mar.' When I said 'No, not good for chop,' he grunted and walked away, thinking me mad, I suppose.

On Saturday morning I thought I would go and see what there was in the market, and do my own shopping, thinking I could do it cheaper by going myself, à la Mrs Leslie Roberts. I started forth in great style, with my holland umbrella and Mormoh behind with his stick and a basket. The market was a great sell: nothing in it but spoons, shells, plates etc. and a few green bananas. I wanted a pumpkin, so Mormoh said he knew where I could get one so we walked out behind the town a good long way, cottagers all along all rushing out to look at me, and I could hear great talking, something about the 'Doctor'. At last we came to the cottage with the pumpkin plant growing in front of it. Mormoh told me it was where he lodged! They brought me one out and wanted 6d for it. I said 'No, 4d,' but he turned round and walked into the house, so I came away. Another woman had one and was going to let me have it for 3d, when evidently she heard the others say 6d. I offered 4d, but she wouldn't sell it, so off I walked. On the road opposite they were building a new house, and I saw a queer flower growing. I was going to pick one, when the crowd yelled for 'Lucy!' Lucy appeared with no clothes on above her waist, and demanded a penny! I was so disgusted. Mormoh said 'It's because they see white face.' I came on, Mormoh by this time walking by my side, walking, walking through sort of waste land covered with a jungle of grasses and flowers. There were quantities of a small yellow flower, marguerite. I brought home a bunch and arranged them in a brass bowl on the table, but they wither in a day. I got home very disgusted with my marketing, the only thing I bought was 1d of green peppers. After I had been in an hour, they brought the pumpkin for 4d! It's awfully good with stewed beef.

Mr Boddy came to tea yesterday, and afterwards we three took a long walk into the bush. Lovely it was. He showed us a splendid colony of excellent pineapples that will be ripe about Christmas. I was gathering grasses, and he would bring one saying 'The British Museum will give £10 for any specimens of this!' He and Charlie are going out this afternoon at 3.30 about an hour's walk through the bush after guinea fowl. I have advised them to take an extra hammock to bring home the game! But Mr Boddy says he has a very strong boy who he thinks can manage.

I sent Mormoh out this morning to buy fish. I told him to try to get 'Spanish' and sole; he came back with mullet, saying 'No sole live, Mar, moon too strong.' It's too funny, if they can't get a thing, they say it no live. I saw a rather well-to-do nigger arrive by boat on Saturday rowed by two men. He disembarked with his luggage; amongst it was a yellow tin bandbox with a band of red, white and blue paint round it. They are evidently the fashion here. He came up the pier and started home. Soon I could see him running back, shouting to the boatman, 'You see papaar in bottom of boat?' They didn't hear him, so he yelled: 'White paper in boat?' 'It no live, Sah,' shouted back the boatman, and began looking in the sea as if he could find it there. By this time the man was flying down the pier and began searching among his luggage, and I suppose found it, because he came walking back apparently at rest. They are so funny to watch.

Yesterday after breakfast a Chief came to consult Charlie dressed in native dress, but his son who was with him was in European. The chief was troubled with his liver, the result of too much gin! He was sitting in the bedroom off the drawing room, and saluted me as he went out. I took up a convenient place near the window where I should not be seen to see him disappear. His suite! were waiting for him under the house, about four men. His bottle of medicine was handed to one (a huge black whisky bottle full) and a parcel to another, and he sailed off, with a look of deepest sulks on his face! Carrying his umbrella across his shoulders behind his back, an expression of despair on his face, due I fancy to his gin being stopped.

4 November

Thank you, my sweetest Belle, for the little mahogany frame. It's really too sweet of you to give it me. I don't like taking it because you found it, and thank you, my darling, so much for the promise of a cake. It will be really lovely to get one. I have made a few Paisley buns, but they are such a bother to make here, and one does enjoy something rather nice for tea. As we only drink tea once a day now, that ½ lb with the scented taste is still going. I shall be thankful when it's done; although in a way one gets used to it.

After Charlie and Mr Boddy had gone the other afternoon, I told Sam I should want him at 5 o'clock to come out walking with me. Just as I was on the step starting I saw the Roman Catholic priest and another asking if Charlie was in. They came up and the strange one introduced himself as the Bishop O'Gorvan! – the Roman Catholic bishop of Sierra Leone. They came in and stayed half an hour. I then started off to meet Charlie and Mr Boddy and met them quite a good way out, not seen a bird! How I laughed. They sent their hammocks and guns home and walked back with me. They had picked up a man at one of the *fakais* who said he would show them where they lived, no signs of any bird, so Mr Boddy said 'Where them bird?' and pointed his gun at him. The man edged round and round, Mr Boddy following still keeping his gun on him till he got near a native hut, and he jumped through the mat wall of it and disappeared into the bush and they never saw a sight of him after. They simply roared. Mr Boddy asked his boy why he ran away, and he said 'He fear for die, Sah!' We had a big tornado that

Charlie being carried by the hammock boys, from a family album

night, the wind roared and the house shook; but the thunder and lightning was not very dreadful.

Yesterday being my birthday we had the duck killed, and in the afternoon Charlie went to return the bishop's call, but he had hardly been in the house a few minutes when he saw a big tornado coming, and thinking I should be frightened he came back and we sent a note asking him to dinner instead. He wrote back a nice little note saying he would be delighted, and he arrived at 7.15. We had sago soup, fried fish, roast duck (excellent) and rice boiled with some native plums, which the washerwoman, Sarah Peters, had brought me on Monday with some oranges, and coffee. He was such an interesting man. He has been out nearly a year, travelling all over the country; and he is so interested in everything he sees. He was talking of the Leopard Society, and Charlie was saying from the nature of the wounds it must be an adept at the work, that he thought one or perhaps two must be doing all the murders. And the Bishop said the knife that makes the fatal wound is sacred and is always supposed to be in the care of one man, and that it is supposed always to be kept in condition with human blood. He was coming here the other night on the mainland from Moyamba on the railway, and sitting passing round through the outskirts of one *fakai*, he saw a hut with five or six men sitting round a fire at 3.30 a.m.; he said it looked very suspicious and if he had been a district commissioner and caught them he would have had them all up.

I was so surprised to hear you were going to Glen, but so very glad, I'm sure the change would do you good. I'm thankful Clerke has at last found something that would account for your toothache, but are you taking that medicine Charlie prescribed for you, you ought to, and take plenty of vegetables. I've now got a slight pain in that tooth he filled for me, at the back, he evidently didn't do it properly; I'm afraid he is past his best.

I'm really going to try to take the photos tomorrow a.m. and send them off to Dr Keenan.

We finished the little biscuits for tea yesterday, and I am trying to make some plain scones for tea today, the bread is so doughy. Could you, my wee Belle, send me in a newspaper some dried sage leaves? I can't buy them here, and I see some very nice geese strolling about that would be very nice with sage stuffing in them. Please put all these things, hairnets, postage and all down in your account for me.

5 November 1908

I shall have to send this letter off in a hurry, as I took the opportunity of Charlie's having gone to York Island to have the hammock boys in to clean the windows, and they have been at it an hour. They look awful. These hammock boys nearly drive me frantic, they are so dull and so stupid, and they are actually afraid of standing on the window ledge. Charlie had quite a busy morning before he started. The Chief came again at 8 o'clock feeling better, which is a good thing for him to own, as they never will. It appears he was on his way to Freetown to see Dr Kennem, the black doctor there, and came to Charlie instead. He pays £1.1.0 a visit, so I hope his cure will be sure but fairly slow! Then came a family party, father, mother and wean; and a man from the Swiss Company with a note from the manager to say his pony had run away in a *fakai* and kicked a little child, but he thought it was only a scratch, but sent the child to Charlie to satisfy the parents. The poor little thing's arm was broken, and I had to help while Charlie set it. I hated hearing the poor little thing cry. During this time the hall was full of people as it was pouring a simple deluge outside.

My garden is really beginning to show something now. The French beans are a foot high, the marrows nice young plants planted out, and I have sown two rows of French beans straight into the ground, the others are the tall ones, and I have sticked them. Could you, dear Belle, get me two packets of parsley seed from Ryders, St Alban's, and four packets leek seed, and two of young onions for West Africa. Also dear Belle, buy for me and send it if you will be such a dear in the Christmas box you so sweetly said you were going to send, a gunmetal watch for Sam like that one I gave Charlie, only I think you can get them for 12/6 or 15/6. I don't want to give more; also a little strap chain, I think you can get them from the saddler's. I am sending a blank cheque, also a tea cup and saucer like mine of Indian Tree for Charlie's birthday present. I am sending a blank cheque, so will you fill in what you want after you have paid for hairnets and all expenses for me.

A native chief in Sierra Leone, 1910, from an old postcard by Lisk Carew Bros, sourced from http://knowledgeequals-blackpower.com/post/36352941273/grand-bazaar-1910s-sierra-leone-chief-in

Charlie will send a cheque to dear Father for the silver insurance when we hear what it is, and our grateful thanks for all the trouble you have had.

Now I am going to write a letter to dear Father and Elsie; with my best love and to dear Kate, and tell her I will thank her so much for her nice darling letter, which I hope to answer next week, and with best love to you, my darling, and best to the dear Aunties.

Ever your own Twisty

I was amused about Sambo and the canary. I'm afraid he will try to take him for chop one day! Mr and Mrs Pidgeon went up one of the rivers last week and she got a young leopard given her. He came in while I was calling, he was adorable, but would soon grow a bother, I'm afraid, and their parrot was terrified of him. I hope you will send me a paper with the grand wedding in it! These pens are very bad wearing ones.

To her father

5 November 1908

My darling Father,

How the weeks slip along; we have been in West Africa one month on Saturday, which will be the 7th, and it has been a very happy month. I like the life here very much, it is so full of interest, and never a week passes but we have someone in to call or to dinner. This week we had Mr Boddy the District Commissioner here to tea on Saturday and Monday, and after tea on Monday he and Charlie went off shooting. They had heard there was guinea fowl not far away, so they went off in great style, bags of cartridges, and my parting words were not to shoot one another and to leave a few birds for another day. One of Charlie's hammock boys was to show them the way, and he took them to a *fakai* a good way out. They asked a man in the village if he knew where the birds were, and he led them on but not a feather did they see. Mr Boddy pretended to fly into a rage and terrified the man so much he jumped through the mat wall of a hut and disappeared into the bush, and no calling or anything with else would bring him back. So when I went out at 5.30 to meet them with Sam as escort they were both returning empty-handed. How I laughed!

While they were away the Roman Catholic bishop of Sierra Leone called, a very nice and interesting man. He is Irish, but has spent most of his life in Brittany and the USA and West Africa. For the whole of this year he has travelled about the country walking every step of the way, he never takes a hammock. He came to dinner on Tuesday night and we had a very pleasant evening. I think they are all very fond of Charlie; he saw a good deal of them at Freetown, and they are also very pleased that the sick priest here made such a good recovery from blackwater fever. There was another priest ill at Mogamba in the Protectorate of the same thing, hut he died, poor fellow. They stay here for such a long time before they give in; this one is to go to the Islands for a change.

Charlie has also a chief as patient now from up one of the big rivers; Chief Fatomah his name is, he had a very nice face, and gives me sweeping bows as he comes in and goes out. He comes attended by his son and about eight or nine carriers; he is staying here now for treatment.

The garden and grounds look very different from when we arrived. I am so dreadfully sorry I have not been able to take a photo yet. I had intended doing it today but it poured; they have to be sent off as soon as they are taken; but I will send them to Freetown all being well next week. It is a big square plot of ground like Bronceris garden, so rather difficult to handle, as the Americans say; but down the centre we have planted a double row of banana trees. They are only 4 ft high now but will soon look very nice. Then I have a plot for cucumbers and vegetable marrows, and on the other side a small plot of scarlet runners.

Charlie has gone off to York Island and is staying [for] lunch there or he would

send a message I know; he was very glad to get your nice letter.
With best love dearest Father,
Ever your loving Maida

P.S. I'm afraid our present of a silver fruit dish to George has got lost; we have
never heard from him.

Monday 9 November 1908

My own darling Belle,
No, your letter never came, so it shows that if they miss the 11 o'clock post at
Caernarvon on Friday they will not catch the mail; however I was glad to get
the wee note and dear Father's letter so I know you are all right, and I shall look
forward to two budgets next week. I only got your letters, and one from Mrs Grey
thanking for the little Welsh doll; no letter from Elsie, I hope she is quite well.
Time is flying along with me, the only trouble is that I do so little, I mean that I
get so little done.

Last Thursday and Friday I was busy sewing half-blinds for the downstairs
bedroom; the muslin was narrow but cheap, 10 yards for 2/-, so I had to put two
on each window, that made eight to be made so it took some time. They look very
nice in the day, but last night we made the unfortunate discovery that they can be
seen through, so I shall have to make plain pieces of dark print to put on at night
if we have anyone staying here.

After being for ten days without any boat three have now been in, so they
brought us our mails and newspapers on Friday. The *Bakana* came straight from
England and brought the District Commissioner Mr Page. He called in the
evening (with Mr Boddy) and has been most attentive but he is a holy terror; I
daresay a good servant to the Colonial Office but awful. When we came down to
breakfast on Saturday morning there was a note for me: 'The District Commissioner requests the honour of Dr and Mrs H. etc. to dinner at 7.30. R.S.V.P.! I
wrote back 'Dear Mr Page ...'. At 7.30 we sallied forth. Charlie felt obliged to
put a stiff shirt on and a dinner coat, I went in my pineapple dress. We found Mr
and Mrs Pidgeon there, she in a low dress the bodice hanging off shoulder straps
that were very loose and a short skirt, very messy blue crepe de chine, and an
orange-coloured waist band; she would talk the hind leg off a donkey as we used
to say. Well, we went in to dinner and of course his servants were all new and had
to be howled at, terrible it was, but the worst of all was that a tornado came on at
9.30, torrents of rain, which kept us there tied by the leg till 11.30 p.m.! As you
know my poor Charles gets drowsy after 10 p.m. but by 11 o'clock his face was
a picture, I had not to look at him in case I laughed. Mr Pidgeon is amusing to
listen to as he never bothers about any of his Hs – 'aggling, 'ankering, 'uge and all
that. Killing it is but frightfully common.

Yesterday morning I read the 'service' and then tried to paint a shrub I found in flower; my paintings are not a great success. For lunch we had a queer native fruit called sowsop or some such name; it's like a fat short cucumber with a dull green skin and blunt prickles on it, and you slice it like a pineapple. The flesh is dead white and the seeds this big: [circle]. Jet black; it's very luscious and rather nice. Mormoh also brought a pineapple for 2d, we've not tried it yet.

On Saturday night I walked as far as the Hospital with Charlie and in a little house opposite I saw the native plums growing, a big forest tree with leaves like an ash tree only more leaflets and brighter green, and covered with these big plums. We asked the woman if she sold them and she said 'Yes, three for one copper,' that is, three for a ha'penny. So we got six for 1d. I gave Mormoh two yesterday to stew to make a summer pudding and if it had had a little longer to stand it would have been awfully good. I made a boiled custard on my little spirit lamp and M. watched me and I told him to keep it and pour it over the 'punny'. When Sam brought it up there was only the custard nearly solid. He had taken it out, added sago to it and thickened it, and no sign of the summer pudding! They brought it in and I turned it out at the table and poured the other over it.

We took a walk after tea; I had made some more of those Paisley buns, and put apricot jam inside and Mormoh baked them to a turn and they were 'boach'.[21] Charlie takes two, and they only make four mouthfuls, and they take such a time to make and hot, hard work! Poor me!

Today is a holiday – the 'King's Birthday' – and who came at breakfast time but Mr Page to ask us to go a picnic with him to Bendu on the mainland. Charlie told him Mr Cortie had half promised to take us on the steam launch to the *Sheeba*, the open sea, but however he never came, but after no end of a muddle it ended with in our going off the Coaling Company steam launch with Mr and Mrs Pidgeon and Mr Sharman of the Coaling Company, and Mr Page came too. There was a lovely breeze on the water and we got there in about 20 minutes. The landing was really killing. We had to jump down first of all into an old boat in which two wicker chairs had been put for Mrs Pidgeon and me. The bottom of the boat was full of water, but they bailed it out. It was then found there were no oars, so we had to be pushed along by bamboo poles till we got as near the shore as we could, when we had to be carried ashore by two niggers. Mr Page, always over-anxious to be alert, got astride on the shoulders of a nigger (that's how they often carry men ashore) but the water was so deep and the nigger's legs stuck in the mud, that for a few moments Mr Page's fate hung in the balance, the nigger swayed to and fro and couldn't move, and Mr Page clung on to his head for all he was worth. I was just longing to see them both go over, and I was shaking with laughter, and all the savage niggers on shore were yelling and shaking with laughter too, it was lovely. I wished it would last longer, but no, Mr Page like a cork always floats, and he was

21 Delicious – origin unknown, perhaps an invented family word. M.B.M.B.

landed on the dry yellow sand with a satisfied look on his face, but we had had a good laugh.

There is nothing left of Bendu except a Police Station and telegraph office. It was, before the 'rising' ten years ago, a flourishing little town. I was hoping to find some shells on the lovely golden sand I can see gleaming from here, but there were none. We walked up through the bush as far as the Police Station, sat there for a few minutes on the verandah of a native hut and had a drink of water; it was blazing hot. The flowers are certainly more varied on the mainland, but I don't collect them, it would only bother me. We got back on the launch and had tea on the launch, it certainly was 'the cup that cheers', how thankful I was to get it, and we got back here at about 5 o'clock. We had had a very enjoyable afternoon.

I wrote last night and asked Mr Page to dinner tonight, as he is going off tomorrow on patrol for a month. I'm going to give him a good dinner following Mr Punch's advice of 'Feed the brutes'! Here's the menu – sago soup, fish (kind unknown yet, the little dugouts have not come in yet, I can see them dotted about all round), chicken cream, that is, chicken pounded and mixed with bread crumbs and an egg, and some lean ham pounded, and put into a jam pot to steam, and turned out; fourth course, beef olives with fried potatoes in the middle; summer pudding of native plums; and cheese savoury made of grated Gruyère cheese in scrambled egg; very good; and pineapple as dessert, a beauty it is too. Now isn't that a good dinner for the wilds of swampy West Africa? Tomorrow I'll [tell] you all being well how it all turned out. I hope neither Charlie or I will have to yell any orders at Sam, it quite puts me off to hear servants slated at meals. He never has to be reprimanded so I don't see why he should tonight.

I am now going to write to Emily Pattullo. Charlie is still at the Hospital. He walked there today and I had the hammock to take me to the French Company.

Wednesday 11 November

Just before sitting down to my letters I looked through the window and a black girl was walking along carrying a gourd full of cassada on her head. She looked up and saw me and said 'Mammy Boa'! And last night after tea Charles and I spent an hour gardening instead of going for a walk; and as I was planting tomato seeds with Charlie and three hammock boys I heard someone laugh and say 'Missis, I help you?' and there were two fat jolly-looking Mammies dressed in print gowns and their husbands all watching and laughing. They think a white woman strange enough, but one who works in the garden they think very funny I think. The hammock boys dig the ground with big kind of knives they call machetes, and Charlie rakes and bosses!

Well, our dinner passed off very well. The only dish that I did not care for was the chicken cream, it was dry; but Sam waited so nicely, and it all went off smoothly with one exception: our poor cat cannot get over the evil habit of screaming [and] crying till he gets his soup! We whack him with our napkins but no, he throws himself down full length and looks up at me and says 'I do try, but I can't help it.' I got him too old for him ever to be like Pop, but he amuses us both very much, he is full of character. I was taking my bath this morning when I saw him sauntering down through the garden across the road to two Government sailors. He rubbed himself against their legs and made them take notice of him, then he went on past the customs to a boat-house to look for lizards. In a short time he was to be seen galloping back with a young lizard, and I am sorry to say he only plays with them, cuts off their tails and lets them go.

Then he is very friendly with the hammock boys, and when they are chopping their rice and palm oil under the house he goes down to them and comes back with a streak of palm oil on him. Then after dinner when the servants have gone we sit with the front door wide open and generally Puss goes out for a prowl, when suddenly he rushes and gallops in, his tail huge and thick, and twisty ears, some dog, generally the Coaling Company's terrier after him! Then he amuses me in the morning when it's hot and I just go round the garden: he follows with his mouth wide open, panting!

At 11 o'clock I'm going to make a Paisley jam sandwich for tea. So you see I have heaps to do: in fact the days are not nearly long enough.

We had a baddish thunder storm last night, lightning coming from two sides incessantly, but it was not very near, and I was actually too sleepy to watch or be afraid.

I must now write to dear Father, and I am afraid I shall have to ask dear old Kate to wait another week. Give my best love to the dear Aunties and Bessie and anyone you think would care for any! Very very much love to my own young Belle from Twisty

I don't know what you must think of my letters all about myself, and I have never once hoped you have a jolly time away.

17 November 1908

My darling Trixie,

Very many thanks for your two lovely long letters; they arrived on Sunday afternoon. I was so delighted to get them and one from dear Father and Kate, but nothing from Elsie or George. Letters are always nice but out here they are just lovely. I also got a little slip to say a parcel had come, they would not deliver it till Charlie went there to claim it and declare what it contained. Charlie opened it but never saw the photos. I think the one of you is just splendid, but, Belle, not good and kind of you to get such a waggish hat, there is a proud look on you all over! You know it makes me long to have a hat to perch on one side like that, and that lovely pink [illegible], not good Belle, not good and kind! I have put you in that frame Roderic gave you, and it looks just lovely, and you stand on the pigeon holes in front of me as I write; and then the accounts of those blouses Miss G. has been making for you all sound proud cat.

I am so very very thankful to hear you have at last got rid of your toothache; but here at this safe distance I think I might murmur 'I told you so.'

By now I expect you are home from your holiday spree, the little worm! I can see him wriggling into the drawing room.[22]

I am so sorry dearest Father has had 'India'.[23] I've had a regular bout too on Saturday and Sunday, just the usual 'sickish like' and India pain. I fancy I had been taking too much vinegar in the avocado pears. I asked Sam if he thought them 'good chop for the body', and he said with much stammering, 'If pick off tree ripe they good, Mar. If pick off tree young and leff for ripe they strong Mar.' And that's what we had done, bought them green and left them to get ripe as Father used to do with the tomatoes, I always used to say I thought they were not so good for one that way, so I was much interested to find that in West Africa they thought the same. However Charles gave me a very noxious medicine of Bismuth etc. which is real good for the body! and he has promised me a tonic. As you can imagine it's a real pleasure for me to go and see them made; I think Charlie has some very good receipts in his head for medicines because he has had a wonderful cure with old Chief Fatomah. He was so very bad when he arrived and now he is nearly well and most delighted and thankful. On our walk last night we passed his house and he and one of his sons came out and were so polite. He is quite a nice specimen; some of the chiefs look utter brutes and are tyrants I believe. He is to be here another week or so, and then he will be let loose to go back up the 'Big Burn' river where he comes from.

Well, my dear, on Sunday morning I reduced myself to a pulp (excuse the expression) of heat and nervousness taking my first roll of films which have been dispatched to Dr Keenan. I got so muddled with all the different things that I just clicked them off anyhow in desperation. I am so sorry I forgot what I call the third mouth Charlie has to feed – Mr Puss, he will have to be taken next time. Goodness only knows whether they will come out.

This is a terrible country to garden in. The little plot I first sowed is a rank failure; only two scarlet runners are any use, and only one cucumber is growing at all. A fearful tornado of rain one night helped to finish the scarlet runners and then the hedge on that side of the garden is full of land crabs, which have evidently enjoyed them as a salad. But the plot on this side under the bedroom window looks much more promising. It's about 15 yards square, hedged in with tall palm leaves to act as shelter from sun and rain. Then I shall have four rows of French beans, they look as if they are going to be much better than scarlet runners; a row of cucumbers also

---

22　Rather a mystifying comment, but as transcribed.
23　This seems to be a term for an upset stomach.

covered with palm leaves like little tents, and a double row of the tomatoes planted out with thick palm leaves on both sides, so you have to peer under to see how they are getting on. They spring up so quickly out of the ground and then seem to get disappointed with life, and ask one another that much hackneyed question that one used to hear preachers so often quote, 'Is life worth living?' Apparently to some of them if they have to cope with land crabs, or [illegible] as they call them here, and the climate, it isn't worth living and you go and seek them and find them not, and your dish of scarlet runners or boiled cucumbers looks rather hazy.

But every night Charlie and I and the three hammock boys sally forth with three murderous-looking cutlasses, our only tool for digging, weeding and planting besides a rake, and work away for a good time. The other night we earthed up the French beans and it was as well we did so as we had a tornado and the extra earth supported them; they all look most healthy. Puss always accompanies us and rushes in and out of the palm-leaf hedges wildly with lashing tail till we stop him when he flies off and up a tree, full pelt, and comes down with his mouth wide open panting!

I can't write any more till Charlie comes in for paper.

Wednesday

I forgot to tell you that Saturday and Friday I was very busy making marmalade from the oranges in the garden – four or five bitter ones and I put one sweet one and one lime. I unfortunately did not boil it quite enough, the first boiling, so it had to go on again on Monday, and now it is just a tiny bit gluey, but Charlie says it's very good. It is very sweet, I can 't understand that, as I had 7½ lbs of the stuff – fruit and water – and I put 8 lbs of sugar to it. I fancy the reason is that the oranges have not so much flavour as the Seville ones. In making it I had a striking example of 'Necessity is the mother of invention' as we found no saucepan big enough to boil it in, so we boiled it in a bucket! Although I heard Mormoh mutter that 'the bucket's heart was not strong enough for boil', but it boiled it very well. When pineapples are in season I will make pineapple jam; the sugar is 4d a lb here, that's the only bother.

I find the pressing of the plants a great job.[24] Moving those heavy boxes nearly does for me, and if I have Sam with me it sort of bothers me; and the plants look so hideous after they are pressed. It is wonderful how quickly the days pass, they are too short because you cannot do hard work as you can in England for long at a time, you feel exhausted after it.

Did I tell you Mrs Pidgeon came to have tea with me on Friday? I must write a little every day or else I forget what I have told you. I made some London buns with apricot jam and they were very good. She is a frightful little gas-bag, like Mrs Arthur. After tea we took a little walk with her and called for her husband.

---

24 This refers to the collection of pressed plants she was doing for the British Museum. M.B.M.B.

They are both very common; he is the best of the two in a way. On Sunday night when Charlie and I were sitting on the pier we could see them go off in one of the steamer's steam launches, and today she has sent for Charlie again. She took a chill; I'm afraid she is not very strong.

After Charlie had gone to the Hospital today I happened to look through the window and saw three native women pass; they said 'Boa' and then stopped and asked for copper. I laughed and said 'You got plenty copper' (they were half in fun I think). 'You got more copper pass me.' 'No,' they said 'you got white man, we got black.' 'But look your grand earring and ring.' I said. 'My ring silver, your one gold,' she said. Then she asked if I had scent. I said I never used it. 'You use grease,' they said, and made signs for rubbing my hands and face. I said 'No' but I thought for the fun of it I would get my scent and give them some on their hands, so I beckoned them to come round. Only one had the courage to come and I put scent on the end of her nose and lip and said 'You like it?' and she giggled and laughed. Then I put some on her gown and she said 'Give me the bottle, Missis' and held out both her hands. She really was quite charming. How I laughed and said 'And what I get then?' and she laughed and went. She was a Mendi girl; they dress in the native dress, a cloth drawn tightly round their bodies, and a turban of a gaily coloured cotton or silk handkerchief. The Mammies – Creoles they call themselves – who live in Bonthe are descendants of the freed slaves of Sierra Leone. They dress in trailing print gowns and a turban, and only speak pigeon English. I am told there is great jealousy between the two, and to the great joy of the Mendi tribe two Creole youths are in jail now for three months hard labour for stealing out of the Swiss store and Mr Pidgeon's store; they were clerks.

There is such a charming little brown bird, it looks like a pipit of sorts, and it has such a pretty note, rather like a blackbird, and it can lift a little crest on its head. Sam says it chops peppers; it perches itself on the palm and warbles away in the early morning so cheerily. The colony of palm birds is in great force. They have young now. A boy brought me a nest with four eggs in, but they were all nearly hatched so I had to throw them away. The nests are wonderfully made with little doors to them; but they are aggravating little birds with their eternal twitter. I don't mind the noise now but poor Puss! He sits on a tree, and his jaws quiver to get at them, and they enjoy it and come hopping all around him.

When I went to the Hospital with my man the other day I saw a fine tree covered with the most lovely orange-coloured sort of laburnum, only much closer bunches of flowers. I found it was a leguminous tree and the ground was strewn with the pods, and we find the natives boil and eat them. Each pod contains one bean as big as a broad bean; we are having a dish boiled for lunch, chamby or chambé the natives call them.

Last night after tea while Charlie and I were gardening Chief Fatomah passed with six men walking behind. He saluted and in a few minutes he sailed into

'Leopards climbing a tree', from an old postcard, sourced from http://www.sierra-leone.org/Postcards/SL628670.jpg

the garden alone with one man. I never saw anyone walk with more dignity; he shook hands with us both and called me Madame! I asked him how to kill land crabs, and he said 'Pour boiling water down their holes.' If you could have seen the hammock boys work while he was there, as hard as they could! I told Mormoh when it was dark to try the dodge of boiling water, and after dinner he brought a chader in. He met it out of its hole and threw the boiling water over it and killed it. After the Chief went Charlie and I walked as far as the Hospital. I went in; the women's ward has about ten beds in it and they were all occupied. They were very interested in me.

It's too bad, our newspapers have not come this week, and there is no boat due till 26 November, terrible it is. I was so much interested in your visit to Glenn and look forward to your next letter. How many suitors has Gertrude now?

The average temperature in our drawing room is 80 degrees; when we came down to breakfast this morning it was 75.

Now, my own young Belle, I must stop. I am going to write to Kate and Father. In the next *Punch* would you put me in a couple of rows of white pins medium size. In your account of your tea at the Vicarage you said '___ sang really awfully well.' Who was it? Mrs W. J.?

I went by hammock to the French Company yesterday morning. I wanted coffee and coffee cups.

Best bestest of loves and give my dear love to Auntie Kate. I am so glad dear Auntie M. has gone off to Henley Park.
Your own loving Twisty

20 November 1908

My darling Trixie,
I posted your letter yesterday after I got back from York Island, but I am going to try and write a little each day now.

It is 10.45 a.m. I have been busy since breakfast with my dried specimens. I've been at them for nearly two hours. They are most unsatisfactory; the leaves of the shrubs all turn black and drop off as I press them. Then I have to write little notes inside each about the plant and enter it in a book. If only they looked nicer when they are finished. I've had no time to touch my paints all week.

Yesterday as I told you I went to York Island; we did not stay [for] lunch. I sat on Mr Cortie's verandah, and he sat with me while Charlie went to the other firm and saw the sick people. On our way there we saw three crocs, one a little baby one; he was lying on the mud bank of one of the islands, the other two were swimming. As we came home the sand banks were all up and women on them digging for shell fish which they call 'langer-langer', a white edition of that pink shell we found at St Maxime in two valves. And a heron we saw. Lamina the boatman said there were egrets on the other side of the island. After lunch I helped Charlie with the blood-sucking flies; they seem only to be able to find one kind. They have their wings crossed like a pair of scissors.

At 3 o'clock I made my first lot of crampog and Mormoh baked them. He was rather flurried over the frying of them as he arrived late (they are off duty from 1 o'clock to 3 o'clock) and we all, Sam included, scolded him, so he did not bake them as well as he could do.

After tea I went to see how Mrs Pidgeon was. I found her better sitting in the verandah; at the far end was the leopard asleep. They have to chain him now, but she is not a bit afraid of him and brought him on a chain to me. He rubbed himself on my sunshade and then showed signs of getting a wild cat as he saw I was strange, so she tied him to the leg of a table. It's such a pity they will very soon have to cage him. The captain of a ship had brought her two cakes, one just like a small wedding cake with white icing and silver balls. The inside! It had made them all sickish; it had too much butter in it and was altogether stodgy. I came back and

Maida's photo of Charlie at home in Bonthe, from a family album

then walked to the Hospital with Charlie. The women like to see me. One was enclosed in screens the day before yesterday. When Charlie went inside the first thing she said was 'Where is Missis?' so I went in and she took my hand and said 'Thank God for the Doctor, God bless him, and you too Missis' – and a lot more I could not make out. She was funny. Charlie had been very cross with her the day before as he found her lying with her feet on the pillow!

Last night just as I had dropped off to sleep he was called out to the Postmaster's wife three doors off. He left me alone in the house with Puss and locked us in. He was back in about three-quarters of an hour; he had been very busy this morning too. There are ten more men in jail for stealing palm kernels; and patients coming to see him and waiting for him. I'm laughing as I write this, so like can't you hear doctors' wives talking, you know! But that is the best of this place, there is plenty to do, and being on the road it is so lively.

I forgot to tell you the other day as we were returning from our walk a young man came up to us and asked us if we would like to buy two young leopards. Charlie said he would have taken them if we had been coming back to England but we had only just come out. Charlie was thinking if they had been male and female he might have taken them to the Zoo and seen what they would give for them; if they wouldn't buy them we would send them to Bronceris and Walters could have had one as a pet!

Sunday 22 November

My darling childie, I had a busy morning yesterday. I went first of all by hammock to the French Company, came back and made a Paisley jam sandwich and some scones as we thought Mr Cortie from York Island was coming to tea. However we got a note last night to say he had to go up the rivers so could not come, but he is sending the launch for us at 3 o'clock to go and see one of his men who is ill, so we will take tea before we go. The jam sandwich is good, but this Ideal milk does not make very nice scones.

After my cooking I felt tired so took an orange and then went at my pressed plants till lunch. After lunch I went upstairs and took down my hair and rubbed it with the lotion Charlie gave me; and lay down and slept for two hours and then had tea and went for a walk, had dinner and a game of piquet. After we get in from our walk at 6 o'clock I always have a wineglassful of vermouth and so does Charlie, or else a small whisky. I enjoy the vermouth so much, it's slightly bitter; do you remember how Captain Hankin always took it before dinner? That's all the stimulant I ever take except if I go out to dinner and there is champagne. I've had two champagne dinners! and when we have anyone in we have a bottle of Madeira which I have a glassful of. So that's all my tipple. Charlie is true to whisky, but very often only has it once a day. Oh! we are a most temperate couple!

Then after dinner we have our brass coffee pot brought in and I make the most [illegible – ? delicious] coffee, 1/- a lb; it is 4d a lb if you bake your own beans. We have offered to buy Mr Reaney's coffee mill and if we get it I shall try to bake our own beans. I greatly enjoy coffee for breakfast too. Yesterday our breakfast consisted of porridge for Charlie; while he is eating it Puss and I wait and watch the coffee boil, then we had two fried mullets, then a piece of baked cassada. It is a root, as thick as a parsnip at the thick end; it's baked in the wood ash, then the skin taken off and you eat it with butter and salt; it's awfully good. Cassada is what they make semolina from. Then bananas for our last course which 'go' awfully well with coffee, try it. So we have nice breakfasts, don't we?

Today we had fish curry with a border of rice; Charlie and Puss like it for a change. I've got nine plums in the house; I'm going to try and make jelly with them, but I have a suspicion that jams and jellies have a tendency to turn to syrup in this country when you boil them.

Greenlegs is becoming quite a good servant; he has 'plenty brains' and uses them; and he is so anxious to learn, and just fancy, he was the one of the four hammock boys who was straight from the bush. The other three are a lazy lot; I think Charlie will send them off at the end of the month and get one new one and only keep two hammock boys for a few months.

We are expecting the mails today, lovely. I've had three little dark red roses in an empty magnesia bottle behind your photo since Thursday; I got them at York Island.

Tuesday 24 November, 2.00 p.m.

I've just been in the greatest excitement. While we were at lunch we heard a steamer tooting, and we flew to the window of the medicine room and soon saw a big grey German steamer come in sight. They anchor there just about 2½ miles away, all the German ships do. Soon we could see streams of boats going out to her from here, and now the curtains and cake have both arrived! I'm not allowed to open the cake till our own I made is finished, and I'm just dying to, you have no idea how I long to taste it, and the lovely pleasure it is unpacking parcels from home. Everything is kept, the paper, string and contents! The curtains are *very* nice, their being so narrow is no harm at all here, they are quite wide enough and not so wide that they would [illegible] insects, tell dear Auntie Kate. Sometimes I've written home for things and regretted it before the things arrive, but not so with these, they will be the greatest comfort, as the drawing room is so light with all the windows that it is sometimes trying for the eyes; and I am so glad to have the tea-cloth, I've put it into the linen cupboard. The linen cupboard is my greatest delight. As I told you it stands at the bottom of the stairs, about 6 ft high with shelves, and my little store of linen fascinates me, and on the bottom shelf I have a wooden box with eggs (for eating!) and my store of coffee and rice. One shelf has Charlie's shirts on.

On Sunday we had a very quiet happy day. Charlie does not go to the Hospital so we have a nice lazy morning, although he is always doing something, and he read me the Psalms. The boat to take us to York Island never came till 4.45 but we went; it was a strange feeling being rowed by six naked (except for small loin-cloths) black men. Not one of them could speak a word of English. We got to York Island and just stayed half an hour for Charlie to have time to see the sick man and back again as hard as we could go to get home before dark. Such a lovely sky I shall never forget it; it was 'plums and custard' and then above that pale green, and then a purply glow and on that palest greenish white clouds.

We took 45 minutes to come back and they were chanting some weird African part song. It was just dark when we got back. The home looks always very comfy when we get back with Sam and Puss always there. We were very disappointed when we got back to find the mail not arrived. After dinner while Charlie was sitting smoking I heard oars, and I thought it must be the overland mail, so Charlie and I just walked down to see, Puss accompanying us in a wild mood. The stars were glorious. Out of the dark boathouse emerged the black boatman who said they had taken the mail bags to the Police Station for the night as the Post Office was closed. I was so wild, especially as Charlie had not had his papers the week before and we hoped they would come: and he had been so good to the Post Master's wife when her baby arrived.

However we had the joy of them next morning, a lovely one from you and dear Father and Kate and Elsie, and all good news except poor George and his troubles. I am so sorry to hear of it, and I hope by now that Winnie is better; poor thing, it is such a painful thing – and poor Gertrude Walker too. You seemed to be having a very jolly visit to Hilda's, I am so glad my darling. As I write we have been having the most appalling cracks of thunder, no lightning and now downpours of rain. I hope it stops before we go for our walk. It will do the French beans good.

26 November 1908

My darling Belle,

I've had to hurry with my letters as it's been a busy morning. While we were dressing Charlie espied one of the hammock boys strolling up and down the road not doing work he had told them to do. So the day began with Sam getting a good rating from us both and then the hammock boys were paid and told never to let Charlie see them again. Then I've been trying to make some plum jelly with these native plums; we use them stewed but there is a horrid hard fibre in them so I thought I would try jelly; it looks lovely. I've put a little into two egg-cups for Charlie and me to try at tea. Then I showed Mormoh how to pickle some grey mullet for breakfast; and after I've finished this I'm going to hang the green curtains.

Will you let dear Elsie see this letter as I am sorry I cannot write to her this week, but am going to begin her letter tomorrow. I know you would like to know my 'menu' for lunch; as Charlie is away the dear boy has given permission for tea, then two purple garden eggs[25] boiled, cut in half, the pulp mixed with minced tongue and filled into each half, and a cheese omelette and fruit. Last night we had a fresh beef tongue boiled, 1/8 it cost, and spinach, or rather country greens which are just like spinach.

I'm thankful to say Charlie's last bottle of medicine has taken my 'India' away. I hope dear Father's is better.

We are expecting a Mr Reid here either this week or next. He is in the Customs. We have had a washing table and dressing table made and painted white for the bedroom out of the drawing room, and I'm going to use the Liberty cloth on the dressing table I think. The joiner is also making me a little frame for that photo of you standing up by Ellis and Walker.

With our best love my own darling Belle from your own loving Twisty

P.S. Puss has just come in with his mouth wide open panting! Last night he walked down to the quay with us and sat there with us. The tide was out and he could see below on the sand some little fish the size of sardines jumping; they are called bull fish. They were nearly driving him distracted, and there were some black and white kingfishers hovering over them too, so that he was crying when he looked at them. It was nearly dark when we got in, and I said to Charlie, 'Did Puss come back?' and I looked on the road and there he was with two nightjars tumbling in

---

25 Aubergines. M.B.M.B.

front of him on the road, sometimes within an inch of him and then flying over him nearly touching him with their wings. He was greatly tried!

To her sister Kate[26]

26 November 1908

My dearest Kate,

Very many grateful thanks for all the trouble you took over the curtains, and for sending us a cake. I can't tell you yet what it's like for I've actually been forbidden to open it till a thing I had made was finished! Today when Charlie comes home from York Island I shall have that great pleasure. But this letter has to be posted before 2 o'clock; but you can't think what pleasure I've had just looking at the parcel. I will write again when I have sampled it. What it is to have a husband with strong views.

You are quite right, I am very glad to be here with Charlie, and now we have got the house straight and comfy and cosy it is very happy. It's curious I'm – so far – never dull or bored, and although you would perhaps think that there was not much for me to do yet I'm always doing something, generally I dare say not much use, only it keeps me employed.

After Charlie got back from Hospital yesterday he fixed the outside rush mats on the windows of the side of the house where the afternoon sun strikes it, he did it so well and they are such a boon. I'm going to try as soon as my letters are

Kate Roberts, family photograph, date unknown

done to get the green curtains up before his return. I'm asking Trixie to pay for the material and Miss Parry with a blank cheque I sent her.

Poor Katie of Ceidio, it is a pity she and Hugh have got into such a rut. They will never be any different now I fear.

I was amused at Miss [illegible] being ill with 'heart affec', I should think the Dr's visits would be the best cure!!

I'm sorry only to be able to send a short note this week. Charlie was late starting

---

26 Later known to me as Nonin: M.B.M.B.

for York Island, and I've been making plum jelly from native plums nearly as big as cannon balls! It looks good.

Your loving Maida

Sunday 29 November 1908

My darling Belle

Your lovely long letter reached me yesterday after lunch; it came by the *Axim* which also brought a Mr Reid, an official from Freetown here, and he is stopping with us, so after lunch I went upstairs to lie down and Charlie brought me up my budget – yours, one from Aunt Mary, Katie and dear old Lydia, none from Father, I was so disappointed till Charlie came up and told me he had it so that was all right and I was happy once more.

Aunt Mary was full of the death of old Mr Priestley and whether we could get back to Crûg or not. I wouldn't go if I were paid to, unless I had enough money to buy it if it was in the market, but to ever put my head again under any of the Wynn Griffith[27] or Priestley yokes, no thank you. I have no doubt my head will have to go under many yokes for all that, but that one would be the most galling; 'The House of Llanfair' has no attractions for me.

But before I go any further I must begin with business. It is weighing on my mind, dearest. To begin with I *do* feel most dreadfully sorry to have given you *all* so much trouble, but it is a consolation to me, and I *do hope* it will be to you, that all the things sent have been worth double their value. The curtains are really a great blessing, you have no idea how great the glare was in the drawing room, it was making our eyes ache to read, and now when Charlie comes in from the hot sun outside he finds it delightful. Well, so far so good, but I'm on my last fringe-net! Will you, darling, order me half a dozen small mesh 4d ones mid-brown; that's all I want now.

So far I owe to Father about 6d for the letters sent on after I left, 4/- for the postage of the curtains; I can't remember anything more. Now, will you pay that and Miss Parry and all I owe, the tablecloth, doilies etc., the butterfly boxes and carriage and everything with the blank cheque and £1 beyond for ready money for anything I may send for, or else I must send direct to the firms; but I think I have come to the end of my requirements. If you would care to sell your old embroidered linen dress I would not mind buying it, tell me what you would take for it, but don't send it till I hear because I shall not want it for some little time; I am wearing out the holland and the blue linen, but I thought if you cared to sell we might come to terms!

Tuesday 1 December

The last month of the old year come round, it is wonderful how the time flies

---

27 The Roberts family's landlord at Crûg: see page 1.

along. We have a Mr Reid staying here for the week, he is Assistant Inspector of Customs, a Scotchman, a nice quiet man. He is I think going to take us in the Customs boat down to the promontory of this island tomorrow afternoon and I will take Mormoh with me to make tea.

Please tell Walters the gingerbread cake was cut last Friday; I've tasted many before, made many myself, but *never* have I made or tasted one so good as this. I'm sad to see it go, and it's vanishing with three at it each day; it's the *one* cake Mr Reid cares for! It has got such a nice brown glossy outside and is as fresh and soft as the day it was baked. Thank you all so much for it.

Well, I must tell you Charlie sent all the hammock boys flying on Friday except for Jomendi (or Greenlegs I think you know him by). They were the laziest set of boys I ever saw, and now we have a brother of Greenlegs instead and he helps in the garden.

I have been working each day with my pressed plants and am now mounting the grasses and sedges on to clean paper. All those little labels Gulie Lister sent me have stuck together and I have such a business to get them loose, my hands all perspiring. I have 30 grasses only so far; as I am writing now at half to four and I am waiting for tea, the perspiration stands in drops on my hands, and after lunch when I go and lie down and if I sleep I wake up drenched with perspiration, but I fancy it agrees with me because I really feel very well I'm thankful to say. But in the morning now after I have done the housekeeping and seen Charlie off to the Hospital, and I go and work with the plants upstairs, I very often have to take my dress off after to cool, but I go steadily on and I really don't mind it. It's 85 now in the hall as I write.

Our beans are bearing nicely. Charlie and I work every night for a little in the garden. In fact one or two nights lately after Charlie has had a busy day we have worked there till 6 o'clock and then just walked down to the end of the pier and sat on the crane to enjoy the breeze. Puss loves this; he comes with us, flying along as Pop used to.

I have had to give Sam a great talking to, he has got so lazy! Mormoh has a very good fit on, and does cook so nicely. You never saw, I'm sure, such lovely fishcakes as he makes, I don't know what he puts on the outside with the egg before he fries them but they look lovely. Then I've taught him to make lovely stews with beef and pumpkin (pukie he calls it and so do I now, it's such a nice word!) and boiled rice round. It's curious that everyone out on the Coast acknowledges that this is lovely rice, but they cannot get a market for it as they have not been able to find a machine, or make one, that will take the husk off, so the English prefer white rice with no taste to it in preference to this; and what is grown in the swamps is the best.

Mr and Mrs Pidgeon had gone off for a week up the rivers in a small boat tugged by their steam launch, getting to resting places for the night: the steam launch broke down, and they had to sit in this small boat and be rowed all night and till 12 o'clock next morning! And the leopard with them, they were afraid of leaving him behind; he jumped into the water too and nearly got away and there he was all wet in the boat too! She passed as I was in the garden and stood talking for an hour! She really beats Mrs Arthur B. R.

3 December 1908

Darling Belle,

I do so very much hope that Charlie's[28] coming home will not interfere with Father's trip abroad, and more than that if he goes he will have every comfort and stop to rest on the way. I am so afraid that this will not be in time before he starts; he needs this little change, it's his one pleasure in the year. It's ridiculous for Charlie to come backwards and forwards like this to America, I'm sure we should all like the trip. I'm sure Kate would not at all object to journeying back and fore to America to see her friends.[29] If he pays it all himself well and good; but it's too bad for him to come and worry Father at his age.

Charlie [my husband] and Mr Reid have gone to York Island, and won't be back to lunch. He is a very nice man in the house, so quiet and sensible. He took us yesterday to Mokolo[30] by the Customs boat. It's the promontory of this island, and you get lovely sea breezes there. Such a lovely row it was, much prettier than to York Island. Some places we went down canals and you might have imagined yourself on a slow-running river in England; and Mokolo was very charming, just a nice little bit of silver sand in front, and really the shore was about 20 ft or so above sea level. It reminded me a tiny bit of Llanddwyn. We took our chop-box with us for tea, and had plum jelly sandwiches which I had made here and arranged on a plate wrapped up in a banana leaf; and we opened my last tin of mixed biscuits! We did enjoy it: we had it under a shelter built for a boat right on the shore. Then Charlie went off with his gun and an old native trader, Mr Williams, sent a boy with him: there are guinea fowl there but they don't come down to the shore till after sunset. It *was* jolly. Mr Reid and I tramped after him. Charlie walking with a gun is a different person to Charlie without one, nothing stops him. On we plodded; we crossed a river on two tree poles which were worn to a smoothness like glass. He shouted back to me

28 The Charlie referred to here is not my father but my mother's eldest brother, who was, as I remember, considered a most unsatisfactory individual, due, it was thought, to having been dropped on the head by the nurse when he was a baby. He eventually settled in a very small town on the Welsh Border, not far from my aunt Trixie, but she and my mother completely disregarded his existence. I never saw him, but kind Nonin kept in touch and, I suppose went to his funeral when he died, as I remember her telling my mother that his neighbours referred to him as 'the old gentleman' and said he was a great reader, so he cannot have been too brain-damaged after all. A sad story and not a cause for family pride, but I thought he had better have this tiny memorial. M.B.M.B.

29 Nonin (Kate) had spent some time in America working as a nurse in a town called Hamilton in the Rocky Mountains where her two other brothers Wynne and Llewelyn had settled. M.B.M.B.

30 Maida spells this various ways including Mucalo, but this appears to be the accepted version.

White-bellied sea eagle, photo by Hafiz Issadeen, used under Creative Commons from https://commons.wikimedia.org/wiki/File:White-bellied_Sea_Eagle.jpg

that I wasn't to come, and some little black imp of Roderic's[31] age said 'Missis, you no to come.' I said to Mr Reid 'That settles it,' and I went over on all fours. It was a deep pool underneath and when we came back two native girls were bathing and swimming beautifully in it. Charlie got one pigeon only, but as he got back to the shore he saw a curlew and a fish eagle. He shot them both with one shot to the delight of the sailors.

We are going to chop the pigeon and the curlew tonight and Sam and Mormoh the sea eagle. It was a dull slate grey, very elegant in shape, it was really a species of heron I think, and its legs grey and its feet yellowish green. I thought of keeping the wings for you but they are not a pretty colour. It does amuse me to see the nigger boys go out shooting, they love it, and they go peering into the trees for these pigeon, then they would come creeping up to Charlie, 'You see am, you see am?' Then Charlie would say yes and take aim when they began to dance with their fingers in their ears shouting 'Kill am, kill am.' If the bird fell, shrieks and a great scramble as to who should carry it. If he missed they said 'He done gone, Sah.' I did enjoy it and came back loaded with plants, and some man came with a bunch of lovely pink flowers for me. We never got back till 7 o'clock my dear, moonlight, and we had to dress and go to Mr Page's for dinner by 7.30. No one likes him, he really is a plague. I'm thankful to say he is going on patrol next week again, and will be away till after Christmas. He had a

---

31 Maida's nephew, son of her sister Elsie.

punkah[32] up at dinner and each time the rope went up it gave me a rap on the head!

Now for your questions. I go on writing 'copiously' as dear Father said, can't you imagine how I would talk if you came here!

1. Well, I'm afraid we are not very early in the morning here, we generally have breakfast at 9 o'clock and go to bed at 9 o'clock or 9.30.

3. I generally wear in the morning my holland or blue linen, or a slightly soiled white drill; and in the evening my grey voile and grey crepe de chine blouse or my haik and that blouse with the Breton lace, that's when we are alone I wear these; if anyone comes I wear my white Jane Parry or the pineapple.

9. The washing, my dear, is really awfully well done. Sarah Peters is a brick, I hope she won't fall off; much better done than poor Mrs Jones or that other woman but not quite so nicely as the steam laundry, and we pay £1.1.0 a month

6. You asked about the heat. I hear now that this and April are the hottest months, and Mr Page said 'Well, Mrs Hunter, I hope you think this is hot enough.' I had said to Charlie two nights ago that I felt it very hot, but really I like it; I can't help fancying that all the perspiring suits me; but anyhow so far, and I always thank God and you see I had put touch wood, you know what I mean, I have never felt so well, and I have an enormous appetite; I do hope I shall keep so till the end.

7. My hair is not coming off nearly so much since I've used the hair-wash. I've pushed my fringe all up!

We shall have to go to Victoria next week, the trial of these prisoners is coming on. It's a bother going in a way, I don't like leaving my comfy house! My best love to [left blank] and your own dear self
from your own Twisty

7 December 1908

My darling Belle,
The mail arrived quite unexpectedly yesterday at about 9.00 a.m. An Assistant District Commissioner had arrived by the same boat on his way to a place beyond Mr Reaney, so I suppose the boatmen had to row well with him. I was so delighted to hear you had arrived back safe and well after your nice holiday and that you found dear Father and Kate well and Mormoh a good cat.[33] Fancy Walters having taught Sambo to beg.

Well, genuine hot weather has set in, and mighty hot it is. Yesterday it was

---

32 A large cloth fan on a frame suspended from the ceiling, often moved backwards and forwards by pulling on a cord.

33 This black Persian cat had been so named in honour of my parents' cook, and was later to climb into my pram when I was a baby at Bronceris. M.B.M.B.

really 'drefful', today there is a nice breeze every now and again which is most welcome. I had a very nasty headache all day yesterday, and it's then you feel the heat, when you do not feel up to doing anything. But this morning I'm thankful to say it has gone and from the time Charlie left till he came back I bustled about sending off the laundry, arranging flowers etc. and then I went to my specimens. I'm just mounting the grasses on plain paper I get from the French Company and label them, but you have no idea what a lot of work it means with the perspiration standing in beads on my face and hands; then all the ones pressing have to have their papers changed. But I enjoy it all very much and it makes the time fly.

On Thursday night Charlie, Mr Reid and I went for a nice long walk into the bush behind the cemetery. We saw some pigeon, so next evening we and Mr Reid had an early cup of tea and he took his gun and they both went off. I had to go to the Roman Catholic bazaar; I had promised the Sisters to go. I bought a very nice white linen or calico cushion cover worked by the nigger girls, and some handkerchiefs that with their corners all turned in will make little handkerchief sachets. Then I came back (I had gone in my haik skirt) and got into a short drill skirt and went to meet the men. I met them by a little stream. As we crossed the bridge, which was broken and partly in the water, a man was bathing in the pool. He had the good sense to sit down at the bottom with just his head out of water as we passed, and Charlie must needs ask him if he had seen any guinea fowl! He gave all the information he could, still with his head out!

Mr Reid very kindly said we could have the Customs boat on Saturday to go to Mokolo again, so we all three started off as before at 3 o'clock with the chop-box, and ordered dinner for 7.45 p.m. so that we need not leave there till 6 o'clock and see if there was any guinea fowl. We had a lovely row there, only I was dead sleepy and it was awfully hot, and we had tea in the same place. We found Sam had forgotten the teapot, so we had to make it in the kettle. While we were preparing the tea Charlie heard Coo-oo-oo in a tree and off he went and shortly returned with a plump grey pigeon, and then we started off and walked with no luck. He shot a green pigeon and some other bird and then we returned. It was by this time turning twilight and we were getting near the cotton tree they said the guinea fowl roosted on. Charlie was tramping on in front rather disconsolate, and we were all very sceptical. I called out to cheer him that we were drawing near the promised land! We got to the place and looked at the tree, and as we looked we saw two big fat birds fly up to roost. Charlie was off on tiptoe in an instant, and we shook our fists at the boys to keep them from shouting. We could see Charlie creep near and nearer and then stop, and we waited and waited and the boys said in low voices 'He no see am' when bang! and then bump, bump and down came the lovely fat bird from the top of the tree!

Such a beauty, fat and young. An old man then came out of a cottage just by, and Charlie said 'They come here every night, they come here tomorrow?' 'Ho,' said the old man, 'they no come tomorrow, it Sunday, they come Monday.' It was now nearly dark and the moon shining brilliantly and we took an hour rowing home. It was lovely. Going through the narrow passage between the islands was most beautiful, those are the places the slavers used to lie in wait for small boats and snatch up the slaves.

We got home and bid Mr Reid goodbye as he left at 5.30 next morning to go by boat to York Island to join the *Batanga*, which was to have sailed at 9.00 and never went after all till 10.00. We had the guinea fowl for dinner last night and it was excellent, great big slices off the breast. Charlie has cut the two wings off for me; it has been a nice change to the bill of fare.

This morning when Sam brought the shaving water he told Charlie that 'Jomendi b...y humbug him too much, pain too strong.' Charlie gave him a big dose of castor oil and he has been lying in the hammock under the house all day. Poor Greenlegs, and he is such a good boy too.

We have to go to Victoria one day this week, the Circuit Judge is going there for the leopard palaver. Mr Reaney has written to say the place will be very full and he is afraid he will not be able to find us a house. I am going all the same; I fancy we shall only be away one night.

Wednesday

I finished my grasses off yesterday morning, 30 of them each on a clean sheet of paper, and labelled them all; and now I shall have to go on with the flowering plants. Mr Reid brought home a branch with a bunch of four what looked like dark-coloured peaches the other day. An old man said they were not good to eat but if made a decoction of they were good for the skin. I lay down after lunch yesterday and read *Diana Mallory*.[34] I think I shall like it. To my great surprise while I was lying down a tornado came on. We were supposed to have done with them, and we had begun to have the Harmattan wind which I don't think I shall care for, it is very much like an East wind would be at home I think, with a thick haze. The moon is full these nights and would be grand only the slight haze dims it a little, and there is thunder about all these days.

There was great excitement here yesterday, the prisoners being taken to Victoria for trial, the murderers I mean. The boat had to go with one load; it left here about 10 a.m. and would reach Victoria about 4.00, then it had to come back for the second lot. One of our old hammock boys had to be engaged as rower, it would do him good. Mr Page is away and has the big boat, but he is expected home on Thursday, so I hope we shall get it to go. Charlie thinks it will be Sunday we shall be going. After breakfast yesterday I heard a great drumming from two drums, one doing tum-tum-turn-turn very quickly and the other tum-tum very slowly. I looked through the window and could see a long white boat start off with ten

---

34 *The Testing of Diana Mallory* by Mrs Humphrey Ward was first published in 1908, so this was a new best-seller.

oars, or rather paddles, they were paddling it like a canoe. It was the Paramount Chief of Sherbro going to the Circuit Court; it did sound and look weird. Then in the afternoon it started off again, it had only gone to York Island in the morning, and in the distance I could hear a horn blowing. I thought at first it was a steamer coming in, but it must have been some other chief going along. Charlie says they blow their horn as they go.

In the evening after gardening we took the walk I like up into the bush, and in coming home heard great music of shake-shakes, and saw three men followed by a lot of girls dancing, and we were told they were returning from the Bunda-bush. Do you remember reading about it in Mrs Cator's book?[35] When they are about 13 they have to go into a clearing in the bush for three months with an odd woman for a certain kind of training.

But I have gone this far without ever attending to your dear letter. To begin with you *must not* make me any more things, I do not really want a toilet cover here, honestly, I'll tell you why. On Saturday night I killed a cockroach as big as a small mouse on my dressing-table! and I have on it now white paper that Charlie brought me from the Hospital. It really looks all right. I am sorry to say my silver leaves much to be desired! I'm going to clean it today! It's really sweet of you to make me a tablecloth; you really must not do these things. And before I forget, do you really not want the pineapple dress? I have ordered one and it will be here about January, but if you do not want it I'll give you something else. I doubt very much if they will wash nicely, unless you do it yourself, and really you should make the whole dress yourself, and cream mercerised lawn would be quite as good a match for the bodice. I think if you made a slip of pale tangerine batiste of cheap silk it would look pretty, but remember *there is* no hard wear in them.

What a bother that you have had to join that wretched Badminton. Caernarvon certainly does sound dull. I'm very happy here with Charles, although nothing could be duller I never feel dull; the only time one feels a bit dull is if you don't feel well – get India or something like that. Otherwise I never long for gaieties; but it would be lovely to have you all in to see me.

Don't say unkind things about my poor cat, although he is ugly we are both devoted to him, he is so full of character. Charlie calls him 'Puss' but pronounces it 'Poos' in some queer way of his. You see, he was a young cat when I got him, not a tiny kitten, so it takes longer to get him into your ways, but yesterday afternoon when I was resting he came upstairs to look for me, and flung himself full length on the floor by my side with his tail far out and slept soundly, and I think he is getting to know us quite well.

My own Belle, I'm at my last gasp for a fringe net. I hope this will last my trip to Victoria, and I have no more. They rot quickly here I think.

I have to write a line to dear Father and to Elsie's boys, so excuse a hurried end

---

35 Presumably Dorothy Cator's *Everyday life among the head hunters* (Longmans, 1906).

up for this week. I will leave a note here for you for to post in case we are kept at Victoria. Best best love from us both, and give our love to the dear Aunties.
Ever, Belle, your Twisty

P.S. I've never wished you a Happy New Year and Christmas, my darling, and God bless you and keep you under His care.

That Mrs Latchmore was a doctor's wife; Mormoh was with her. He got ill and had to retire from the Service. I believe she was a nurse.

Would you, my darling, without fail give Roderic and Rob 2/6 each out of my money; it will save no end of bother.

15 December 1908

My darling Trixie,
Such a lovely budget of letters reached me on Sunday while we were at lunch; we had been expecting them Friday and Saturday by the *Egwanga*, but she never came, so we knew we should get them by the overland mail on Sunday. Just as we were at lunch we heard the 'toot' of a steamer, and there we saw the slow old coach going in, and no sooner had we sat down again to the table than the letters were brought in. They had been sent overland. So we sat down to them after lunch, one from dear Father, Elsie and you, and one from Emily, May and Muriel Robinson, and Charlie got a budget too; all good news I am thankful to say, and now this will reach you while you are alone.

I am very glad you have Walters and Lizzie, and very glad that Father had agreed to keep Lizzie, I like her so much, and of course Walters who I hope is a fixture. It is a great relief to me to think of your being there with the three servants: it's very good of Father isn't it? and I am thinking of him and Kate travelling today. I do hope they have a good journey. I shall write direct to Cannes to him.

My darling childie, what are you sending me in the Christmas box? You spoil me, when are you going to give it up? and think more of yourself. You know quite well you spoil me; what would give me real pleasure would be to hear that you are working something really nice for yourself. How does your screen get on?

The *Egwanga* brought us a budget of papers too, many many thanks for the two *Thrones* and all the *Punches*. I've only had time to peep into the latter but I saw enough to make me want to see more. I don't believe I ever thanked you for the *Queen* and *Bystander* you sent me from Glenn.

The *Egwanga* also brought us two gallons of methylated spirits. Mr Reid got it for us. We had to pay 1/6 a bottle for it at the French Company, and the last time we sent for it [they] had none, so I am sure it will be cheaper. He said he would let us know when they returned how much it cost. I have worried so that I never told you I sent my fur collar back with him to post in England; you would wonder, my darling, that I put no word inside: but as he was a Customs Officer I thought I had better do the thing strictly honest! I just enclosed two funny little seeds that grow in a big bean hanging off a large tree; aren't they pretty? But it was so stupid not to tell you in my letter that I had sent it. Fancy, Mr Reid sent me a lovely ham and a Dutch cheese as a present after staying here, wasn't it very generous and nice of him? I had been apologising for not having any ham, I could not get it here, and there he sent me one. He has gone on leave now; I hope he will have a very good time. Half the ham is now soaking [in] a bucket preparatory to being boiled. We are momentarily expecting word to proceed to Victoria.

Fancy, as we were going up for our bath the other night I looked up on to the ceiling of the staircase and said to Charlie, 'Look at that big spider.' Charlie said, 'Look out, don't touch it, it's a tarantula spider.' I could not have reached it anyway, but Sam came up and with a long stick knocked it down and killed it. The natives are very much afraid of them. It was as big, including its legs, as the top of a teacup and the legs all hairy. Father Noirjant was in to dinner last night; he was surprised to hear of one in the house.

Thursday 17 December

Here comes posting day and I have only written two sheets to you, but the fact is on Tuesday evening I went for a very long walk with Charlie. We began with the French Company, then I begged him to take his gun with him to the cassada fields away behind the cemetery, and try to get a pigeon, and we walked as you know I can, awfully quickly to get beyond the little stream where the man was bathing. This is my favourite walk, behind the cemetery you get into the bush and go along a little path with bush on one side and sort of fields and waste on the other and a coffee farm beyond till you get to this little stream and around the little pool marsh plants grow, most fascinating like the marsh at Crûg used to fascinate me, and there I found an orchid standing 4 ft high with long leaves like an aspidistra. Beyond the little pool you walk up

Tarantula, adapted photo, used under Creative Commons BY-SA 3.0, https://commons.wikimedia.org/w/index.php?curid=121946

a little hillock all covered with cassada, and a tiny little house built for the old man who works on it, I will take a photo of it one day. But I'll call this walk the cassada farm walk so that you will know. Well, to return I suppose I walked too fast and ate too big a dinner, but I've had a bilious headache since like I get at home, no worse, not as bad perhaps as 'India' pain!

It was Monday night I remember, and on Tuesday I tried to paint the orchid all morning, such a time it took me, the leaves were awful and in the night after all my trouble cockroaches went and ate the green paint off in patches! That was Tuesday I painted, and lay down in the afternoon. Yesterday I had to attend to duties, darning socks, tidying the house and boiling down some more plums for jelly; and rested again in the afternoon, that's how I left my letter. Then in the evening I did not feel up to walking (Charlie had given me some strong medicine) so he gardened for an hour till the perspiration was pouring down his head and neck. He is very fond of gardening. Today I am thankful to say I feel better. If you are not up to the mark out here you feel very low! A sort of depression seizes you.

My dearest Belle, to return to your letter; many many thanks for the fringe nets, I was at the very last gasp. I don't need back hair nets. I really have lost so much hair I don't do it down ever. I hope you have paid for the nets, dear. All your Caernarvon news was most interesting. Fancy Mrs Wyatt expecting. I am sorry to hear Mr Lloyd Roberts is looking so worn, poor fellow, he is much to he pitied; and poor Miss Hulm too, please remember me very kindly to her, and to the Finchett Maddocks.[36] I am sure you will miss the Preeces; how is Eileen Clemenger? The fair Adrian will soon be expected home, I wonder at what time of day or night he will alight on Caernarvon platform!

I simply cannot realise that tomorrow week is Christmas day, and here we are melting in the heat. Puss is very sweet these days, nothing he likes better than gardening with us, and he loves me to clap. He crouches down as I come near him preparing to meet me! and then off he goes flying down the garden and up a tree at the bottom, and he comes up every morning as we are dressing crying hoarse cries!

Mormoh has just come in with the jelly; it looks a lovely colour. I have left it to cool a little as I have run short of anything to put it in, so have to use tumblers.

I am so very sorry, darling, to hear that you have been having headaches. I wonder whether it is your eyes? I shall have to have mine seen to when I get home I am sure.

We have not yet heard when we are to go to Victoria. Those poor boatmen have been ploughing there backwards and forwards for the last 10 days and they say they are still at the first leopard case. A sub-chief is implicated in it; this is the new circuit judge's first trip too so perhaps he is trying to be very thorough.

The *Olinda* is due today! I don't think she will come till tomorrow or Saturday though. We are hoping our trip to Victoria will be over before Christmas; it would

---

36 Spelled variously F/Pinchet(t) Maddock/Maddox, but this looks right from the web.

be a nuisance if it were not because we are kept more or less on the jump. The jelly has overboiled!

Such a killing letter came for Mormoh yesterday, registered with three stamps on it! It was from the wife he left at Freetown, a most jolly letter saying her first husband had sent her a nice country cloth, and asked if Mormoh was able to keep her. Meantime she has taken Dr Murphy's boy as her third husband, and she told Mormoh he had given her £6, one of which she had given to her big sister. Then she goes on to say 'My compliments to your new wife at Bonthe'! We had been telling Mormoh he was not attending to his work, and Charlie said 'You go look for a wife, that what you do, Mormoh?' and he had said 'No, Sar, I get no wife'! I did laugh, they are so funny; but really Mormoh cooks very nicely. She also told him his best friend was in jail at Freetown for stealing tobacco from the Coaling Company. She had paid someone 3d for writing this letter, Charlie tells me.

I must now, my own darling, write to dear Father, so goodbye for this week. Oh, before I forget, I think it would save bother and muddle if the London and Lancashire sent the div.[37] to the [illegible]. I will fill in the form that way, all my other divs go there. I don't know how I forgot this one; it will save you any anxiety and worry, dear, and thank you for getting this form for me.

Every good wish and prayer for you in the New Year, my darling Belle, and best love from your own Twisty. Charlie sends his love.

Did I tell you Mr Reid sent me a ham and a Dutch cheese by the *Egwanga*? Wasn't it kind of him; also a letter from Dr Keenan to say he could not get the films back, isn't it a bother I ever sent them to him.

P.S.2 Very very many thanks for the sage, my young grasshopper.

[The next two letters are addressed to Maida's father, who was staying in the south of France with his daughter Kate.]

15 December 1908

My dearest Father,[38]

I hope this letter will find you and Kate safely and happily established at Cannet,[39] and that you like the place and the pension; I believe you will feel obliged to end up with St Maxime, all the same.

We are daily expecting the summons to go to Victoria. The judge is already there. I expect we shall be going tomorrow or Thursday at latest. Mr Page is very kindly letting us have the big boat so that I can lie down in it; that will be a great comfort, as the heat is pretty bad now, this month and May are I believe about the

---

37 Presumably the dividend on some savings or investments.

38 This letter and the next to Maida's father are written with noticeably more attention to composition and punctuation than the spontaneous outpourings to her sister. M.B.M.B.

39 Unclear in the original, but presumably the family were at Le Cannet, near Cannes.

worst in Bonthe. Except [for] the great discomfort of perspiring, I am as well as anything.

I was so amused on Monday afternoon. We were both sitting in the drawing room, Charlie in a place where he can see the front door, when a knock came and he went and I heard a voice saying 'Good afternoon doctor,' and Charlie in a 'sychlid'[40] voice answered 'Good afternoon'. I then heard him begin to say he belonged to the Wesleyan Mission, and after a great deal of talk Charlie said 'Are you coming to call?' He said 'No, I'm coming to beg.' 'Ohh,' said Charlie, 'that's another matter. Begging is a bad thing; but I don't belong to your church.' 'Well, doctor, I don't approach you as a member of my church, I approach you as a Christian.' Another prolonged 'Ohh' from Charlie, who said he would think about it, so the Minister said he would call again. 'No, don't waste your time, go somewhere where you will get more' said my poor Charlie. Then he left. Charlie found me in roars of laughter because he is so like you over subscriptions. I've 'a deal of trouble' with him.[41]

I was thinking of you very much on Monday and Tuesday night, and hoping you were having a comfortable journey. Please tell Kate that I heard from Dr Keenan last mail to say he had given my roll of films to a man to develop and he had gone away to the bush, and his assistant could not find them. It's a great bother, I shall send the next lot straight to Trixie.[42]

I've had a little 'India' or I would write a letter to Kate. Tell her I send my love. With our united love to you, dearest Father,
Your loving Maida

P.S. I expect you will see in *The Times* that there is a Commission to enquire into the emoluments, duties etc. of the West African Medical Staff.

18 December 1908

My dearest Father,
I posted my letter to you yesterday, but I found after it had gone that I had not told you about a fine fish we bought. On Wednesday morning after breakfast they came to say a man had brought a fish to sell. We went to look at it, and it was huge, over 16 lb it weighed. They called it cassada fish. It tasted like halibut which we pay 10d a lb for at home, and it was a lovely grey colour. We asked him how much he wanted for the whole fish and he said 1/- so the servants agreed to take half. I had a good laugh over the dividing as Mormoh held the knife and Charlie stood over him while he placed the knife where he thought half would come.

40 A Welsh word meaning as far as I can make out 'dry' – M.B.M.B.
41 In spite of this rather discreditable anecdote, I remember my mother telling me often that my father never charged any priest or minister of religion of whatever denomination if they were ill. M.B.M.B.
42 There follows a repetition of the letter to Trixie written on the same day, not reproduced here. M.B.M.B.

When he cut it we weighed it. *Our* half weighed a little over 4 lbs and theirs over 16 lbs! So we had a thick steak off theirs. It lasted us two days, the steak for lunch, the tail end boiled for dinner, fish cakes for breakfast, fish pudding for lunch, and warmed up for dinner, so wasn't that a wonderful 6 d worth of fish?

We had tea early yesterday and Charlie started off with his gun and Greenlegs to try to get some pigeon. He went [on] the walk up behind the town and through a little cassada farm, and Sam and I followed in an hour. Sam knows so many of the trees (sticks he calls them) and their uses. He pointed to one shrub like a laurel with green berries on it and said 'It got milk in it, if it go in your eye it spoil it, you no see', and then added that it was also used for catching birds, and what was it but birdlime? We met Charlie and Greenlegs with one pigeon, and we are having it for dinner, and we had a lovely walk home.

We hear they are still on the first leopard case, so most likely we shall not go to Victoria till after Christmas. It is a bother, because it keeps us on the tenterhooks. The *Olinda* has just tooted and passed down to York Island; it will bring our letters and I believe our Christmas box from home.

Sunday 20 December

I hope by today, dearest Father, you and Kate are beginning to feel rested after your journey. I shall be very relieved to get your letter, the one you write after your arrival. I shall get it about the middle of January I hope. I am enduring great tortures! The Christmas box is in the medicine room, and I'm not allowed to open it – or rather unpack it, the lid has been taken off – for two reasons. First, Trixie told me I was not to open it till Christmas, and second, she forgot to send an inventory, so it was a favour of the Customs official here to let us have it out of the office until we can declare its value, I think it was awfully good of you all to send it, I will enlarge upon its delights when I've unpacked it.

The head of the French Company has come by the *Olinda* and a Colonial official, Mr Tingelly, who has come here on business is, or rather was, staying at the French Company. They both came on Friday by the *Olinda* and Mr Tingelly (funny name, isn't it?) goes back on her today. They both dined with us last night. Mr Dubois (the French Company) is also French Consul at Freetown; he is Swiss and the image of Brynteg Mademoiselle to look at.

We have been much interested in the papers the last week or so. The clipping of the German Emperor's wings will, I hope, have the desired effect for Germany. As far as we are concerned, it has only given us another leg up. I greatly enjoyed Mr Asquith's speech at the Mansion House too. All this will seem ancient history to you.

I got by this mail a heavily sealed (eight seals I think there were) letter from Edith Capron. I opened it expecting at least a £5 note, but no! a tract Christmas card, a sort of text! But a very nice letter from her, dear old Edith. I gave the text to two little nigger boys who came with their pockets full of seeds for me, funny little boys they are, one is called Alfred. He was *simply delighted* with it, so it gave what it was meant to do, pleased, and I hope some good, no harm at any rate. I also had two very nice letters, one from Auntie Kate and one from Bessie. I wrote to Auntie Kate last mail, and I had written to her from the Canary Islands, I wonder whether she ever received it.

I had also a nice long letter from Elsie and a short one from Kate enclosed; they had been revelling in crampog teas!

Goodbye for this week, dearest Father, and take every care of yourself. I don't think you should walk too far by yourself so near Cannes as you would do at St Maxime. Your last letter was very interesting. *All* our good wishes to you for 1909. Ever your loving Maida

Christmas Eve

Darling Father, I have only time to send my loving thanks to dear 'Grandpère' for the lovely bottle of lavender water you sent me. It was very very good of you, and Trixie sent me a tiny little frame with your photo in. We both thought it so good, and I am so glad to have it. Charlie has gone to York Island or would send love with mine.
Your loving Maida

20 December 1908

My darling Belle,
Very very many thanks for your nice long letter which arrived on Friday afternoon while we were at tea. We had heard the *Olinda* toot while we were at lunch, and we ran to the medicine room window to see her pass down to York Island. And I knew on board was my Christmas box that you had taken pains and care and thought over. It did not arrive here till yesterday after tea, the Customs man very kindly let us have it out, but we can not unpack it till Charlie gets the list from you my darling, or we may unpack it about Wednesday and give him the value. We had to take the lid off for him to see, and I could not resist taking my table-cloth out, thank you, darling, *so so* much for it, it is a beauty, and so beautifully worked, the cotton is so glossy. Sam likes 'plenty cloths' too. I am so delighted to have it, there's no doubt Aunty Kate is quite right, I am pampered. Also on top was Sam's watch chain which I think he saw. He can't do enough these days, but I am afraid once he gets the watch he will slack off. But it's terrible hard not to go this very minute and unpack it. I'm trying to persuade myself the ants may be going to them etc. I've also seen the beads! I could not help pulling those out too! Do you remember when Elsie and the children came to spend Christmas at Crûg, and the two boys got into her box and ferreted out all their presents? Well, I feel *just* like that; it's a delightful agony or rather an agonising delight prolonged!

The mail brought me besides your dear letter a very nice long one from Elsie saying she is sending us a box of mixed biscuits for Christmas instead of a card. It's awfully good of her; I'm afraid I'm getting downright greedy! [And] a short and rather cool note from my poor Kate. I do hope she does not mind sharing Father's letter, but really she will have not to mind, writing is done under difficulties here, it makes one perspire so much. Also a long envelope with about eight or nine seals on from Edith Capron. I cut it open with bated breath and found a text! but a very nice letter too. The text I gave to two little nigger boys, one is called Alfred. He has been picking me some rather pretty grey seeds; he was simply delighted with it, much more so than with a penny I had given him another day.

A Mr Tingelly from Freetown, a Colonial official, came on the *Olinda*, also Mr Dubois the head here of the French Company and French Consul at Freetown. Mr Tingelly stopped with him as Mr Page is away, but he goes back by the *Olinda* today. They both dined with us last night. I know you like me to tell you what I gave them to chop. First, groundnut soup, boiled fish (a big grey mullet, the tail end, very good) chicken cutlets with tomato sauce round, very good; then beef olives and fried potatoes; pudding and cheese savoury. The only flaw was that Sam had a lapse of memory and brought the savoury in before the 'punny'! And also I had taken the bother of making a pie-dish frill of white paper, as Sam will entwine one of those glass cloths round the pudding dish, and if he didn't go and put it outside the frill. I could have wept. The chicken cutlets were really very well made. He killed the chicken after tea, and plucked and then boned it in such a way that he got about eight cutlets off, each with a bone that looked like a leg bone in.

But the casual way in which he does his cooking – he was wandering about the garden with the ground (or monkey) nuts that he had browned on a plate, shelling them in the most leisurely way; the pudding was good too; we had got some apples off the *Olinda* which we stewed and added a little madeira to, and put it at the bottom, and fine sago stewed in milk and eggs poured on the top; and spoonfuls of plum jelly decorating it. The table looked very pretty too with just two brass bowls of those lovely pinky red lilies, and a sort of feathery leaf, and the pink curtains in the window; but the room is absolutely bare of furniture, and the sideboard is a deal table with a country cloth on it! Still it looks very nice because the whole of one side of the room is open, and you can see the hall with the long table with green baize and the pigeon holes above, and on that all my photos in frames. Do you remember that one I brought of you taken by Ellis and Walker? I've had a little [illegible] wood frame made for it, it looks really quite nice, and you inside of course sweet, my beloved seal. I wonder whether you will feel dreadfully lonely without Father and Kate; I hope Robert will cycle over to see you very often, and Elsie will go I hope. I only hope you will all keep well.

I've not been to church here yet, Charles reads me the service on Sunday in his *own* way, beginning with the Psalms, funny isn't it, nothing will prevail upon him to alter! And I enjoy that very much. I think I will try to go on Christmas Day though, that is if I'm not at Victoria.

Fancy, those butterfly boxes have never come yet, they are at Freetown. Elder Dempster stupidly put it on a boat that did not come to Sherbro, so it got put out at Freetown, we have sent for it but I don't know when it will arrive.

I'm much interested in all you and Auntie Kate and Bessie have told me of the illustrious bride;[43] such an effect it had on me that last night my slumbers were disturbed by dreaming I had gone to call upon her and she sent a note in to tell me she was too tired to see me; and I had come without cards to leave upon her, such a jumble! It will be nice for her to have a car of her own by which to escape from the worthy people of Caernarvon!

Tuesday 10.00 a.m.

I've just been pressing plants, a most exhausting job. I shall send the first batch home at the beginning of the year, and I expect they will arrive all mouldy. As far as I can make out there is nothing particularly new or interesting about them; of course they are all new to me, and many of them I cannot make out at all.

Yesterday morning I made some little buns and tidied up the home here and there and lay down in the afternoon, and at 3.00 we had tea and Charlie went off at 4.00 to try for guinea fowl. One of the labourers at the Hospital said he knew where 'they live'; and at 5.00 Sam and I went to meet them. He is splendid for telling me about the trees, 'sticks' he calls them, what they are used for and so on. One bush we passed with green berries turned out to be full of bird-lime. Will you read up in the Encyclopaedia about bird-lime and tell me what it says, and before I forget, will you send me a recipe for kedgeree. We walked a long way before we met them; not a bird had they seen and been such a tramp, most disappointing.

I am going to wash my stays this morning, all the perspiration makes them nasty.

Charlie came back from the Hospital very early this morning and we are *now* going to unpack the Christmas box!

Wednesday

Many many thanks, my darling, for all the lovely things you have sent. It was too sweet of you to send two cakes, you have *no* idea how we shall enjoy them, they look lovely, and the Christmas punny. I'll let you know how they all taste and how we eat them and everything. At present I am luxuriating in the feeling of plenty; and of a change of diet, one gets a little tired of the same thing all the time. I felt like unpacking a stocking taking all the things out of the tin box – the dear little photo of dear Father, I will bring the frame back for you, Kate's jolly little cloth and dear Father's bottle of lavender water. It was too, too good of you all, especially you, my darling, who took all the pains and trouble.

---

43 It is not clear who this might be. There were no royal weddings around this time. The Welsh newspapers mentioned the wedding of Cicely Horner, brother of Mrs Raymond Asquith, and the Hon. George Lambton, a brother of the earl of Durham, so that is a possibility.

The only thing that I have to return is Sam's watch. We cannot see how to turn the fingers: it has not got that little 'twisty tail' that keyless watches usually have, and to take the glass off each day is too complicated for Sam. Could you, dearest, change it? I am so sorry to trouble you, it's the thing for moving the fingers I mean.

We had a most awful thunder storm last night, I was terrified; it came on after tea. I had gone to call on Mrs Pidgeon and to lend her *Diana Mallory* (which I enjoyed immensely) and I had to come back, it got to look so black, and we had a thunder storm then before dinner. Then we went to bed and I said to Charlie 'There is a fire behind the village out towards the cassada farm.' But he made light of it, and I got into bed when we heard the church bells go. It was a house on fire; the woman had a lamp near her bed. All these Sierra Leonians have their lamps lit all night. It was evidently quickly burnt out and we got back into bed, to be awoken at 11 o'clock by bad thunder, but three of the flashes came with the thunder, such a terrific noise I never heard in my life, and as if the heavens were opening and floods of rain on top of us. After one of these flashes I could smell that smell of gunpowder. I really was terrified. It returned again at 4 o'clock in the morning but not so terrific. Isn't it funny, as regular as clockwork they have a tornado at Christmas. Charlie says we shall get them like this in May. All evening I had been enjoying the lightnings, they were a lovely rosy pink, but in the night I saw nothing but terror in them. I was telling Charlie in the night I hoped you had one of the servants sleeping on the landing with you, dear, *be sure you tell me.*

Thursday

Posting Day! I suddenly thought I would try another roll of films today and send them to you, but I must tell you that such agitation seizes me when I begin to touch the camera that I am sure they will be terrible. The first is the view up the road opposite the drawing room window and that lovely tree is the African oak. The house you see in the trees is the house of a black doctor, Dr Jarret by name. Second is the view out of our bedroom window. The palm tree has been spoilt by the palm birds tearing the leaves for their nests. Third, Charlie and I on the steps. It's difficult to explain the steps; as I walk out of the hall I go down about twelve steps with trellis on each side and a roof, and at the bottom the steps turn and go down either side. Four, Sam, the little one, and Greenlegs or Jomendi as he was christened. Fifth, Puss going up a frangipani tree after a lizard. Six, the house taken in a terrific hurry. Charlie was off to York Island, and I wanted to finish them off at once. In the next roll I will take an interior. Your dear little pictures look so sweet on the wall, and in one of the recesses I have your photo in the new frame, and the little round frame (black wood) with the one you took of Roderic in. Rob adorns the long wall. If any of these photos of mine are a success, will you, darling childie, order a tin of platinotype paper and do me off a few; also if you could get some light (in weight not colour) mounts, and send them out to me I

Pooz (visible towards the bottom right) goes up the frangipani tree after a lizard. From a family album.

should be much obliged. Of course I can trust you to put down all postage you are spending for me or else I shall feel vexed cat, and it will worry me.

Everyone thought the storm the other night terrible; it was right over us, but no harm done fortunately. I had Mrs Pidgeon to tea yesterday; she is really a terror. She evidently came out here a common little thing and got a lot made of her, and is evidently very puffed up. *Not one word* can you get in edgeways: and she boasts of her husband and what a lot the firm think of him. You never knew anyone like her. She has asked me to go to the recreation ground tomorrow to see Bonthe play York Island at cricket! All these common trading people, it's a great trial. She was speaking of Mr Dubois as 'Jewboy'. I never took in she meant Mr Dubois, I thought he was one of their men till Charlie told me. They are asking us to dinner next week!

I am going to make the mince pies this afternoon as Mormoh will have the baking pot hot then. You, dear dear childie, I have not thanked half enough; I had your new cloth on my table (the big table with the cakes and a pot of jelly on) yesterday and that wretched little Mrs Pidgeon was clawing it with her dirty fingers. I am naughty, am I not?

Chief Tucker's wife came to see Charlie today; she will stay a week or ten days for treatment.

One of the features of the West Coast is terrible dreams. I had a horrid dream last night that dear Father was not well. I do hope he is all right.

We heard from Mr Reaney today that we are not wanted for at least another week. On Sunday evening when Charlie and I were returning from our walk we saw a policeman and a small crowd round the Hospital. And there was an awful-looking old woman having her head washed. The people had brought her from the Imperi district the other side of the river, and said a cannibal had tried to kill her. It was an awful sight. It had been done ten days ago and she was skin and bone. Charlie does not think it is a leopard case; the wounds don't look like it.

For this week all my love from your own Twisty

P.S. Poos! sends his love to Mormoh and says it no good for send him lizard, as they no good for chop. He begs him not to get too fat cat as he might die of apoplexy.

28 December 1908

My darling young Belle,

I shall have to try to write in a smaller hand as my paper is showing signs of finishing too quickly. *Very very* many loving thanks for your long jolly letter. I am sorry to say the gossip you give is – sad though it sounds – revelled in by me. I get a little envious when I think of your tea parties with the dear Aunts. How I used to love seeing them, I am going to write to Auntie Kate this mail, all being well.

Well, my darling, Christmas is passed very peacefully and most happily. Your lovely Christmas box arrived before Christmas, and your Christmas letter on Christmas Day, so nothing could be better than that. I had a lovely budget of letters, dear Father's, yours, Elsie, Mrs Chas. Rees, Miss Clemenger and a card with Cefn Hendre[44] on, Ann McCharlie, Amy Daniell, Aunt Annie (such a very nice kind letter), May and a card from Jess.

We had breakfast on Christmas Day at 8 o'clock and at 8.20 I sallied forth to Church. I must tell you I trimmed that white hat we bought at Chester for the occasion; I undid those frills of spotted net, and swathed the crown first with tulle and then the spotted net, and put on the left-hand corner the cluster of moss roses – *most successful* considering that all the trimmings were sticking to my hands as I did it, and the moss off the roses! But it's a very sweet hat. I reached the church door and saw no one to lead me to my pew, the congregation had partly assembled, and I could see were agitated by my arrival. A huge Mammie came up the steps and volunteered to usher me into what is supposed to be the Government pew right under the pulpit, as it were where Mrs Finchett Maddock sits. A lovely little

44 A district of Caernarvon.

church it is and no wonder when I tell you later on how they get their things. I sat down and soon a black gentleman (Dr Jarret) seeing that nature had not made my legs long enough to reach the ground very kindly brought me a hassock.

Well my dear, as you know a knowledge of Church ritual is not a strong point with me, but there were some killing things happened. Two men in black robes stood one on each side of the aisle at the top, and waited for the clergyman and choristers as they walked up, each holding a staff with a brass knob on top of it. The children evidently were not coming quick enough, so they were beckoned to hurry up. I must say they looked sweet, little black cassocks and beautifully got-up surplices, and bare feet. They looked as St Augustine said I think angels, but their voices were much, much too loud. The service then proceeded, really wonderfully well done, only too slow. Then, when it came time for the sermon, the beadle who had a wonderful black gown trimmed with velvet stepped forward, met the parson at the chancel steps and walked in front of him with a black ebony rod with silver knob, and ushered him to the pulpit. The whole proceeding lasted two hours. I got home with a splitting headache, the singing being too loud and the sun rather hot. I came back to find Charles halfway through the drawing room window, and he greeted me with 'You have had two hours of it!'

For Christmas dinner I had arranged to have soup and fish and stewed beef and pumpkin, and given strict orders to Mormoh how to boil the Christmas pudding. Well, I saw Sam stagger in with it still steaming in the bowl, and the bowl on the dish. How I laughed, but I quickly turned it out, and it was excellent. I had it turned back into last year's bowl which was smaller, my young Belle, and said we

United Brethren Church, Bonthe, a postcard of 1904, sourced from http://digitalcommons. otterbein.edu/archives_sleone/18/

would have it again for last night for Mr Laurent; and if you please Mormoh sent it up cold! I had beaten butter sauce with it. Charles and Mr Laurent ate it cold! and liked it.

I found in my dressing bag this morning the list of French books Mrs McLehose gave me to read. I am copying it for you.

Our first set of beans are over; we have had six or seven dishes from them, and they have been a great pleasure, the only things that have done well except those convolvulus Mrs Bodvel Griffiths gave me. They as I told you came on at once, and then after growing about two inches stopped until now they are growing up. I have a pot of them one on each side of the front door; I can't make out whether they are going to flower. The zinnias are flowering, but they are poor weakly little specimens. Gardening is most doleful work at Bonthe; there seems to be no nourishment in the soil.

Wednesday 30 December

Mr Reaney arrived at 1 o'clock today and is staying with us, also his dog, a huge white bull terrier with a long tail, hideous, and he is frightening my poor Puss! The nuisance is that we have to leave Mr Reaney here while we go off tomorrow to Victoria, and go into his house. We have to be back on Friday as Charlie has some business with the District Commissioner on Saturday. How the weeks fly along.

I didn't tell you about Charles presiding at a treat to the poor on Saturday. It was given in a temporary long tent made of poles and green palm leaves. Charles was asked to take the chair at 10.00 a.m. We both went, I in my solar topi with that white spotted net scarf round it, white drill skirt and blouse. We arrived there ages too soon; they had collected £12, wasn't it good, and each poor person (they could only take up 50) received an enamel mug 6d, ditto dish 6d, four heads tobacco 1/4, 3 lbs rice, 1 lb meat, a pipe, a little lamp with a wick in it, 3 biscuits, a 1d loaf, and a bottle of paraffin oil, altogether 4/6 or 5/- worth. Charles took the chair, and by this time Mr and Mrs Pidgeon had arrived. The chief clerk introduced Charles, 'our worthy and beloved doctor'. Charles made a nice little speech, he was a bit 'nervous loike'; and then Mrs Pidgeon and I were asked to hand [out] the things. And then two got up to propose a vote of thanks to the chairman and me, and another seconded. It was too killing. They alluded to Charles as 'Charlie B. Hunter Esq. M.B.', then 'our Medical Officer of Bonthe' and goodness knows what else. I could hardly keep grave. Then he (one of the men) proceeded to read the list of subscriptions. One was 'Mr George Williams 1/- but he hasn't paid'! Wasn't it lovely?

Thursday

We are leaving at 10.30. It is rather a bother leaving Mr Reaney here and his three servants all messing about.

I am so sorry to have to send such a poor letter this week, my darling, I'll write a longer one next.

Thank you so very much for all you have paid for me. I am especially glad you paid Miss Hopkins. She was on my mind, and I was forgetting each week to send the money. I will send you a cheque of Holt's next time for any little things I want.

All my love, my darling, from your own Twisty

P.S. A *very Happy New Year.*

Dr Hunter to Trixie[45]

Sunday 27 December 1908

My dear princess,

It was very nice of you to write me such a jolly Christmas letter, and I was so glad to have it. It came most appropriately on Christmas at midday; a ship had come down from Freetown that morning, and brought all the papers and letters, with yours of the 11th so it was pretty quick of reaching us.

I send you my very very best thanks for the lovely box, which came in good trim the week before, the variety of the contents was most exciting to 'pull' one by one, and the cost of them which I had to give to the Customs was not far off the list you sent two days ago. The box itself was brought from Liverpool by the steamer free of charge, one of Sir Alfred Jones' little attentions to those on the Coast at Christmas. Well, we have been tasting the different nice things and they are all much enjoyed by my Maida and myself.

Maida keeps so well and jolly and full of buck, which is a blessing. I really think better than she does at home, no colds and chills you know, and she chops well and enjoys her time here very much. The life is so free and easy, and she bosses the 'boys' fine, and looks after the 'chop' in good 'fashion'. She says I'm getting fatter but I don't think so. She was so frightened the other night when we had a strong tornado, but she will get accustomed to them when we get more of them in April and May. There was a cricket match between the York Islanders and Bonthe on Christmas afternoon which we went up to behind the Hospital. Bonthe won to the great joy of the natives here: and yesterday forenoon there was a distribution of various articles and chop to the poor at which I presided. £12 or so were subscribed. Most were old women. They each got an enamel basin and mug and spoon, a small tin lamp, a bottle of paraffin oil, 3 lb rice, 1 lb beef, two boxes of matches, 1 lb tobacco leaf and a pipe, a couple of big biscuits and a loaf of bread – quite the best poor treat I've ever seen.

We are both as fit as possible, and send plenty love and best wishes for a bright and happy New Year.

Your loving Charlie

---

45 My father addressed my Aunt Trixie as 'Princess', which was his name for her for some reason unknown to me. The word 'chop' occurs frequently, as it has done throughout the letters; it seems to be used on the Coast as a verb or noun meaning 'to eat' or 'food eaten'. M.B.M.B.

Maida to her father[46]

28 December 1908

My darling Father,

I will only write a short note this week as Charlie has given you all our news.

We hope you and Kate have had a very happy Christmas; we have had a very quiet but very happy one; and our budget of letters arrived by the SS *Boma* on Christmas morning and we had them at 3 o'clock in the afternoon. I kept them until we returned from the cricket match and then when I came I had a feast; but I shall have lots to do answering them. I expect I shall only have one more letter from Bronceris, then I shall hope to hear of your safe arrival in the south of France.

When we got down on Christmas morning all the Government boatmen and the Customs boatmen were waiting on the steps for Charlie! When he came down they wished him a Happy Christmas, of course a hint for a Christmas box. Charlie gave them 10/- between them: they were delighted and gave him three cheers.

At 8.20 I started off for church and was shown into what Mr Page told me was the Government pew. I sat down and took all in: it's a lovely little church, and such a nice little organ, surpliced choir, and the little black boys with bare feet. To say the service was hearty did express it, they 'yelled' the whole service through.

Yesterday at 10 o'clock Charlie and I sallied forth to the distribution of Christmas fare; I wish you could have heard the speeches. The chief of the District Commissioner's office introduced the chairman as 'our worthy and beloved doctor', then Charlie went into the chair and looked really lovely sitting in it. He made a nice little speech, and then Mrs Pidgeon and I distributed the gifts. Poor old things, they were dazed with the handsomeness of the gift, most of them; but some of the Mammies made all sorts of blessings, really very nice; then two more speeches from Government clerks, first proposing a vote of thanks to Charlie and second, seconding. They called him Charlie B. Hunter Esq. M.B. and so on, the Medical Officer of Bonthe and every honour they could. I could hardly keep from smiling. Then they thanked Mrs Pidgeon and me, and Charlie returned thanks. It took two hours. Tomorrow is a public holiday too by order of the Governor, rather ridiculous when we have already had Friday, Saturday and Sunday.

I am very glad the Georges and Charlie[47] seem to be settling down together, long may it last, and I really hope prove successful. I am so relieved to hear George wrote to acknowledge our little wedding gift; I never got the letter, and feared Owen had not sent it properly addressed. I gave it to Roberts and Owen to send.

In every letter I believe I say I shall write to Kate next week; but I know she is

---

46 Mr Robert Roberts would have been interested to hear about the trial, as he was himself a JP. M.B.M.B.

47 Her brother – M.B.M.B.

kind and generous enough to take this for her as well. I hope she will find some congenial friends at Cannes like she did last year.

My best love, dearest Father, to you and Kate, from your loving Maida.

3 January 1909

My dearest Father,

Here we are in the New Year. I wish you and Kate again a very very happy one: it is nice to think that I can now say I shall be looking forward to meeting you again *this* year.

We went to Victoria on Thursday and only came back yesterday afternoon at 2 o'clock, very hot and very tired. The letters arrived soon after we came. Trixie seemed rather low after your departure, and it was a short letter from her; she will have settled down by next week I hope, and next week I shall be anxiously looking out for your letter announcing your safe arrival in the south of France.

We had a very nice row up to Victoria, although very hot, and it is rather tiring sitting for five hours in the blazing heat. We left Mr Reaney here in possession of the house and we went into his when we got there, a sort of exchange is no robbery sort of thing. Charlie went into the court house as we passed, a big round mud building like this: thatched roof, the dots are the heads of the people sitting all round the court house. I went on and got tea ready, to find Sam had not packed the teapot.

After tea Mr Justice Townsend came and called. He had very kindly sent a message by Mr Reaney asking us to dine with him that night. He is quite a young-looking man, an Irishman but exceedingly nice. We walked down the village to his house (a native mud one) in brilliant moonlight, and he was waiting outside. He has two very nice fox terriers, one called Twopence and the other Mrs Wiggs.

Next morning Charlie was up at 6.15 and off after bush fowl. He got back at 8.30 with two, and two pigeon. Then he dressed and went to court and gave evidence. The man was 'let off', and when Mr Reaney came home in the evening he was disgusted; but the Judge did not think there was sufficient evidence to convict, and nor did Charlie.

We stayed the whole day there, and Charlie went after bush fowl again but was not successful. I went with him and the vegetation on the mainland is *really* tropical, of course much more so than here because this not so long ago was mangrove swamp. But at Victoria I could hardly get along after Charlie, it was so interesting. We left the road and took a little path through the bush to a little clearing (a farm they call it), just a sort of [illegible] with thatched roof reaching to the ground so that we could hardly stand up in it. They live in the town and just come there for the day. The first we came to was empty, they had gone home;

they collect the palm kernels, that is their business. We walked on down another little path and came to another: there the father was sitting at the door taking the husk off the kernels, and inside was the mother stooping over the three-legged pot of boiling rice. While I sat at the door while Charlie went off after bush fowl they took no notice of me; she went on attending to her rice, and her little girl ran out and picked cassada leaves which were laid on the top of the rice, and then the lid put on and left to finish. That was all their evening meal. They had a hen and four chickens which also go up and down with them.

We came back and left next morning at 8.20. It's a great business getting everything packed. When we started everything was enveloped in a cool grey mist just like a fog, lovely and cool, and I thoroughly enjoyed the first part of the row down till it got too hot. Charlie shot a curlew and it fell into the water and a little canoe with two men coming behind picked it up. Then he got a pigeon and then a snipe which made the soup; then as we got nearer home we came upon the little fishing 'dugouts', each with one naked man in. He sits with one leg over each side and a line attached to the big toe of each!

We bought a big cassada fish weighing about 10 lb for 9d so we brought our dinner with us! I was very glad to get home and sleep in a comfortable bed and house. I had had a bad night at Victoria; there were rats in the bedroom, and the camp beds are so near the floor that I kept jumping up all night thinking they were on the bed. Charlie was very kind and patient with me.

Yesterday we went to Mokolo the promontory, no luck as far as birds go, but very nice tea picnic there, and a lovely row home by full moon. It is very weird coming in and out of those mangrove islands at night, with six black men chanting their weird African melodies.

Goodbye for this week, dearest Father; Charlie has gone to York Island or I know would send his love. Trixie is sending *Punch* here still. Charlie thinks she ought to send them to you. Please tell her to do so, dear Father.
Best love from Maida

5 January 1909[48]

My darling Trixie,
Begin the new by calling you by your proper name! We got back from Victoria at 2 o'clock on Saturday, very hot and tired but we had a very nice time there. As soon as we turned a certain corner, we saw a German boat at anchor, and another just steaming up, so we hoped our letters would have arrived, and they came just after we got in. I am now longing for the next as I am a little afraid you might have influenza as you had such a bad head. You seem to be getting headaches so often, and I am rather afraid it's because you are straining your eyes too much over your

---

48 There is a good deal of repetition in the next letter, but some amusing extra details, so it is reproduced in full. M.B.M.B.

The countryside near Bonthe today. Photo by Redmond Shannon.

work. Now all I can say at this distance is *don't be silly*. I get headaches too, I had quite a baddish one coming down from Victoria, but I must tell you about our trip.

We left on Thursday at 11 o'clock, such a bustle we had packing, and Sam is a noodle at it. Of course he forgot the teapot! Mr Reaney had brought a message from Mr Justice Townsend asking us to dine with him that night, so that was very nice. When we reached Victoria we found the court was sitting. The court house is a big round building with thatched roof, and you can see the people sitting in from the outside. Charlie turned in in passing, and at 5 o'clock the Judge came to call. He is very young-looking but very nice indeed; he is Irish, comes from Galway. We hope he will spend a night with us if he passes this way on his return. We walked down to his house (a mud house) by brilliant moonlight, I in a white blouse and white drill skirt, and Charlie in dark blue flannel. He was waiting outside for us. We had dinner at his camp table, the size of a large table napkin! But it was very jolly, and we came back shortly after 10 o'clock.

It seemed impossible to realise that I was in West Africa and that I should spend my New Year in a mud hut. Well, that night I slept the sleep of the just. Our little camp beds are put close together so that the one net will cover them and the one pair of sheets do also. But the following night I realised that there were rats in the room! It was awful for us both, because I would jump up in a fright all the time thinking they were in the bed. Poor Charlie, it was too bad.

On New Year's morning Charlie was up at cockcrow and off shooting, and came back with two bush fowl and two pigeon; we sent one bush fowl to Mr

Townsend. I spent New Year's Day quietly in the house resting, and after tea Charlie and I went off again after guinea fowl only to be tantalised to distraction by the wretched things. We had brought Jomendi with us as well as Mormoh, and he came too, but the bush is so thick that although they were calling within a few yards of us we could not see them. It sounds most unsporting but here you have to catch these birds on a twig or a stump and shoot them as they sit, or you can never find them. The vegetation on the mainland is lovely, much more luxuriant than here; at least I ought not to say much more, perhaps that's not true, but of course this is comparatively new growth on the mangrove swamp.

The District Commissioner here, Mr Page, wanted us, I think, to come back on Friday. He never said, so, but he cast out hints. He is always off on patrol himself, they complain that he leaves the place too much; but he is so utterly impossible that I am only thankful he goes. He is not a gentleman, and is most disliked. He is very nice as far as he can be, poor thing, to us but it's only because he would not dare to be otherwise, but to his Assistant District Commissioner, Mr Reaney and Mr Paling he is a holy terror. Fortunately he has nothing to do with us; but it's a pity because in a way he does not keep up the position of the Government officials, and in a place like this where there are so many traders it is necessary. But we are very happy here, as we are quite happy together, and we like all the trading people very much, they are most nice and obliging. The Assistant District Commissioner here is a black man, Mr Metzer,[49] and really so *very* nice, much more gentlemanly than Mr Page.

We left Victoria in a dense fog on Saturday morning, it was lovely and cool. Mr Reaney walked down with us to the boat, and as we were leaving Mr Townsend came running down to say goodbye. We could not wait as the tide was turning. It was simply lovely going down the river in the mist: all along beyond the mangroves tall palms rose up, and every now and again we came to a corner where the palm and tropical vegetation had extended right to the river bank, and you would generally find there a little sandy path leading to a little *facki* of about four or six native huts.

As we came along down the river with the tide husband shot the dinner – first a curlew flew over us, bang and down he went into the water. We had just begun to turn the boat, which was no easy matter, it's such a huge thing with six oars, when a little dugout came along with two men in, and they paddled off to get it for us and brought it. I persuaded Charlie to give then 3d, rather silly, I dare say, as they never expected anything, but the boy was so pleased. He handed me a big bunch of bananas and some oranges.

We continued our voyage when next a pigeon fell to the gun, and fell into the mangroves, but the little dugout again came to our rescue and fetched it for us. We next overtook a most weird dugout. One man was standing up behind

---

49 Maida also spells this Metzler and Metzger, Metzer is the most common version.

paddling it and in the very front was a man enveloped in a shiny black mackintosh sitting in the bow, which, I may say, had been broken off. How the thing kept afloat I don't know, with alligators all around. He turned his back and kept it so the whole time we were in sight (the man in black). I fancy the other canoe had told him who Charlie was. The boatmen summed his conduct up like this: 'He do some bad, he fear.' I wonder who he was.

We stopped at the usual little stopping place, and I boiled a cup of tea and we had a hunch of your lovely Christmas cake, Belle, it's very good, and we had some bananas with it, then the boatmen came up and off we started again. We saw a most lovely heron, huge it was, a lovely blue slate grey, and under its wings and a little down its breast was magenta coloured. Charlie had a shot at it as the sailors wanted it for chop, and I wanted the skin, but alas, we were too far off. Then Charlie shot another sort of snipe which made the soup but was rather fishy. The curlew was excellent. Then we came near York Island, and came upon a little fleet of fishing dugouts. We told Kong, the coxswain, to steer us into the middle of them, and we soon had them all around us. The fishermen dispense with all clothes while they fish. We bought a 'Spanish', a big fish weighing about 12 lbs for 9d, beautiful fish it is like very excellent cod. Then we reached home.

Pooz was on the steps, and did not seen to realise for about 10 minutes that we had returned, but when he did he was overjoyed. He comes up with hoarse cries every morning to awake us. We had a quiet day on Sunday, but yesterday Charlie hardly sat down the whole day, it always comes in rushes.

Every morning now there is a thick fog, it's lovely. I stand in my nightdress in the dressing-room, drinking in the cool air; then about 10 o'clock the sun bursts through and it gets hot. That convolvulus exasperates me; it grows and grows but won't flower, and now I fear it's in too small a tin and may die before it ever flowers. The other couple are in a porous country pot, smaller than the chatty, and they now look the healthiest. The zinnias are flowering nicely now too.

I must write to May. I told you, didn't I, that the butterfly boxes have been carried by mistake down the coast; but the butterflies all seem to have disappeared! We saw two most lovely little birds as we came along on Saturday. The first was as big as a blackbird and brilliant cardinal with just a black head, and shoulders; it was hopping about in the mangroves. The other was a little kingfisher, smaller than those in my hat, a lovely metallic purple. Then there was a kind of fly-catcher, its back and head are green, the green of verdigris, and under its wings is bright chestnut colour and it has a long tail.

I had such a nice letter from Mrs Finchett Maddock, I must try to answer it; and also such a nice one last week from Miss Clemenger; my letters are getting dreadfully into arrears. I've been busy mounting my few plants since I returned, and have not nearly finished. I had such a killing letter from Dr Keenan the other day. They have found the roll of films, but only one or two are any good. They have not come yet.

'Making a canoe', undated old postcard, sourced from http://www.sierra-leone.org/Postcards/
SL887927.jpg

7 January 1909

They've just come this morning; they are not at all good. I evidently had not got the camera straight in the one of the house.

We went to Mokolo yesterday afternoon; the tide was against us so we took nearly two hours to go. We started at 2 o'clock and took tea with us. It was a disappointing trip for Charlie as he got no birds, but I enjoyed it awfully . I found an orchid growing on a tree, it appeared common. Do you remember Mrs Finchett Maddock giving us a spray of little yellow orchid? Well, it was like that only smaller and more dingy looking. It's beautifully cool this morning, temperature down to 76°.

We had very nice fish-cakes for breakfast made of boiled fish and rice mixed with an egg and fried. Last night coming from Mokolo the moon which was full was rising as we were getting down to the boats. A beautiful red it was as it rose through the mist; it was lovely.

My young seal, did I ever thank you for the *Punches* and *Tatler*? It is so very good of you to send them to us; but does not dear Father want *Punch*? Charlie thinks it ought to be sent to him. I am anxiously waiting the post from the south of France with news that he has arrived safely. Charlie has gone to York Island; I would have gone too, only I had not finished my letters. I've written to May, and I have to write to Elsie so I must stop. I've begged Charlie to get off on one of the mangrove islands to see if there are eggs in a bird house (that's what they call a nest!) I saw as I was returning from Victoria. They tell me parrots build in the very top of high palm trees and their nests are impossible to find.

I am asking Mr and Mrs Pidgeon to dinner on Saturday, rather a fag, but we think we ought to.

All my love for this week, my own own Belle, from Twisty

P.S. We begin our fourth month today. We landed three months today.

9 January 1909

My darling Belle,

I am beginning my letter today as I expect the mail will he in today, a boat is expected. I want to hear from you as I rather suspected by your last letter that you were in for influe,[50] but I hope not. I also shall be very glad to hear from Father of his safe arrival. When Charlie came back from York Island on Thursday (he sees the daily telegrams there) he said you were having terrible snowstorms at home, unprecedented the wire said. I do hope you are all right; he also said there had been a terrible earthquake in Sicily, and that Naples was awful with the dead bodies being brought there.

I immediately thought of Father and hope they would feel nothing of it at Cannes. It might unnerve Father; we shall he anxiously awaiting the papers.

Fancy your having such snow. I always think a big snowstorm is so romantic, until it begins to thaw. When Charlie was telling me about it, and how trains were snowed up etc. I was muttering 'How lovely, how lovely', but Charlie did not agree.

I was so glad you had driven to Nazareth[51] with Father. I am sure you miss him. You said in one of your letters that Elsie once thought of selling that bracelet of Mother's. I wish she would sell it to me, I always liked it.

At last, my dear, there are buds on the convolvulus, but unfortunately the bottom leaves seem inclined to turn yellow; that may be its nature. It has grown right up the trellis work of the steps, and if it opens will be a great pleasure. We have dug up another little plot and fenced it in with a hedge of palm leaves and sown some more beans. We had our last dish from the first plot the night before last, and now the second plot is beginning to pod, they really have been true to their name, 'Canadian wonders'.

I have finished *Marcella* by Mrs Humphrey Ward and have now begun *Robert Ellesmere*. I enjoy her books very much, but I did not like *Marcella* nearly as much as *Diana Mallory*.

I went for a short walk last night with Charlie just round by the Hospital. I've been feeling rather limp and headachy, it may be I've been eating too much Christmas cake. We have the two going; I keep them rolled up in the greaseproof paper and cut wedges out of first one and then the other.

I wrote to Emily Pattullo yesterday. I'm trying to take a letter a day to finish off

---

50 Presumably influenza.
51 Presumably a local chapel. M.B.M.B.

the budget I had: so please tell Mrs Finchett Maddock that I am taking them in rotation, and give her and Lucy Potts my love.

At Mokolo the other day I got my white Island blouse (the dress Charlie gave me) so stained on the arm with some plant. I can't find out which plant it is: Mrs Faunce told me to beware of it. I also found the other day that my black evening skirt which was in my box was all mildewy, irreparably so I fear. I must have my blue serge dress out for inspection, it is in the big wooden box. We asked the Pidgeons to dinner tonight, but they are going to the court at Victoria on some civil case of his, and won't be back in time.

Charlie is expecting a big case of drugs by this boat and I am almost hoping my butterfly boxes will come; but as it happens the butterflies have disappeared for the time being. Charlie says they come on more in the rainy season. I've mounted 59 plants; I expect I shall have about 70 to send off next week, and 30 or 40 grasses all mounted on nice paper; they look rather toney! I am now going to attend to housekeeping duties, it's Saturday. The butcher came last night to say they 'kill cow' today, so I ordered 1½ lbs fillet and gravy beef and this morning Mormoh came to say 'They no kill cow Mar, I go 5 o'clock time, cow no kill, I come back make porridge, and go 8 o'clock time, no cow kill.' I wonder why the villain changes his mind. However Mrs Jones, another butcher, volunteered to kill a mutton, so we ordered a leg which has come.

I was amused to hear that Mrs Morgan Lloyd had dressed three times to go and call on the bride!

I saw such a jolly country basket the other day; it belonged to one of Mr Heaney's Court messengers. He said he would try to get me three but now he tells me they don't come from up his river but from up the Kittim River. They are not made here. I also saw a very pretty one the shape of that one we brought from Algiers only done in coloured grasses; it belonged to one of the boatmen. He wanted to sell it to me, but Charlie told him to bring me a clean one next time he went up the river. The chances are I'll never see the dirty one again or a clean one!

Going to Mokolo the other day I saw something move near a bush on the beach. I thought it was [illegible]. I looked again and saw it was a monkey with a long tail. He then marched along the sand. I thought he looked sweet, Charlie thought him 'loathsome'!

Monday

The mail came yesterday bringing a nice haul for me, one from you, one from dear Father, Elsie, Edith and Katie of Bryn Teg, and Dr Ballingal, very nice, all good news. I was so thankful to hear of Father's safe arrival but so sorry he had such a disappointment over the rooms. He sounded tired, poor old darling, and his brollie had been broken on the journey. The mail arrived overland. Just after lunch I had gone up to try to put an india-rubber filling into the tooth Clarke filled for me before I left, when I could hear Charlie call 'Maida, the mail!' Down I flew and let my fillings go to the winds. You had ended your letter up in a hurry after being out with the beagles. I am *always* so glad when I hear of your being out, it's so good for you; and dearest Trixie, could you for my sake give up either your early morning tea or the cup you have after dinner. I only take it once a day now.

Mormoh seem to be a darling.[52] Pooz has a cool fit on these days.

Last night after tea Charlie and I set off for a round, first to see the old Chief who has come back again, his heart is bad; then on to the Hospital. There is such a nice little girl in now with curvature of the spine and an abscess on her spine. Charlie operated the other day and she is much better. When I went in last night she was reading her Bible. I sent her by Charlie this morning 'The World and his Wife' and the two coloured pictures of the *Graphic*. He says she was very pleased. We came back and Charlie went to call upon Mr Page, and I took Pooz on the wharf, then we came in and had our bath. As we were dressing after I heard a great noise and we looked out and saw a big fire, a house as big as this with a zinc roof belonging to a Chief. He is brother to a large native trader here, whose warehouse burnt up under suspicious circumstances a few months ago. You never heard such yelling, waving their arms shouting 'Lord a mussy'. I got Charlie to take me to see it and Jomendi came too as escort. Then we got back and were at dinner who walked in but Mr Page – such cheek it is of him to walk in like that. He is a most unpleasant man. He is anything but a gentleman and tries to be familiar, and yet one feels he would always do one a bad turn. He is most heartily disliked, but to have him stalking in like that is insupportable.

It's now 2.00 p.m. I've just packed a pair of socks for dear Father for his birthday. I've not idled a minute of today, all morning doing the laundry list, putting out clothes to air in the sun (it's a dull day though) and I've been at my plants, and am going at them again as I want to send them home by the *Axim* on Thursday. I've wasted a little time since lunch teasing Charlie!

Tuesday

I regret that the palms I had got and planted died so I sent Jomendi for another. He brought first a small one, then a beauty, and I have it in a big Kerosin oil tin with water; I think it will do better. A woman has just come selling oranges. She comes regularly: eight beauties for 1d and six bananas for 1d. The pineapples are not yet quite ripe, and the new crop of avocado pears is growing; they are now the size of hen's eggs.

Pooz has caught two palm birds this morning. He only hurls them down, doesn't eat them; he is so interested in his game (he is under the big mango tree) that he has not come in for his milk.

---

52 This must refer to the Bronceris kitten. M.B.M.B.

We heard last night that two little piccins were burnt in the fire, poor little things. They were lighting a lamp and it fell over and took fire, and one of them was blinded so could not see the door. That's all I could gather from Sam.

Darling Belle, you must not send me any more papers, one a month is really too many, please don't, darling.

Another dull morning but delightfully cool. We hear Mr Reaney has to proceed at once on leave so he may be here today or tomorrow.

13th

Yesterday afternoon Charlie and I were sitting on the front door steps, Charlie joinering! and I laughing till I could hardly stop. He always breaks his tools, the strongest iron implements break in his hand! How I laugh. He was fitting up wooden wedges for the box taking his blood-sucking flies to England.[53] Well, up came a parcel for me with the stockings hanging out! They tear them open at the Customs at Freetown. Many many thanks, darling Belle, for the pins, pens, sealing wax (I'd nearly finished mine), the four little mats and the stockings: have you put down all postage? I am enclosing a cheque for £1 for postage etc. I will give 3/- for the linen dress, and if you can find that old cream mercerised lawn blouse of mine you might send it. I may have given it away, I think I did. Put on the outside 'Used or half-worn clothing'. Will you get me enough chiné ribbon for a belt to twist round and 1½ yards for a panama hat of 6½ or 8¾ stuff, all postage to be taken out of the £1 including postage of parcel: I think 3/- mean for the dress, so take 4/-. If you don't I'll not ask you to do anything more for me! Will you also get me 1 dozen neck supports 2½ inches and 1 dozen 2¼ inches, with no metal about them as they iron-mould. I am sorry to trouble you, dearest Belle.

I am so distressed to hear the dear Aunts have not heard from me. I have written three letters to Aunt Kate, one from the Islands and two from here, and I will write again in a week or so. I think of them *so* much, and wonder what Aunt Kate would think of my housekeeping!

At last Mrs Bodvel's flowers are in bud. In two days I think two will be open. We planted beans on Saturday night, they were up Tuesday morning, and we are having nice dishes from the others. It came on wet yesterday and rained nicely all night; today the Harmattan is blowing, a nice cool wind with haze, and today our washing water was quite cold.

I've at last got mounted on yellow paper with labels with notes of soil, height etc. etc. finished of 70 flowering plants, 12 ferns and 34 grasses, and they are to go today to England.[54] It sounds nothing, but it's been 'sweat of brow' work, and

---

53 These were mosquitoes collected in the various West African rivers to send home for the research into malaria which was then being developed. M.B.M.B.

54 Note (1989): The list of plants and two letters of appreciation of her work were preserved with my papers. I think the contact with the Natural History Museum was made through

Charlie at Bonthe: Maida's photo from the family album

I don't fancy they are particularly interesting, so excuse a hurried ending; in case I go to York Island tomorrow I'm finishing my letters today. Best best love from us both,
Your own Twisty

P.S. One of the missionaries from Freetown who came out on the *Karina*, Miss [illegible] came to see me yesterday. She and another had come by the *Axim* and were returning today. Sister Stephens of the Nursing Home had been very ill with dysentery. I've written to ask her here for a change.

Miss G. Lister, niece of Lord Lister and a distinguished botanist, who was a great friend of my godmother, May Bradford. The papers are now with the originals of the letters at Rhodes House, Oxford. M.B.M.B.

18 January 1909

My darling Belle,

Your dear long letter arrived yesterday; very many thanks for it. What a cold Christmas you had; and even Father says they had snow in the south of France. Poor darling, I've been addressing my letters c/o Thomas Cook, Cannes, and I sent a postcard to the pension he told me they were going to, to say my letters were at Thomas Cook. I am so distressed about it thinking he will have thought I had forgotten him.

Everything has been going on just the same. I felt rather lost without my poor old pressed flowers after I sent them, but I must try and set to and get more. On Saturday two of the Sisters of Mercy came and had tea with me. One is the one who is always here, the other came from Freetown to relieve two others who have gone there. The one from Freetown I liked, she was so straightforward and honest in everything she said; the one here is quite unfathomable. They enjoyed the tea very much, poor things, they lead such an unselfish colourless life. The one from Freetown has been out 18 years and only back in Europe once, and then not to her home in Ireland, but to France, and she never wants to go home again. It's terrible, isn't it?

Such a sad thing has happened here. A young man in Mr Pidgeon's firm has died up the river, quite a lad, he was down at Christmas time at the cricket quite well, and now is buried. Mr Pidgeon has two others ill, and no one to relieve them, so they are in a fix, poor things.

My poor cat, Belle, is so ill. Yesterday all day I thought he was dying. He seemed ill on Saturday afternoon and could hardly crawl after us to the wharf, and when we came back we gave him a dose of castor oil. He couldn't eat his dinner, and next morning when we came down he had crawled into the pantry, but when he heard my voice he struggled up, poor little thing. We gave him more castor oil, and in giving it it got all over the poor thing, and all the dirt has stuck to it, and he has not the strength to wash it off. He is sleeping all day today, but looks frightfully ill. I felt convinced he had been poisoned, but the servants think he has fever.

Tuesday 18 January

Don't read this letter to Auntie Kate because she would scorn me writing so much about Puss! Today when we came down he seemed so glad to see us, and actually was able to jump on Charlie's knee, but so tottery, poor little thing, and when he jumped down he nearly fell. But he made a good breakfast and has tried to wash himself, poor dirty little thing. It's dreadful for him because it's all castor oil and dirt. It's all I can do to do things for him because you know what a horror I have of castor oil, but by tomorrow he will be a clean cat again I think. I tried to wash him yesterday with hot water and cotton wool, but was only successful round his mouth. I fancy he has had fever for all round his mouth was harsh and dry, and he likes the hot water there very much. I should have been so sorry if he had died, because he amuses us so much, he is so odd, and he looked such a pitiful little object on Sunday morning. Sam said all along in a most cheerful voice 'He no die, Mar,' hut Jomendi said 'Johnnie (the garden boy) he say Pooz go for die.'

Fancy, it is difficult to follow the workings of these niggers' minds. A man came to say yesterday from the Mendi country that Jomendi's mother was ill. I asked him if he wanted to go and see her, hut he didn't understand that (he is only just beginning to know English) and he said 'My brother come and say my Mammie sick!' So I said 'Well, don't you want to go and see her?' and he said, 'When Master done go to England, den I go back to my country,' but his face all worked for a moment. I turned to Sam and said, 'Doesn't he really want to go?' and Sam asked him in Mendi and said, 'He say No, Mar!' All Sam's sentences are shot out like pistol shots because of his stammering.

My darling Belle, such a disappointment, after all our waiting the convolvulus have come out white and dark blue! Not that lovely pale blue shade at all; but the one creeping up the lattice of the front door is blue, and it's a fine purplie blue I must say, and now covered with bloom; so I hope it will be a great pleasure once the disappointment is over.

Wednesday 20 January

We are gathering such lovely dishes of French beans, they have been marvellous. Just one or two here and there of the onions you sent me the seed of have peeped up; they may come on though; and at last one tomato is beginning as well. Charlie would have knocked them off, but I knew if they were not able to stand my gentle pushes that they were no use, and the sooner the better they relieved the tree.

Dearest, yesterday afternoon the *Boulama* came in bringing our newspapers. Childie, all the papers you have sent have come, but darling you are too good, you know you are, and I must ask you to pay for them with the money I am sending because I feel it's too good of you. And you wrote such a lovely long letter this week. I love hearing all you do and all the people you see.

I had felt so distressed that I had not warned you I was sending my fur by Mr Reid, and to tell you I was putting in no letter. I am so afraid you were disappointed; but I think it is better in parcels not to put letters as they all have to go through the Customs, and the Customs officials have been so extremely obliging to us.

I am sorry to say Mormoh is seedy; Charlie thinks he has influenza and neuralgia, but he is better today.

We heard, I think I told you, that Mr Reaney was to be relieved by Captain Hodding of the WAFF[55] and that he was going overland; so he wrote me a note of goodbye, and sent me some jolly kak wood, I think I told you, also an old desk of his. Was it not kind of him? And we have been expecting Mr Townsend down

55 West African Frontier Force.

every day from Victoria. However Captain Hodding arrived here yesterday by the *Boulama*, and Mr Reaney arrived last night at 9 o'clock. They both put up under the District Commissioner's house. Mr Page brought Captain Hodding to call after tea yesterday; we were in the garden. He was a very jolly sort of man [of] about 45. He said he had been made to sign a paper that he would not take his wife with him nor allow her to follow! It's because they think it keeps the District Commissioners from doing their patrolling properly. He said he had heard that Mrs Faunce has not been well this time, and she may go to Mrs Hodding at the Hill Station till he goes back. I've not seen Mr Reaney so far, he cannot leave now till the *Batanga* comes in Saturday or Sunday unless he goes overland, but I believe that will suit him. If he left before the 24th he would not have completed 13 months, and for every full month over time you get ten days extra leave; but the Government won't recognise less than one month's service.

I am reading *Robert Ellesmere*, ancient history for a great reader like you, but Mrs Humphrey Ward's books are well worth reading. It's rather a melancholy story though, isn't it?

I can hear you ask how Pooz is. Much better, thank you. He is now I might say quite out of the wood. But he could not bring himself to wash, so this morning I got some hot water and ammonia and washed Charlie's hairbrushes and then put him into it as far as I could. He was furious, and yet something seemed to tell him it was for his good! I got his chest and front legs well washed with soap, and then rubbed him with a dry towel, rather too energetically as my way is, dear Belle, and I heard one low growl! But ever since he has been hard at work washing 'hisself'.

Here are the French books:

Le Crime de Sylvestre Bonnard – Daudet
Le Nabob – Daudet
Les Rois en Exile – Daudet
L'Etui de Nacre – Anatole France
Samuel Brohl et Cie (Cherbuliez)

I've put them down as they are written by Mrs McLehose, but I'm ashamed to say I am not quite sure which is title, which author, except Daudet, I know his name. But they are all good books and I know would not corrupt your or Miss Clemenger's morals! I think if Mrs Wynn Jones joined it would spoil it, she is a fine intelligent woman warped!

I've had my half-blinds washed. They looked very toney when I put them up, but with this Harmattan the dust blows in the day, and a *very* heavy dew at night, [so] that they get dirty so quickly. Mr Page has evidently been much struck with them, because he said yesterday, 'Mrs Hunter, I must let you into a great secret. I've been hemming curtains!'

What a jolly lot of presents you got. I like my little calendar from Nellie so much, I must write to her, and dear old Elsie has sent me three such nice crochet mats. I had been keeping her mixed biscuits till the cakes were finished, and yesterday I opened the tin (I have kept two wedges of cake, I want to ask Mrs Pidgeon to tea) as the Customs had knocked a hole in, but I had filled it with red sealing wax. But no, those wretched little red ants had got in. They will be no worse; in fact, I remember Lucy Knox recommending me a tonic made of ants' blood, and these are the ones I fancy. They are full of formalin, Charlie says!

Childie, I hardly like to allude to your promise of another cake; it's too good of you, dearest. I hope your children's party went off well. This, I know, is a dull letter, I've felt a wee bit dull, nothing very definite to do, but I'm bucking and will I am sure be full of buck again next week.

My very best love to you and to the dear Aunties and Bessie, and also to Mrs Finchett Maddock.

Ever, my own Belle,

your Twisty

21 January 1909

Good morning. I am going to York Island today for the sail, back to lunch. Mr Reaney and Mr Page [are] dining here tonight.

25 January 1909

My darling Belle,

Your nice long letter came by the *Batanga* on Friday, just after lunch. I was so delighted to get it but, my darling, you are surely not sending me another box of cakes. It's too good of you. They did not come by this boat [and] I suppose got left at Freetown. It is a dreadful post office: but I shall have it to look forward to next week.

I did so enjoy your letter and I love to hear all you do, but before I go any further, my pet, what a shock I had with the Waterloo House bill. To begin with, I never had any batiste in August, you know I had nothing made, not did I have 6 yards of sateen, or braid. I know nothing of them, I never had them. It must be that unscrupulous Miss Hopkins who got them for herself. Now don't do anything but look on the paid bill from Waterloo House. If you remember I drove there and paid the night before I left home. Also send me Miss Hopkins's receipted bill. There are only 12 yards val lace on my dress and 6 yards insertion, and if there is any bother about it I will return the dress for them to see as I can do without it. It's most annoying. I think on the file too you will find Hamley's receipted bill, as I have the counterfoil in my cheque book.

Really Bessie is a most annoying person. I should not bother to want to play with her; she is always the same, is she not? She has her good points in other ways

I suppose. Does Eileen Clemenger play now, and was the fair Adrian home for Christmas?

I am so glad your Christmas party was such a success. I am sure the children enjoyed it.

I am glad to hear the watch and films arrived safely. I wonder how they will turn out. I was so amused when I was writing home the other week, Sam came and stood by me, and after much stammering I found he wanted to know whether the watch was coming and how much it cost! They are killing, but he has been so good this week. Mormoh has been home ill for two days. Fortunately he was able to come back yesterday as the Judge arrived in the evening. We had been more or less expecting him all day, but he never arrived till the evening. He is a most gentlemanly man, but oh so nervous, he has a sort of St Vitus's dance which convulses him every now and again, and it may be he is landed here for a week or so! He was to have gone on to Shugi tomorrow, but it appears instead of finishing at Victoria on 12 January, and afterwards the date was altered to the 20th, it is now the 25th, and Mr Page told him he would find no one there.

It also appears that he left his address at the Post Office at Freetown for all letters to be sent to Victoria. None arrived. He wrote and wired to the Postmaster General who wired back that they had been sent, and now he finds that by mistake they have sent them all to Shengi, and no doubt all official letters as well. He is terribly heavy company. Charlie came to bed more dead than alive last night! He has the most angelic little wire-haired fox terrier called Mrs Wiggs and she has three puppies three weeks old. I should simply love to have one, only I should have to leave it behind and that would be too painful. I have not seen the puppies because he is very nice in that he sent his dogs with his servants. Mr Reaney used to annoy us by bringing his dog with him. Any other dog I really should not have minded but I did not like that one.

He came in to dinner on Friday night. He asked if he might. We were very glad to see him, and he sent me two big bags of Liberian coffee. I wish I could send you some; I will bring some with me, though I wonder whether you will like it.

I only had letters from dear Father, Kate, Elsie and you this week. I must try and get some more letters answered. I am not doing quite so much plant gathering these days: I don't know how it is, we don't seem to get so much time for walks. Charlie has been busy, and also I took a little rest; but I must begin again. Mr Page has lent me *Pride and Prejudice* and Carlyle's *Past and Present*. I am so glad to have them. I did not care very much for *Robert Ellesmere*, I was interested in it but it was so depressing. I am going to send to Lees for strong cambric this mail for making drawers. I do not want to send my good ones here because Mrs Peters has rather fallen off in her washing (but has been warned!), and also all the perspiring makes them rot. I shall have them made by Kate's pattern, they are so delightfully cool. I shall also get a little cambric to be making into camisoles to have something to sew.

Belle (Beatrice) Roberts, from the family abum

Mr Reaney left by the *Batanga* for Freetown today but goes home by the Villa boat tomorrow. He is a queer fish; he would like to bring one of his daughters out with him next time.

27 January

As you say you can always tell by my letters if I'm not well, I may as well tell you I don't feel very fit today. I forgot to tell you about a week ago I found a jigger in my toe which Charlie took out for me. It was not painful but a very nasty and queer feeling. It's a tiny insect that burrows into one's foot and there makes a nest. In about ten days it begins to wriggle (horrible, isn't it?) and you can see a black head under the skin, and you have to cut it out with its bag of eggs about the size of a sweet pea seed. Well, now I have another, it's more painful and made me seedy, bilious and bad throat but no fever. I hope it will be ready to take out tomorrow, when I hope I shall feel better. Charlie has gone to play tennis at the French Company. I of course cannot walk.

I am such a bother, darling, but I think I shall have to ask you to send me my strong black boots if you can find them. I'm afraid I get these jiggers by going out with boots with holes in, and I've worn two pairs out, they were old when they came. Charlie has been so busy, there is a lot of illness about, and he has had two big operations at the Hospital. If it had not been for these Mr Page had asked us to come with him and Mr Townsend up to Shengi but as it [is] I'm very glad we did not go.

These palm birds are having their second nesting since we have been here, it's when they are building they make such a terrible noise.

6.30

Charlie just came back, and a letter waiting him on the steps wanting him to go to

York Island, so he has just changed and gone off, and won't be back till 9 o'clock or so. Another man very ill with fever.

9.00 p.m.

Sam is hanging out of the pantry window and I out of the bedroom window watching for the boat. There is a lovely half-moon so it's light outside. Pooz is perambulating about the garden quite restored, only about six spots of castor oil left!

Thursday

Charlie did not arrive till 9.45. I was listening to hear the splash of oars come round the island when instead I heard a snorting, and they sent him in the steam launch. He made them toot the whistle to show he was coming.

I am thankful to say I feel better today. The jigger is quiet and will be ready to pull tomorrow; but I don't know what gave me the bilious attack; everything is different when one is well.

I am at last sending £1.10 of Holt's money. Will you take 5/- for the dress and the remainder for all little expenses of postage etc. Pay yourself back for all you have spent 'di lol!⁵⁶

Charlie saw Mrs Pidgeon as he was going to the French Company last night and she said she was going to call today. She told him she was coming last Friday, and I stayed in and she never came, and I heard she had gone on to the ship, so I shall tell her so! I hear they have been asked by the firm to stay till July; they were going home in March.

Oh, I've been wanting to tell you, perhaps I have already done so, but the chocolates Mr [illegible] gave me at Christmas were lovely, and I came to the conclusion that the insides were made of almond, sugar and a little bit of chocolate mixed with the white of egg. Well, that's common enough, I can hear you say. Yes, but the almonds had been browned first before being crushed! That's what it tasted to me like, I will try [it] I think when I get home. I made a little lemon (or lime) curd the other day, it's very good, but I was telling Charlie I think with limes I must use a wooden spoon to turn it, as the metal spoons are inclined to taste.

Mormoh is having a slack fit these days, and I gave Sam a piece of my mind yesterday, and the washer-woman on Monday. She brought me a present of mangoes today! With all my love, my little pet, this is a dreadfully dull letter.

I am so glad you and Elsie see one another's letters.
Ever your loving Twisty

---

56 A Welsh expression. M.B.M.B.

Do let me know by return whether I shall buy you the pineapple dress. The Indian may be here any day!

1 February 1909

My darling Childie,

Your dear letter reached me yesterday evening. Charlie and I had just finished tea (we were expecting the mails overland) and I had gone to the pantry to make a custard as Mormoh is ill again, and I looked through the window to see if I could see the little boat coming when, lo and behold, I saw a German ship in the act of anchoring. She had come up without tooting; but there was no sign of the little boat with mails. So we went for our walk first up to the Hospital. Charlie called to see Mormoh on the way and found him very bad. Charlie took him into the Hospital. He never told the boys he was not feeling well, and I fancy must have gone out dancing on Saturday night, and has now, I'm afraid, got pneumonia. Then we went on to the French Company. Charlie wanted to see Mr Dubois. One of their men died here two years ago, and his people want the remains home, but they have to wait two years before they are exhumed, and now the two years is up. Charlie has arranged to go and see it done tomorrow morning. He gets £5.5.0 for it! and the grave-digger gets 25/- and the cemetery clerk £1.1.0, a great haul for them.

Now before I go on, oh but to finish first, we heard at the French Company that the letters had arrived, and there they were; for me, a very jolly one from Father, really a wonderful letter, one from George, Elsie and Jess, and one from the Sister at Freetown to say she could not come. Charlie got letters from Captain Bond, Jess and his lawyer. So we set to and read. I read all the others first, then I took up a very fat rubbishy-looking one which turned out to be from a vagabond at Bronceris! In the middle I was hauled off for my bath. Thank you my pet for all your loving messages, and for getting me Sam's watch. I wish you could have seen his face, he was simply delighted. I think he thought it wasn't coming. While we were bathing we found the German ship had disgorged her parcels, and there was that lovely box for me. I have not opened it yet, I am waiting till Charlie gets back from the Hospital. He likes a finger in every pie! And I like to keep it somehow to feel there is something more from you still to open.

Now before I allude to your letter I will give you an account of my doings since my last letter. I was feeling very flat in my last as I expect you saw, but I am thankful to say I felt better on Friday. On Wednesday we had a great time, and Thursday afternoon, unpacking a case of drugs for Charlie, £8 they cost. The boys loved the job, and the medicine room looks so nice and tidy, so different from when we arrived. I forget what we did on Friday. On Thursday afternoon Mr and Mrs Pidgeon came to tea. I thought they would never go. Charlie left after tea, he had to go and see a German who was ill, and he said he would come back for me, and there he found them still here; so they walked up to the Hospital with us.

They asked us to dinner Saturday night. We went! I put on the dress Flora McDonnell made me, and found Mrs Pidgeon in a high washing blouse. We waited and waited for dinner and at last we went in, very messy. I've given an account of it to Maude Clemenger. Poor Charlie did not enjoy it at all, nor did I; they are too common for anything. We first had Scotch broth, that was good; then beef olives done nearly black. Oh before that fish done in a pie dish, and fancy, the pie dish had been burnt black. If she had only taken salt to it and had it cleaned. Then the beef olives, then duck, and by this time she was calling the boys for port wine. At last it came and he poured me out a glass when [there was] a shriek from her, 'He's poured out Madeira!' All the time pickle pots were flying round. Then a boiled pudding, not bad, then apricots filled with cream, not good. After dinner we sat on the verandah and coffee came, ditch water, then I could see her asking the boy for something and at last she said 'Great Scot, bring the liqueurs!' I nearly laughed. Then Mr Pidgeon asked Charlie to play a game of billiards, and she sat at her piano and strummed, you never heard anything like it. At 10 o'clock we bid them good night. In crossing the yard I was so busy watching two geese hissing at us that I nearly fell into a gutter, but saved myself by catching hold of my poor Charles and gave him a bad blow! It was a lovely moonlight night and we enjoyed the tiny walk home. I shall ask them back and then I hope we shall have done our duty.

Yesterday Mormoh never turned up, and we got no fish all day, so poor Pooz was very grumpy. He comes up every morning to call us, but Sunday morning we closed the door at the top of the stairs as he insists on our getting up at 6.30. Charlie heard a melancholy wail at 6.30!

Last night we had a tornado. It began with a great wind howling all around, they terrify me, especially coming now in the dry season. The thunder and lightning were not very bad, but downpours of rain. I kept poor Charlie awake for an hour and a half, so he says, and he says he is going to put me to sleep downstairs so that he can have a night's rest! But I maintain I did sleep off and on, for at one time I dreamt the German Emperor was attacking us with his cannon which turned out to be the thunder.

Just now I went into the drawing room and had an orange. I happened to look through the window to see under the big mango tree my poor Pooz with the prison dog at his nose, and he daren't move or he would have been caught. His tail was arched and huge. I sent Jomendi and Johnnie to the rescue, and Pooz flew in and came in crying bitterly!

Dear Belle, I am so sorry to hear of poor Aunt Mary's illness. I am afraid they have a sore trial in front of them, and I fear poor Aunt Mary is in a bad way; I am so very sorry. I am going to write to her this week; and Mona's friend dying, Elsie told me about it. You know I think the strain of going in for a medical degree is too much for most women.

1 p.m.

My little pet, we have just opened the lovely box of cakes you have sent us. Wee Belle, you spoil us; the Aberffraw cakes[57] might that minute have come out of the oven, *lovely* they are, and to think that your dear hands have made and punched them makes them all the dearer. Now, sweet childie, no more, or I shall begin to think dear Auntie Kate was right when she said I was pampered. You are the kindest sister anyone ever had, and I do nothing, absolutely nothing, for you.

2 February 1909

Fancy, it's only half past 8, and I have come in after taking Charlie halfway to the Hospital. We were called at 6 o'clock as Charlie had to be at the Churchyard at 8 o'clock.

Last night after tea we walked along to the French Company and had a set and a half of tennis. I have bought a pair of rope shoes, 1/-, the smallest pair they had, but it's all I can do to keep them on my feet. I enjoyed the tennis though very much.

I told you Mormoh is at the Hospital and we have an old cook of Dr Dawson's. He has been with the French Company. He is not nearly so good a cook as Mormoh, I shall be thankful to have him back.

And now about the photos. The one of the house is really quite decent, you will have had my others now explaining the rooms, but for further explanations, these windows are, beginning from left side, pantry, two medicine room windows and two spare bedroom windows; the drawing room windows are behind the tree. This tree was bare when we arrived but is now covered with lovely leaves, a beautiful green and veined with very dark red and brown. The three windows upstairs are where we dress, our dressing and bathroom. If you look on the pantry windowsill you will see Sam's leather and the silver pepper pots. They are always put out in the sun all morning, to keep dry I suppose.

My poor Pooz – I told you he were a fright, but a dear puss and very kind to me. Charlie is awfully fond of him. I am sorry to say Charlie has torn up the picture of us standing on the steps. He says I looked like a housemaid.[58]

Your work sounds most interesting. I am sure it will be lovely when it is done.

I call the Aunts' bill of nearly £16 exorbitant. Surely they do, that does not include the nurse does it? Ours is bad enough I think. Who is it for? I fancy he has put me in too, the brute! Has anyone been successful in finding Mrs Lloyd Roberts at home?

The reason you get my letters earlier now is that they leave Freetown on Saturday instead of Monday.

---

57 A classic kind of Welsh biscuit, often cooked in scallop-shaped tins.

58 History repeated itself. Thirty-six years later my husband John took an oil painting of me done by Felix Harta during the war, and put it on the bonfire. M.B.M.B.

3 February

We had a very jolly walk last night. Charlie took his gun and we went up to the cassada farm, and then turned off to the left by a path which led us into very nice parts, large patches of cleared land. I found a most curious plant, at first I thought it was a fungus; a thing like this: The dotted top is a big brown head. I am sending it to Professor Bower at Glasgow to ask what it is. Charlie got two pigeon which we are having for lunch today done in the baking pot and haricot beans baked with them. It was a lovely evening. We had our dinner and were just beginning piquet when a knock at the gate, a man come for Charlie, his sister-in-law very ill. I went with Charlie just as I was, up the road and turned to the left. Charlie told me to stay outside, but a Mammy came and asked me in, and I was dying to see inside. I walked in through a small room with a tiny wooden bed and a hammock in it and sat there. In the kitchen six Mammies sitting all round the room with turbans on, quite still. One would now and again mutter 'La!' To my grief I could not see into the bedroom, but the woman's mother, husband, brother-in-law and sister-in-law and Charlie were there, and it was the size of the bird-room, not so big, at Rodney Street. She had fever, a temperature of 105–7°, and was in a torpor. After Charlie had examined her and found it was malaria, I could hear him issuing orders for windows to be opened and for the Mammies to clear! He sent her medicine and this morning she is better. A killing sight, I shall never forget it; there were two doors to the house, and people were coming in through the other door, walked into the bedroom, had a look and went out. As they came in they said 'How do?' and a chorus of low 'How does' [came] from the Mammies sitting round.

Darling, we had the yeast cake for tea last night, lovely it is. I like it better than the Christmas cake, but Charlie doesn't, although he thoroughly enjoys this one. Little Belle, such a dear to think of Twisty.

Poor Mormoh, we went to see him last night. His temperature was 105°C. Charlie thinks he has a little malaria as well. He is a great rascal but I am longing to have him back.

I've been trying to make pineapple jelly. I took three pines and boiled them down, but instead of juice pouring out they seemed to soak it up. I only got half a pint of juice, and I put in half a pound of sugar and it's got treacly in the boiling I think. I started boiling it on my spirit lamp in the drawing room, stirring it and reading an article on 'Socialism' in *The Times*. All of a sudden the lamp all blazed up, and I shrieked for Sam. We put it out and the saucepan was sent to finish its doing in the kitchen.

Goodbye for this week, my young Larkspur! Ever your very own Twisty

Darling, thank you so so much for the *Ladies Field* and *Punch*. We have just had dinner and after a glass of Madeira and Aberffraw cake, lovely.

One of Maida's
pictures of
Bonthe, from
the family
album

Went the same walk this evening, lovely. I dug up the root of that plant, one huge tuber like a huge potato; it's evidently an arum lily of the Lords and Ladies type. Charlie got two pigeon. Those two we had for lunch were boach, the liver chopped up in the stuffing.

Thursday

I am going to York Island with Charlie today, so I am afraid I shall not have time to write to Elsie, so will you let her see this. A great tornado of rain last night, but the thunder not very bad.

10 February 1909

My darling Belle,

Very many thanks for your nice letter which came last Friday. I do not like very much the mails coming on Friday as it makes the week long waiting for the next. But this week I want the steamer to come as soon as possible as she is direct from England, and we get fresh butter from them, in jam pots kept on ice, and only 1/6 a lb.. Here we pay 1/3 for a half-pound tin of train oil! So it makes such a difference.

Thank you too so much for the *Ladies' Field* and *Punch*. We do enjoy them so much, it's very good of you to send them to me. I have lent a lot of the back numbers to Mrs Pidgeon. I am expecting Mr and Mrs Johnson the Colonial Treasurer here this weekend. We heard from him that he is bringing her. The bedroom is rather small for two so he may sleep at the French Company. It will be nice seeing them, I hope she is nice. Mormoh is getting better, I am thankful to say, so I hope he will be back. This cook is so dirty and a wretched cook.

I have an atrocious cold in my head, I haven't an idea how I caught it, but I am hoping it's only a three-days one, and that I shall be all right when the Johnsons come.

We had another awful tornado of rain the night before last; you really never heard such an appalling noise. Charlie awoke to hear the wind start and was just in time to go and close the three windows upstairs that you see in the photo. The storms come that way. There was a tremendous wind and then torrents on the zinc roof above our heads, and continuous lightning, but the noise of the wind was so terrific that the noise of the thunder was actually drowned. Six inches of rain fell in four hours, which to those who know is pretty well, as Uncle Hugh would say. It came on at 2 o'clock in the morning and the tumult lasted for 1½ hours. It is so strange coming now because the tornadoes don't begin till the end of March. It may be the earthquake that is accounting for it all.

My poor Pooz was out, but came up punctually at 6.15 to awaken us! He is in great form these days. Charlie says he is a most methodical cat; he comes up to call us every morning, and after seeing we are well and getting up he goes down and waits for breakfast which consists of milk and fish, and after that he goes out on 'his rounds' through the garden and under the big mango tree where they are now building a boat. He goes there and sits near the joiners, afraid of no one. Then he comes in and sleeps on the steps till lunch, fish or meat, and goes after that and sleeps again on the steps till after tea, when he comes and plays in the garden while we are there. Isn't he a happy cat?

The other night I happened to look at the tree that you see against the house and saw one branch covered with huge hairy caterpillars. I thought if I could keep them they would eventually turn into fine butterflies or moths, but if they had been left there they would spoil the tree, so I got Johnnie to cut the branch down and kept about 23 of them in two boxes. Unfortunately the rain got to the cardboard box and it fell to pieces, and I demolished that lot and kept eight. They eat a great lot and I look after them religiously, although it's rather a sickening business. And now they seem to be flagging and not inclined to turn into cocoons, a sell it will be. My butterfly collection gets on but slowly, and they are not very handsome kinds. My plant collecting is also at rather a standstill as I am waiting to hear if the plants are any good. Anything new of course I pick.

We went on Monday evening [on] that lovely walk past the cassada farm, Charlie after pigeon. He got one only, they have got shy, and I fancy not so many come. This country is so curious in that way, things come and go almost before you realise it. These pigeon come to feed on the berry of what I take to be a species of willow. Christmas, the old man at the cassada farm calls the berries, and when they get ripe the birds come 'plenty, plenty' and eat them all up, and I fancy we shall now see fewer and fewer. It was awfully stiflish walking home that night, it was before the tornado.

One awful trouble in this country is keeping your food free from red and black ants; they swarm. Sometimes you find your sugar basin swarming; you open a pot of jam, [and] inside [are] red ants. They are very minute, and one must eat hundreds, but it's horrid. Then cockroaches come, they fly through the window at night. I hung a pumpkin up in the medicine room, [and] next morning they had been at that. Last night when I went to my bedroom [there was] one nearly 2 inches long on my powder box. These are some of the joys!

Charlie has just passed on his way from the Hospital and has gone to the District Commissioner's office to find out how long it will take the Johnsons to get here without letting them know they are coming, because Mr Johnson's business is to pounce unawares! Mr Page is away; he came back last Saturday and was off on Monday. He is very little here. He very kindly lent me *Pride and Prejudice* and *Past and Present* by Carlyle which I have enjoyed very much; he is so satirical.

We are now reading the papers with the Charlesworth case and can make nothing of it; I fancy she is in hiding somewhere.[59]

Our tomatoes are at last beginning to fruit, and Charlie is delighted. He has supported each plant with about three big sticks each, and tenderly ties the plants to them with strips of pineapple leaf. But I must say only for this they would have been ruined in the storm the other night. We have also got a pile of rubbish and stuff making a sort of manure, and we have put that on the roots and it has been a great help.

Posting Day, 11 February

After lunch yesterday I went to lie down and while I was upstairs I heard an English man's voice, I had such a fright, I thought it was the Johnsons arriving, hut it was Captain Hodding from Victoria. He had come down with money for the District Commissioner's office, and found Mr Page's house locked up. The bottom part is supposed to be left open as a sort of rest house. So he came here. He is very good company, and only for this wretched cold I should have enjoyed myself. The Johnsons are going to him first so will not be here till Monday. I am so glad as by then Mormoh will be quite fit I hope.

It was so funny last night. I said something to Charlie about Stokes Bay, and Captain Hodding said 'Stokes Bay, I live near there.' I said 'Perhaps you may have met Captain Nicholas out in South Africa.' 'He is my second cousin.' He only said that his mother was a dear old lady, and had married Mr Nicholas who was a wine merchant and died leaving her very badly off. Was it not funny? Captain Hodding himself had had a funny career. He entered the army as a Tommy, then left and went on the stage, then volunteered for South Africa, and has now got this billet in the West African Regiment. As soon as he got the billet he had his banns put up and was married in three weeks, left for West Africa and she followed four months after. She has been out four times, and they have one little boy nearly two years old. Mrs Faunce is now staying with her at Hill Station, and Mrs Johnson had gone to her before she came away as her husband has been away some time. I expect I shall hear some gossip from Mrs Johnson! Captain Hodding told me his wife and Mrs Haddon-Smith had got white drill (from some ship I don't quite understand that comes out with materials for the Government) for 5d a yard and made themselves skirts. He is going to get me 10 yards and I'll get them made here.

Captain Hodding (I told you, didn't I?) found that Peter, Mr Boddy's dog that he had left with Mr Page, was his. He had left it two years ago when he went on

---

59 This was a notorious case of a young woman who pretended to be an heiress, ran up large debts, then faked her own death in a motoring accident. The accident happened on 2 January 1909, and made headlines the following day. A couple of weeks later Violet Charlesworth was discovered alive on the island of Mull, living under an assumed name. A court case followed. See e.g. http://www.derbytelegraph.co.uk/bygones-derby-focus-sensational-tale-heiress/story-26606706-detail/story.html (accessed 9 June 2017).

leave and when he got back found it had been given to Mr Boddy, and now when he came here he found him again. Mr Boddy will be furious. He brought Peter with him and he has had an accident on one of the new mats in the bedroom! Pooz is very funny with these dogs that come, he follows them about with his tail puffed out defying them.

Little Ropey, Goodbye for this week. Charlie has gone to York Island or I know would send love. My cold is much better today, I'm thankful to say; all my love my own childie, and best love to the Aunties.
Ever your Twisty[60]

14 February 1909

My darling Belle,
Your lovely long letter came yesterday and also one from Father and Kate, not one from Elsie? I am so very sorry to hear poor Richard has been ill again, no doubt that is why she does not write.

Mr and Mrs Johnson came by the same boat and tell me the mails have been altered again, and now leave Freetown on Friday, so this will have to be posted tomorrow. Fancy, we have had no notice from the Post Office, so if they had not told me you would not have got a letter this week.

It is so unfortunate that Mormoh is still away, this temporary cook is awful, and poor Jomendi has had to give up his pantry work as he has a rash on his face, and Johnnie, the other boy, is not nearly so good. It's a great worry, and Sam, who does all right when we are alone, gets quite helpless if anyone is here. That is the great drawback of these black servants! However I should not mind a bit, only Mrs Johnson is not easy to entertain, as heavy as lead. She was a nurse at the Nursing Home, and got married out here. He is very nice-looking and very nice in a way. She is tall, very good features, grey eyes, but a heavy inanimate face, and really I may say never without a cigarette in her mouth. I cannot help feeling thankful I am not at the Hill Station. Although I may sometimes think Bonthe may be a little dull, and I am sure everyone else thinks it deadly, but I like it and am quite happy in my own way. But fancy, it has such a bad name in Freetown they were all advising Mrs Johnson not to come. Such a malarious place, and so on. She has two little girls, and she has left them at home at a kindergarten. One is six and the other four years old. She and her husband are due for leave in a fortnight, rather jolly for them. But I never knew anyone so blasé.

Yesterday a boy brought a lovely greeny-blue bird to sell. They tie them with string to a stick and bring them to the door like that. I said I had no cage, and he said he would bring me one for 'a copper' – that is, 4d – and sure little enough he came back with such a nice cage, about 1½ ft square, and a little door to slide up and down. But

---

60 Maida wrote another letter containing the same news to her sister Elsie, which is not reproduced here.

I can't find out what the poor bird eats, they say 'he eat Christmas', that means any kind of berry, and he does eat that, but he won't eat rice and the berries will soon be finished. He is bigger than a blackbird and smaller than a jackdaw.

Monday

Please excuse this terrible smudge, the blotting paper must have been damp. This will be a very short letter, as they have to be posted before 2o'clock.

Things have been going better. Sam seems to be more himself; but today Johnnie is away ill, 'his belly humbug him' that's what Sam told me. But Mormoh is coming back today, I am so thankful.

The bird is picking up. I've at last found he eats bananas, so that's a mercy. His arrival has quite upset Pooz, he never came upstairs this morning. I have put the bird pro tem. on the top of the linen cupboard at the bottom of the stairs, and Pooz sits at the bottom looking up and crying, but he is not very well again today. I expect he has been eating a lizard or cockroach. The bird is such a lovely colour. I hope he will live.

I was called down just now (I'm writing in my bedroom) by Mrs Johnson, and sat for a few minutes, and a boy came in. I said 'Is this one of your boys?' and he came on smiling – it was Mormoh! How glad I was to see him. I feel now I shall have no anxiety.

Your Rajah dress sounds lovely. I hope it will be a success. Your last letter was so interesting, wee Belle, all about the Clemengers and Uncle Grif saying 'What did he see in her, I wonder.' I think from what I remember she must be very like Mrs Johnson.

Mr Williams, the CMS[61] parson has just called. He had been to the Hospital and Charlie had told him we had some papers for him. He says the Bishop is coming down soon, and he also says he and his wife are coming to call. She was a teacher at the Wesleyan School at Freetown, black of course as ink.

Do you remember those drawers Kate sold me with rather pretty needlework? Mrs Johnson is going to cut me out a paper pattern of them, they are so beautifully cool and comfy. She appears to be very clever, as they say, with her needle.

I had a very nice letter from dear Father and Kate. I must write to them, so you must excuse more for this week, darling, as there has been a change in the Post Office arrangements.

Best love, my little pet, it's *your* cakes we are having for tea, the one W. burnt which is excellent (cakes with fruit need rather a cool oven) and the Aberffraws.

Ever, Bellerope, your Twisty

I have no time to write to dear Elsie.

---

61 Church Mission Society.

19 February 1909

My darling Belle,
Your lovely long letter reached me yesterday by a German boat; it arrived at
2 o'clock.

Mr and Mrs Johnson left at 5 o'clock to get on board the *Accra* which sailed out
at 7 o'clock this morning. I was rather glad they were obliged to leave last night
and not early this morning, as it is so upsetting. They said they enjoyed their stay
very much, and we very much enjoyed their company. She improved so much on
acquaintance, and after the first day or two things went more smoothly, and of
course I felt much happier when Mormoh came back, he is a most cheerful and
competent rascal! He came back so smiling and jolly and immediately started
cheating me over the accounts! Sam is a terror if anyone is coming, he is so slow
and dignified and sulky. But a week is quite long enough for visitors here, women
I mean, because there is nothing for them to do and Mrs Johnson was a poor
walker. She would have died of dullness if she had to live here; and, of course,
their spirits were 'set fair' the whole time as they sail next Friday for England.
She told me a lot about Hill Station, but was not a bit of a gossip. She was really
very nice. Unfortunately she got a cold with leaving the window open behind her
head at night. Mr Johnson is a very nice sensible man, and young to be Colonial
Treasurer.

My dear Belle, I am wasting hours these days (as I have not done much
collecting, the flowers are more or less over, it's the dry season) watching this bird.
Did I tell you he is the colour of the eye of a peacock's feather? He is a weird bird,
I can do anything I like with him, he eats off my hand, and I have to put a piece
of newspaper at the bottom of his cage each day, enough to frighten any bird out
of his wits, but he does not seem to mind. But these berries he eats are nearly over,
and too much banana I don't think is good for him, so it's a great puzzle what I
shall feed him on. It's such a pity he does not eat seeds. The only noise he makes
is the noise a cat makes when you tread on its tail. When I heard it first I thought
it was the Johnsons' servants teasing my poor Pooz! So it is not a musical bird like
his English brother. Mr Dubois came the other night to pay his respects to Mr
Johnson, and I took him to see it, and he said 'He will die, but it will be nice in
your hat.' We call him 'merle métallique'.

It's awfully amusing, at the beginning of the year the Colonial Office sent out
a new ordinance on the travelling allowances. Up to now, each man when he was
travelling was allowed so much a day travelling allowance, but he had to find
his own carriers. Mr Reaney and Mr Page and all those will lose no end over
it, but fortunately the Medical Officers are the only ones that don't lose over it.
It's too complicated to explain, I hardly understand it myself, but it appears Mr
[Johnson?] had found Mr Page is still drawing the old allowance! So he will get a
reminder from the Colonial Secretary! Don't mention this. Mr Page is still away

and, fancy, Mr Johnson says he gets £50 a year 'Duty Allowance' with which to entertain, and there he is never there. And if anyone comes like Captain Hodding on his way through he is hustled off!

Yesterday the boatmen told Charlie that poor little Peter, Mr Boddy's dog which Captain Hodding had taken to Victoria, had been killed by a leopard. Fancy, the leopard came on the verandah of the house and carried him off, Mr Reaney's house! He was a dear little dog, I am so sorry, and I am sure poor Captain Hodding will be distressed; he was so good with the gun. (I got up to look at the bird which I have got in the medicine room, and the paper blew away, hence the smudge).

It's getting very hot now; it's very hot up to half past 10 or 11 a.m., then a lovely breeze crops up, but yesterday it was 85° in the coolest part of the house at 11 o'clock.

Thank you so much for the *Ladies' Field*, dearest Belle. I will keep all the recipes, there are some very nice ones in this number. Wynne[62] has sent me a bundle of papers too, isn't it good of him? Poor little Willie, he may grow stronger as he grows up.

Monday 22 February

Posting Day and I've only written two sheets, but having had Mrs Johnson here we didn't do anything very much, so there is not much to record.

I had such a nice letter from dear Auntie Kate by the last mail, full of news. Their drawing room must look very nice with the new Chesterfield, you never told me they had it; she says it's by the fire where the blue chair was – that is, by the coal box isn't it? Really young Mrs Lloyd Roberts must be most extraordinary; the older one grows though the funnier one finds people, I think.

I must send the white muslin dress Miss Parry made to the wash; it has been a great success and looks so nice, in fact my clothes are exactly suitable for this place. I just want one or two more drill skirts, that's all. I have worn my brown holland and blue linen alternately week about in the morning, but the holland is on its very last legs; and the only hat I wear is the small panama. I am afraid I shall run short of boots though, I ought to have brought another pair of brown ones.

Mr Page came in to dinner last night in his most aggravating mood. I think he was furious with Mr Johnson. He is a most unpleasant man, but he is off again in two days so he doesn't bother me much. I wish there were one or two decent officials here always, there ought to be.

Our tomatoes grew so much after the big tornado, but the sun has been so hot it has shrivelled the leaves so we have had shades put over them made of palm leaves. One tomato is just turned red and I think will be gathered today.

I cannot get these boys to get berries for this bird. I myself think they are nearly

---

62 Another of Maida's brothers.

finished, so I shall have to let him loose. It's so annoying. I am so sorry too because he has done so well so far; but as he will not eat seed he would always be more or less of a bother.

Just as I was writing two boys and a girl came with a young deer they had caught to ask Charlie to buy it, 7/6 they wanted for it; but it was too young, poor little thing, it was awful to see it. They have such lovely eyes and a nice yellow skin with white lines and squares all over him.

When I got this far I went upstairs to see what Jomendi and Sam were doing. I had told them I wanted the landing scoured and they were only sprinkling it with water, so I have had to stand over them for an hour and a half and am dead tired. Sam is really no use for work, and the boys won't obey him.

I wrote to Lady Roberts this mail. I was so sorry to hear of the death of Mr Hobson; I saw it in *The Times*.

I am sending the order to Joseph Roberts today for more tea and some tobacco. It's very nice tea, everyone enjoys it and it seems to blend with the water so well.

The butter is running like oil these days, in the middle of the pot is a pool of oil. We get the butter off the ships that come direct from England in 1 lb jam pots, it's quite nice. There is a boat due on 4 March, it will come about the 6th, I suppose.

I had two nice long letters from Elsie this mail, and I was glad to hear Richard was better. I had a letter from Emily Pattullo too; I have never answered Amy Daniells or Mrs Finchett Maddock. I must do so next week. This is a wretched letter, my darling, two poor ones one after the other.

My very best love to you, darling Belle, and give my best love to the dear Aunties, and to Mrs Finchett Maddock and Mrs Darbishire if you see her.
Ever your loving Twisty

Don't write me short letters in return, young Seal! Forgive me for these short ones. The cake with the burnt top was lovely, it was so useful when the Johnsons were here, and I have the Aberffraws still going.

I have just had two more of those birds sent me! I have put them in the cage; the new ones are young ones, very frightened.

The photos are awfully good; thank you so much.

23 February 1909

My darling Belle,
I am beginning my letter today so that I need not be rushed next Monday; it is so funny to have to post on Monday.

I have had a very quiet week having had indigestion and the weather is very hot, and next month will be still hotter, so I am just going to take things very easy. So my letters may be uninteresting; you will know why, just because I am not going about much. I think I was rather tired after Mr and Mrs Johnson's stay.

To have to make an effort for a whole week, in one room with the same person, is too much in this climate. We heard from them yesterday. They had had an awful night on board, mosquitoes and nothing to eat, and both their letters were much more full of that than anything else.

Charlie has gone to York Island and has taken his gun with him hoping to get a curlew. They are very good eating. He is very well, I am thankful to say. I expect you will think this letter begins rather dismally but just as I sat down to write Mrs Peters the washerwoman came to say 'a thiefman came in the night' and stole a lot of our clothes, all our towels, my white drill skirt, and I don't know how much else. I have sent her with a note to the District Commissioner, the black one, Mr Page is away of course, he always is, but the black one Mr Metzer is very nice. I do hope we shall catch the thief.

Mr Metzer has just been here; he is so very nice and obliging. He says he has sent two policemen on the track, and he said he came over to tell me so himself as Charlie was not here. Nice of him, wasn't it?

I don't think I have ever told you what funny little shops there are all up the different streets. Just a little shed the size of a kitchen table and a little table in the front of it, with groups of the following on it:- groups of four peppers, three green and one red one on the top; five lumps of sugar, ginger roots, five sweet potatoes, a handful of the small red peppers, two lumps of blue, and that's a little shop. I love peering into them. I got a very nice native-made mat the other day, with black in lines throughout and a tiny red border, so nice for a bathroom. They are made up the rivers and are not always to be had, so I shall keep this one and if I get a chance buy some more. All the groups I have mentioned cost one copper, that is 1d or 2d.

These green peppers are about the size of a bantam's egg, and are terrifically hot. Charlie likes them, and I often say how Auntie Kate would like them. I have implored Mormoh to use them sparingly, but I very often have to sit with my mouth open after them, but they are supposed to be wholesome. I have also been meaning to ask you if Williams could grow what they call here garden eggs,[63] I think you will see them in Sutton's List. They really are awfully good. Now last night for dinner I had only a leg and wing of cold fowl. Mormoh minced it up fine, cut the garden egg in two, filled the two halves with the minced fowl, the inside of the garden egg, a *little* chopped green pepper, and [you] either bake them or cook them somehow. I will ask him how he does them, they are so good, I can eat them when I can eat nothing else. He does small green paw paw the same way. He says he fries them, but then he has no oven, so that's why.

I've just been making a small cake, and while I was in the middle of beating Sam said he and Mormoh wanted me to order 'Good' cloth for them from England to have gowns made of! 'Good one, good one' says Sam with much spluttering. They spend all their money on their clothes. I asked Sam if he wanted it a wide cloth

---

63 That is, aubergines.

Victoria Road, Bonthe, old postcard sourced from http://www.sierra-leone.org/Gspostcards-7.html

and he said 'Yes, double yard', and, fancy, he has only just had the dark green one trimmed with black braid. I'll tell Charlie and he will storm at them for not saving their money!

Fancy, Belle, I've only just realised that nearly all my towels have gone as the Johnsons had been here. Isn't it sickening! And you might as well look for a needle in a haystack as look for a thief in Bonthe; they are all thieves. It's a fact that cannot be denied. I don't fancy anyone will steal our sheets as you can see through them! But the bath cloths were very good ones if you remember, big and thick; and my white drill skirt, what shall I do without it? I'm short of them as it is.

The night before last I went with Charlie on the cassada walk, and coming home through the bush we both saw something move on a palm stem. We waited and two small monkeys tumbled down, babies they were, very small, longish tails and walked with their backs well arched, adorable they looked in the distance.

I am sure you will think me good for nothing not having taken any more photos. I will try and take the drawing room tomorrow, and if I can a native hut. The thing is I must take them snapshot, and it is so hot to go out in the sun. I have just been writing to Amy Daniells and the perspiration is standing in beads on my hands.

Friday

I've just dispatched Jomendi with a note to Sister Felix: (the woman Romans, I had to tell him it was) to ask her to tea, and the two other sisters. I've had a very successful cake-making expedition, ten little rock buns of Paisley flour mixture, and one plain cake the weight of two eggs and so on, but they disappear like snow before my poor Charles!

Sam came to me yesterday and asked me, oh I told you about the black cloth! He asked me again today if I had written. Whatever they have got into their heads to wear black gowns for I can't imagine.

I took the bird in a cardboard box yesterday and allowed him to escape near the Hospital, and he did not seem at all in a hurry to go. I bought another for 3d today, very wild he was, poor thing, and Charlie chloroformed him to death and is going to skin him for me; so I hope to show you what he was like.

Cooking, Bonthe style: Maida's photo from the family album

I am sending an order to Ryans today for some more beans, and I'm going to try melons and garden eggs, and also a packet of balsams and petunias.

I've heard from Sister Felix, two of them are coming to tea.

Saturday

They came and were very nice. I lent them a book of embroidery Wynne sent me. I think I shall send to Robinson and Cleaver for some fine linen lawn and let them make me half a dozen handkerchiefs in drawn thread.

There are some such queer hats the men wear here sometimes; they are made at Lagos. They are plaited straw, white and black, fez shaped. Mrs Johnson says they make rather nice workbags They are 1/- each though. I'll bring one and more if you think they would be nice.

I've just been superintending the cutting up of beef steak and kidney for a pudding for tonight. I have it done in the pantry under my eye as it takes careful preparing. The last I made with Sam's aid when Mormoh was in the Hospital, and it was a gigantic success. They are boiled for nearly four hours in the 'punny' bowl you sent me. My poor Charles is extremely attached to them!

You have heard me speak of Mr Cortie, York Island, the kind man who got me tea on my way back from my first trip to Victoria. Well, when I was last at York Island he gave me such a queer pair of native slippers, more weird than beautiful. I sent him some avocado pears by Charlie last week, and he sent me yesterday two lovely bunches of pink oleander. I have them on the top of the pigeonholes and they look very nice. He is quite one of the nicest of the traders. He is going home next month and is going to be married to a nurse, a Scotch girl. He showed me her photo, she looked so nice and sensible. I'm afraid he won't be back with her before we leave. Mr Dubois, the head of the French Company, whom I said was so like Mlle Gzell, is quite nice too. The rest are so so.

Yesterday morning as I was dressing I was bitten on my ankle by some fly of sorts, and it is swollen today as big as an orange! And hot and itchy, a mosquito I suppose. Charlie will be late today, he is operating on a huge tumour as big as a large orange in a man's mouth! It's grown all over his teeth. How he will do it I can't imagine. I don't know who to feel the most sorry for, the man or Charlie!

If you have finished with any of those drawn thread books, would you send me one, fairly advanced, for the sisters.

Monday

Your dear letter came last night after tea. I will not answer it in this except to say we both think Williams' complaint most unreasonable.

Fancy, plenty of potatoes, apples and vegetables, of course they can have 3 lbs of butter a week for four people, it's ridiculous. They should come to West Africa. We can only get meat now once a week, and have to eat sweet potatoes and bananas to fill up the gaps in our appetites. And 1 lb of butter lasts Charlie and me a fortnight. And look at the holidays they get. You can't have everything in this world.

You will be counting the sheets of this letter and saying 'She's only written four sheets', but look again and see the size of the writing! I'm short of paper.

My dear, I sallied out this morning in the blazing heat to take a photo of a native hut. I got one and a woman washing, and was just going to take it when she saw me, and flew screaming with laughter into the house. Three more followed her and all I could get was shrieks of laughter. I called 'Mammy, come out,' but no. At last two came and I took them in a terrible hurry, the sun was so terribly hot, and three interiors. The first [is] the drawing room, second, the same from the other side, the third the hall and writing table; four, the house from the wharf; five, the women; six, the native house. Will you send me three more rolls of films, or tell the man to. Will you also, without fail, send me a recipe for making guava jelly and guava cheese? Mrs Acton perhaps or Mrs Beaton, or perhaps that famous old book of Mrs Darbishire's.

Best, best love, Ropey, from Twisty

The letters arrived last night by overland mail, so I have not had the parcel. It was cheap ribbon I wanted, dear. I shall be thankful for the linen dress as I have had a white skirt stolen.

Dr Charles Hunter to Trixie

Sunday 7 March 1909

My dear Trixie,

Just a line to tell you that Maida has had her first 'go' of malarial fever. It came on on Wednesday morning and she has had it up to this forenoon with varying temperature continuously, but I am very glad to write and tell you that since 2 o'clock today she has been quite normal. The temperature never went very high (103½) but the sickness and retching and uncomfortableness was terrible. Her stomach is terribly tender, and most of the time she might have been competing with the blasts at Llanberis,[64] poor dear. I was sorry, and nothing would stop it. But I am so relieved and glad that she is very comfortable this evening, and very bucky and chirpy. There has been no sickness or pain or uncomfortableness all day, and she is enjoying her chicken soup and barley water and biscuits with great gusto, and I feel that she will soon pick up and be downstairs in a couple of days.

---

64 Llanberis has a famous Welsh waterfall, tarn and quarry; Charlie seems to be referring to explosions at the quarry (see opposite).

But it's taken it out of the wee woman in the meantime.

I hope you will he able to read this, it's written after dinner, and I'm hurrying to go up beside her and have my smoke!

Goodbye Dear,

Best love from Charlie

[*This letter had enclosed the following note:*]

8 March 1909

Dear Dr Hunter,

I suppose your ice is finished so I send a small piece for Mrs Hunter. I hope Mrs Hunter is much better and will soon be all right again. Will you present her my compliments and wishes for a prompt recovery.

Yours sincerely,

E. Dubois

[*Pencilled in very weak handwriting is the following pathetic little letter:*]

Monday

My darling Belle,

I am thankful to say I am ever so much better. Charlie has been a perfect darling, no one could have been gooder or kinder. It's quite horrid, malaria, like influenza only worse; and the dreadful part was I could not sleep. Last night I had a lovely night. O such 'India' and awful wind to which I see Charlie has cruelly compared Llanberis Quarries, very naughty of him. Forgive me for [illegible] a little note from Mr Dubois of the French Company, kind isn't it, so I took it to write a line on. Charlie is operating at the Hospital today and may be late and the post goes at 2 o'clock, it's now 12.30 and he hasn't come, so I will end this up my darling with my best love, and don't worry about me.

P.S. The parcel not come yet, delayed in Freetown I suppose. I've ordered my little birthday gift for you darling to be sent from Truslove and Hanson. I had intended sending a little note to put inside it, but can't do it.

P.S.2. 1 p.m., temperature still normal! So thankful, poor Charlie has just come, so tired.

[*The next letter is undated but was evidently begun before the malaria.*]

My darling little Belle,

I am so dreadfully distressed to find this morning that my letter will not be in time

The perfect husband for a sick woman – from the family album

for your birthday, and yet when I look at the calendar I believe it will just arrive in time, but not my present; I wrote about it weeks ago, but have never heard. It's not the pineapple dress, I've not bought it as you have that one from Barker's, and I'm afraid you won't like it, but I wanted you to have them. I won't tell you what it is till I hear all about it. But please accept, my darling, my very best wishes for a very happy birthday, and for a year full of joy and happiness and prosperity. It's lovely to think I shall see you, all being well, before the year is out.

I am beginning my letter today as I believe I am going on patrol with Charlie and Mr Page up to Victoria on Friday, not getting back till Sunday. They will make a march from Victoria to a place called Matru to choose a new site for the District Commission quarters. I don't know whether I shall do the march, I am having very bad indigestion these days. I don't know what it is unless it's the heat; so I am sure the change up to Victoria may do me good, especially if we get a breeze on the river.

Mr Page is expecting a Mr Bailly to relieve Captain Hodding so he may be in the boat too, but another boat is coming with the servants. Mr Page has heard, from Captain Hodding I suppose, that the Chief at Victoria has been away some days, so they expect to get news of another leopard murder. They are sure he is deeply in it and yet they cannot get evidence against him; and Mr Townsend let them all off with such light sentences that I expect they feel they can venture another.

We have been without newspapers since Saturday, so poor Charlie has felt very lost. I tell him it's a good thing as it makes him talk! I should have been so glad of the linen dress to go to Victoria in, but there, this wretched boat does not come.

Did I tell you, oh no, it was just after your last letter went off. After lunch I went upstairs to rest and woke up at 3 o'clock to find the front bedroom quite dark, and looked out and saw a big tornado coming. In about a quarter of an hour it was blowing a hurricane and a thick sand-storm, you never heard such a noise. Pooz was terrified, poor little cat, crying all over the house and following me about. We had the shelters moved off the tomatoes and hoping the rain would not get blown away when down it came, nearly 2 inches in three hours. It has done the garden so much good and has filled our water tank which had got very low. Sam had told me the day before there was not 'too plenty' in it.

12 March 1909

My darling, I thought Charlie had sent you these two pages in his letter, but I find he never knew I had written them, so I will just continue.

I am sure you will be glad to know what a good recovery I have made. I feel ever so much better, really quite well now, only I feel I must be careful. I can never tell you how good Charlie has been to me, I never knew a better nurse, and so, so kind. I really have thanked God for giving me such a kind husband, and it was so providential the first five days I was ill there was not much doing, so he was able to come back to me straight from the Hospital, but on the sixth day, Monday, I hardly saw him. I was practically well by then, so I was quite happy, but he went to the Hospital in the morning at 9 o'clock and never got back till 1 o'clock, had lunch, and had to go off to Messrs. P. & B. He came back, poor boy, so tired, it was awfully hot, had tea and off to the Hospital to see his cases. Next day was nearly as bad. When he came back from Messrs. P. & B. he did make me laugh, he said he had met a fellow countryman of mine, and from Caernarvon too! It turns out he is one of their hands, and has been up the rivers. He is an oldish man, and in a bad way, I am afraid. He told Charlie he lived in the next house to the Norman Davies, a cottage near the barracks. Charlie says he is quite a nice man. He had to tell him last night he will have to go home; I don't think they look after them very well there.

I've just had a visit from the black parson, Mr Williams. He came to return some *19th Centuries* we had lent him. He stayed 20 minutes, and my voice went, I could hardly speak! He is quite a nice little man.

Charlie used to be so sweet when I was ill, bringing me little bits of news. One day he told me one of our poulettes was going to lay and was looking everywhere for a nest. He made her a most comfy spot in the place they sleep in, and she tried it, but no, it was no use, and now she is sitting in the oven in the kitchen! How I laughed. It's an old disused brick oven. She did not lay there but chose a spot behind the door of the place they clean knives. She laid her eggs, and then some rascals killed her so isn't it too bad.

Poor Charlie had such a time with me when I was very bad. I could not take the tinned milk, not even as Benger's; so I just took barley-water boiled and boiled till all the nourishment came out of the barley, and chicken broth, and I have drunk quarts of them. For the first two days I used to beg Charlie to give me a medicine to clean my tongue but I had to take some powder instead, then he gave me a mixture. Well, Belle, as you know I have had many 'stomach' medicines in my time, but never a bottle like this one, it literally cleaned my tongue in two days, and was so comfy to take, warmed me 'loike'! I'm still taking it and quinine, and still 'swilling' (!) barley water. Dear old Charlie when he came back from York yesterday found Sam hadn't told me there was barley water, and I had had none. He did storm at poor Sam, but he deserved it, he has got utterly lazy, and it's done him a lot of good.

I write a little but then I go and lie in my long chair; I'm going now, but before I go, and before I forget, let me thank you my darling for your lovely letter. It came while I was ill; and thank you for waxing my kist etc., you are a brick. Your story of the Holmes amused me vastly, such impertinence! Personally I should not have thought Miss Frater too young to come home alone with the gallant Dr J., nor should I consider him fascinating enough to be in the least dangerous. I always thought Mrs Herbert Humphreys a much over-rated woman, and now I think her positively silly and interfering. I should like to see a stand-up fight between Miss Frater and Miss Edith Hulm in the Castle grounds, and would take a front seat on the walls, and pay for a seat for you on one side of me and Auntie Kate on the other!

Very many thanks for the *Ladies' Field* and the *Bystander*, it's too good of you, Seal, you know it is. Wynne sent me another *Young Ladies' Journal.* There is such a tricky blouse pattern in it, if I can remember I'll cut it out and send it to you.

Saturday 13 March 1909

Last night was the hottest night we have had. Charlie could not even bear the sheet over him. Thunder was rumbling all around when we went to bed but it never came on to a tornado. Mormoh was taken ill again last night after tea with a sort of colic; Charlie has told him to go to the Hospital this morning. He came to cook the breakfast; he does not seem strong, it is such a pity, for with all his rascality I am so fond of him. He will do anything for me, and try any new dish, he is like Walters in that he loves experimenting.

I am wearing my holland dress every other week with the blue linen (the latter is very hot though). The holland has been a marvellous dress, but if I were you, Belle, I would have yours bleached before you have it made up, because they are such a hideous colour at first.

I caught such a weird what they call praying mantis or some name like that in my room this morning. They are sort of flying grasshoppers, some are two inches long; they often fly in while we are at dinner, light green ones and brown ones. This one is only an inch long, pale green and this   on his back. I have killed him and hope he will keep.

Monday 15 March

Well, I was lying down upstairs yesterday when Charlie brought me the letters; all I can say is how thankful I am you went and found dear Father better; and I hope you won't leave him till he comes home. I was so thankful to hear he was better, but he must be careful and not return to England too soon. Childie, what a journey you had, and what an experienced traveller you will become. Perhaps as you are so near Marseilles you could cross over to Algiers and hire a camel and come here! Poor Kate too, I am sure she had an anxious time, and being ill herself, I hope she is quite better.

I forgot to tell you such a funny little anecdote which happened the night before I was ill. Charlie and I were returning from the French Company when a native girl overtook us and said 'Boa' to me, then said she would like to buy me. 'Well, how much will you give for me?' '£4' she said, quite pat. 'Only £4!' I said. 'How much you give for him?' – pointing to Charlie. '£10 because he is a man.' Charlie was too delighted; this is no place for Mrs Pankhurst, is it?

Well now, if this finds you at St Maxime give darling Father a good hug from me. Best love to Kate, kind remembrances to all old friends, and plenty, plenty love to Belle from Twisty

I did enjoy your letter so much. I got a letter from Katie Bryn Teg, rather a sad one. It was nice for you travelling with Auntie Kate and Margaret, then seeing dear May and Lewis.

Monday 22 March 1909

My darling Beatrice!!!
There, I've got it out, it looks very nice, doesn't it?

Here it is Monday, and my letter not begun to you. I don't know how it is but I've not written a line all week till yesterday when I wrote to dear Father. It's been so very hot and stuffy, everyone is complaining of the heat. I've given the temperatures to Father so you can judge what it is like.

But before I go any further, let me thank you my darling for all you have sent me. The cake is lovely, quite the best parkin I have ever tasted. Walters has got to make them beautifully; she seemed to have put coarse sugar into it which I think a great improvement. The boots arrived safely too, also the dress which I am dreadfully sorry to find in such good condition, I had no idea it was so good. I'm afraid you could have worn it next summer, but it's invaluable to me; it's so short, no need for me to hold it up which is such a comfort, I can't tell you what a blessing it is. I sent it off that very day to Mrs Peters and she let me have it back next day, and I went to York Island in it. The only mistake you made, my own Lizard, was to get the plain ribbon for my waist, I wanted chintz, but it doesn't matter in the least. Charlie said I ought to pay you 10/- for this dress, so if you like to be such a donkey as not to take more than 4/- what am I to do?!

I must begin to give you what news I have before I get too hot. I have been feeling quite well all week, and such a good appetite and very happy, enjoying myself in a very quiet way. Thursday we went to York Island. I always like Mr Cortie. He had a big glass dish of chocolates brought for me. He goes home this week, I believe, to be married; he has been out two years and needs a change badly. It was terrifically hot coming home, and I was awfully tired that night as we took a longish walk after tea.

Wednesday night Mr and Mrs Pidgeon dined with us. I wore the white muslin, it's so cool and comfy. I am sending it to the wash next week. I showed it to Mrs Peters today. I'll give you our menu: soup, cutlets of fish (sort of fillets), cutlets of beef – and do let me tell you I have them put at 1 o'clock into the mixture for Wakefield steak, page 59 in the King's College Book; boiled potatoes and boiled Spanish onions (rather plebeian, you will say) then chicken cutlets and a salad composed, my wee Belle, of a tomato out of our own garden, banana sliced and avocado pear, the tomato in the middle and sliced white of egg as decoration, very good, a nice dressing with one hard boiled yolk in it; then boiled Cabinet pudding, and scrambled egg with cheese in it on fried bread. A very nice dinner it was, and Sam waited beautifully. We had exactly the same menu on Saturday night for Mr Dubois and Mr Rupli, only tomato in the savoury as well. We have only had nine or ten tomatoes, but we have simply gloried over them.

On Saturday evening Charlie and I went down to the wharf with that fishing tackle. [We] sat with our feet hanging over and fished for an hour – result, one bite at my red india rubber worm!! Pooz of course came with us and thought it great sport, catching the line etc. We had gone on the wharf the night before too. The tide is just nearly full in now between 5 and 6, and he walked down the steps and after much hesitation drank some water, then sat on the lowest step not knowing that his poor tail was floating behind him in the water! We roared; but he paid Charlie out by coming up and rubbing against him and lashed his tail on him!

Sunday mornings are a great spree now; we have a tray brought up at 8 o'clock with bread and butter and marmalade and fruit and coffee, it reminds us of St Maxime; and we have a lazy morning, not arriving down till about 9.30.

The two priests called on Saturday to say the Bishop was laying the foundation stone of their new church at 4 o'clock yesterday. They said it would be a long ceremony but we half promised to go, but the mails never came in till after 3, and I could not get Charlie up to the point of going, and we could see a tornado brewing at York. No sooner had they all got seated on benches in the garden (we could see them from here) than the storm began. We had one lightning that fizzled around us and the crack with it, and all the congregation had to fly. I was so sorry for them. It's too amusing on these occasions (tornados) to see little absolutely naked boys running with an umbrella up and another under their arms for their masters. The rain came down a deluge, and after it was over Charlie and I went to call upon Mr Page to take back *The Queen's Christmas Book* he had lent us to look at. It's so interesting, have you seen it?

The heat even then was terrific, and the humidity was really something dreadful. All I could do during pauses in Charlie's and his conversation was to say 'Oh, it's hot,' and he would say 'It's awful.' He groans about the weather much more than Charlie. Charlie never grumbles about the weather or really practically anything. He has a good fling at the Colonial Office or the Liberal Government now and again, otherwise he is so equable and very good to live with. If I grumble he says 'Well, I'll send you home!'

I bought another otter skin today for 3/6, do you think they would make a nice coat? They are a very nice colour. At any rate they would make a nice lining.

I shall be so thankful when I hear you have all got home safely. I was most relieved to get your letter yesterday, but we both think it risky for dear Father to go home so soon, as we see by Reuters how snowy and cold it is in England. I shall have a weight off my mind when I hear you are all home again.

This place is terrible for dreams. I dream *so* vividly of dear Mother and so often, till I awake in the morning feeling I have seen her, but they are distressing dreams. But they say it is quite common on the Coast to have bad dreams.

I am so very, very sorry to have such melancholy news from Bryn Teg. It is very sad to think of poor Aunt Mary, who was always so bright and fond of life, to be tied to a bed of suffering. I am very sorry for poor Uncle John, it is a terrible time for him, and for the poor girls.

I have been trying to make camisoles, it's a little change, only the needle has to be emeried every two minutes.

I am glad to hear my poor weeds did arrive at the British Museum, because they have not had the politeness to even acknowledge them. I may get more in the cooler weather, but now I cannot walk, really it's too exhausting. Charlie got an acknowledgement for his which hadn't taken half the time to do; but it was through the Colonial Office.

I have a glass of barley water every morning with my quinine, and I am going to have it now; so goodbye for this week, darling Belle. My best love to dear Kate, and please tell her I am told the kak wood I've got for her is very good and polishes beautifully. Please remember me to Walters and tell her we both thank her for making us such nice cakes, and best best love to you
from Twisty

I am only writing Elsie a postcard this week so will you send this on. Please keep any stamps you want and send the rest on to Rob.

From Dr Hunter to Mr Roberts

29 March 1909

My dear Mr Roberts,
We were very glad you had such a comfortable journey back from St Maxime, and that you didn't feel fatigued, it's wonderful I think.

Poor Maida has had a pretty bad week of it with fever, but I am glad to say she is on the mend now. On two nights the temperature went rather high, but yesterday there was very little, and since last night she has been quite normal, and a solid night's sleep, and she is looking more like herself again today, but of course weak. Her stomach and liver I think are the cause of all the trouble, and in this country any ordinary illness is always accompanied by fever. I don't think there is any malaria about it. I cannot find any parasites in her blood. If she gets another attack like this I think it will be best for her to go home. Although she won't hear of it, I think I will have to insist. We have done nearly half time (six months).

Maida had a bit of fish yesterday, and this forenoon she much enjoyed a poached egg. She has taken her chicken soup, beef tea and barley water very well all the time, and I'm sure she will soon pick up. The weather is at its worst, it's very trying, very hot, then a tornado will come along and it gets cold.

I am in my usual rude health and glad to be able to look after Maida as I can. Best love to all,
Yours affectionately, C. B. Hunter

Monday 29 March (*Enclosed with previous lette*r)

My darling Belle,
You will be sorry to see me writing in pencil to tell you I've had another go of fever, and am still in bed, although I'm thankful to say my temperature is normal today and was so on Saturday, but yesterday it went up again although not high. I am so distressed about it as Charlie threatens to send me home, and it would be such a disappointment not to stay here the year with him. I have been so happy, but if I get fever again I shall have to come.

Maida, undated photo
from the family album

You understand, don't you dear, that it's not because I don't love you all as much, because I do, and I am always thinking of my homecoming, but I would be so sad to leave Charlie here all by himself.

Everyone says the season is unusual, *great* heat, and then a tornado and cold wind. These cold winds they say they have never had before, they only last perhaps a very short time, but that's enough to touch the liver up. This is the worst time of the year too for Europeans, the making up of the dry season. It's this wretched stomach of mine that is the trouble.

Please give dearest Father my best love and thank him so much for his note. I was so glad and thankful to find you had all reached Bronceris safely, it would be a great relief.

I am greatly shocked about poor Lucy Knox. Charlie read my letters first, and kept them till next day because of not exciting me, and I was very thankful. Poor girl, it is sad, and for her husband and little Peter.

Charlie is so good bringing me all my food and trying to make me eat, but it's been a great strain on him, poor boy. I do hope I'm on the mend now; my tongue has cleaned up so that's a great blessing, and when the fever comes it isn't much.

Now I know you will forgive this short note, not that I couldn't write lots to you, but it's better for me to be quiet. I enclose a poem I made on Saturday afternoon.[65] Dear old Charlie was resting by my side asleep so I had to use Kate's letter (I hope she forgives me).

My best love to darling Father, Kate, Elsie and your own dear self from your loving Twisty

The fever came on as I was finishing your letter last Monday, that's why I couldn't write to Elsie; I sent a postcard. I thought of you on the 25th, my darling Belle. I am having a poached egg on toast for lunch.

5 April 1909

My darling Belle,

Very many thanks for your nice long letter which I was delighted to get on Friday, also one from dear Father and Kate. It's a fortnight today since I was taken bad again, and I've had a bad pull; but I've had no fever for a week now so I'm very thankful. But I've been taking at first 12 grains of quinine and then 9 grains and now 6, but whether it's that or not I don't know, but I've had a go of depression that has been awful and must have been dreadful for Charlie. But now I am up and about again I shall soon get strong again I'm sure, and by next mail I hope I shall be quite myself again.

This month is pretty hot so far, but we are getting tornadoes which cool the air. Fancy, on Wednesday, all being well, we shall have done six months of our tour. I hope I shall be able to stand it all, but if I don't pick up now I shall have to come home I fear, and I know you would give me a welcome, but I should be sorry to have to give up because I've had such a happy time here.

How dreadfully sad about poor Lucy Knox, it really is terrible. I never knew the poor girl was expecting a baby; I can well understand what a grief it will be to Sir Owen and to her poor husband.

I did not know Louis Darbishire was engaged to be married, who is it to?

Thank you darling so much for the *Ladies' Field*, I do enjoy it; and Wynne has

---

65 Sadly the poem has not survived, nor is further information available on Lucy Knox.

sent me the *Home Journal* Spring Number. I have not been able to thank him yet, I do so want to do so.

The cat has been most disappointing, not coming near me; and he has now a bad habit of going to the mud on the beach.

I was so amused by your arrow in the *Ladies' Field*.[66] I kept reading the first column advertising canaries, and could not see what you meant; who could the woman be who wanted to part with her boy I wonder?

The Circuit Court sits next week here; it will be nice to see Mr Townsend again.

The 'Sisters' want to come and see me, I must ask them now I feel better. What a mopish letter this is to be sure. Next week I hope to write a better. Give my love to Edith and tell her I've not forgotten I owe her a letter, also Mrs F. Maddock; and please thank Miss Clemenger for sending me the papers when you were away. With our best love, my darling girl, to you and Kate, and forgive such a short letter.

Ever your loving Maida

Just had lunch, fish, cold chicken, and am feeling very comfortable. Charlie has given me a tonic which I am sure will do me good.

8 April 1909

My darling Belle,

I wrote to you on Monday a most gloomy letter I am afraid, but I wrote just as I felt, as I know you like me to do; and I've been waiting till I felt really better before I wrote any more.

Today I really do feel better, since the fever my liver has been out of order and you know what that means; and I do hope you have none of you been worrying too much about me.

I am not going to write very much today; it's Thursday and Charlie was to have gone to York Island this morning, it was his day, but there was difficulty over getting the boat, and the poor thing has gone now, 3.30 p.m. We had an early tea which was lovely at 2.30.

Mr Page has been away ever since the middle of my being bad, he was very nice while he was here, and last night the black District Commissioner Mr Metzer came to see me, otherwise the traders have never been near me. I've seen no one but Charlie for nearly three weeks. I have written to ask one of the Sisters to come and see me now.

Saturday

I find the ink is finished so I am obliged to go on with this in pencil.

It is 5 o'clock. Charlie has just gone out to the French and Swiss Companies, and I thought I could continue this to you. I ought to have put a line in yesterday,

---

66 Presumably a marker to point Maida's attention to something in the journal.

Good Friday, but I was too lazy. We had a very nice day. We have come down to sleep in the bedroom off the drawing room as there is less noise during tornadoes, so I got up to breakfast and enjoyed it so much. Then in the evening we went a walk along the shore, Charlie with his gun. This morning I had a little fever again so stayed in bed till after tea, and have just dressed and feel all right I am thankful to say. It's just indigestion I get accompanied by a little fever, but I feel ever so much better and stronger.

Did I tell you that the Assistant District Commissioner Mr Paling died of dysentery while I was ill? He died up country, it was quite a shock to us all. So Mr Page had to go to Shenge[67] (where Mr Paling was) and has not come back yet, and tonight Mr Townsend is to arrive for the Assize, and the bottom part of Mr Page's house is locked up, it's supposed to be left open as a kind of rest-house; and he can't come here, so where the poor thing will go to I don't know.

The tornadoes are over it seems, but the heat is still very great, although I never go out in it yet [as] it affects my poor 'India'! Now I will stop for tonight, dearest. I wonder how you all are. Tomorrow we expect the mails, it's lovely to think of it.

Easter Sunday, 10.30 a.m.

Just come down dressed! In a nice clean white drill skirt and clean blouse, and look decidedly better and I feel much better, but until the hot weather goes I am afraid I shall have to put up with 'India'. But I am getting to feel stronger, and that is the great thing.

This is a wretched letter, but you can understand I have not had much to write about. I felt baddish yesterday, just dull like!

Charlie came in last night after calling on the firms, and only found Mr Ryff, one of the proprietors of the Swiss Company, at home. He leaves next week for Paris where he lives. He just comes out now and again to overlook his managers. A very nice man he is. When he was out starting the business about 18 years ago he had his wife here for over a year, I believe; but she of course does not come now as he only comes inspecting.

My dear, this morning such a lovely haunch of venison was sent us by one of the young men at the French Company, the one who plays tennis so well (for a Frenchman). It will be so nice as I am not taking beef so far; and Mormoh got a very nice Spanish weighing 5 or 6 lbs, so we shall have nice fresh fish too. Spanish is exceedingly good. Charlie is going to ask Mr Townsend to dinner tonight, the first person in to a meal for nearly a month. I hope I shall stand it; it's when anyone comes I feel so weak.

This poor Circuit Judge arrived last night at 11 o'clock, [and found] Mr Page's house all locked up. He sent his boy to look us up but we had gone to bed. Between you and me and the door-post, I awoke, they made such a noise, but

67 Maida spells this various ways (here, Sheening) but it appears to be the town of Shenge.

he was able to get an empty house at the French Company. He is a most helpless man. [I don't know] why he did not write beforehand and see about a house, that is what everyone does out here.

After lunch

Just a wee line as things come into my head. If you get the chance of seeing the *Spectator* March 6th, do read an article called 'Snow at the zoo'. Also I forgot to tell you, dearest, that the week you had flown over to St Maxime, a *Madame*, *Ladies' Field* and two *Punches* came for me. Did you pay for them all or ought I to thank Miss Clemenger?

Easter Monday

Mr Ryff and Mr Townsend came last night, only Mr Townsend to dinner. He is such a nice man, with all his dreaminess, and a gentleman which is refreshing. I have a wee hit of fever today but it's wearing itself out I hope, and when it comes only stays a very short time.

All the dear letters arrived after tea yesterday, and one from dear Elsie; please ask her to forgive my not writing to her this week, I shall hope to next week.

My darling you are spoiling me with the cake, the drawers and the dress. It's far far too good of you. They have not come yet because no parcels come by overland mail, but we hope a German or some kind of boat will be in this week and will bring them. I do thank you for all your kindness to me, you are far too good; and now I have to ask you another favour. Will you send me three pairs of my woollen summer combinations, dearest? If they have not been worn, will you wear them, and so be able to put 'Worn clothing'?

Thank dearest Father for his nice letter; I hope to begin to answer my letters sooner this week. I was amused by Mrs Darbishire's message, give her my best love when you see her.

Goodbye for this week, my sweet Belle, best love to Elsie and Kate and yourself from us both.
Ever your Twisty

A boy from next door has just been trying to steal two of our fowls! Charlie gave him a good fright. The two little fowls have laid 24 eggs between them, and now both want to sit. They are all kept for me, lovely eggs they are, and there are only eight left.

Friday evening, 16 April 1909

My darling Belle,
I am just going to write a wee bit to you as I still feel as weak as a rat. I fancy I ate too good a dinner last Saturday night when Mr Townsend came in, because

my temperature went up again on Monday, not high but still my tongue was very bad, and I have been in bed until late in the day till yesterday and today when I got up at 1 o'clock and my temperature has kept more or less 99° and I feel better, only weak. But the heat has been intense today, 90° in the drawing room. I am keeping very quiet. I do feel so sorry as I should have enjoyed so much going to the circuit court. There are three big chiefs sitting, and they go past with a man carrying a big staff with a sort of gold top in front of them. One of them is very tall and [has] a long narrow nannygoat beard, and he wears a white gown, and a most beautiful shade of red coat or rather cloak, which falls in folds from his shoulders.

My darling, before I go any further a good ship came on Tuesday bringing your lovely cake. All I can say is that you and Walters and the oven have excelled yourselves! It's lovely.

I asked Mr Townsend to come in yesterday, but court does not rise till 5 o'clock, sometimes later. He has been so nice coming in every day to enquire for me.

I was delighted with the pins, and drawers and ribbon, you do spoil me. I can't think how I shall get into the drawers, it looks as if one would have to sit on the floor to get into them. It was simply sweet of you to make them for poor Twisty.

I wish you could see the way I do my hair, parted in the middle, plastered down straight and my back hair in coils on top! So as not to wear a pad.

Mr Dubois came last night to call when Charlie had gone for a walk with the Judge, and I told him you thanked him for sending the ice. He was so nice and said I might have the loan of their steam launch to tow our boat to Victoria if I thought the change would do me good, was it not nice of him? I did so enjoy my lavender water that dear Father gave me these days, it is so refreshing.

Saturday 17th

Please excuse this dreadful smudge. I have just got up. My temperature [is] normal this morning so that is very cheering and the day does not seem quite so hot, but the night was awfully hot, Charlie said the hottest we have had, not a breath of air. The servants are all as lazy as they can be too, my having been laid up so much and not getting up to breakfast disorganises everything too.

Charlie went to York yesterday and came back at 11 o'clock with two curlew, one a splendid bird, its bill measured about 8 inches, the other was younger.

For tea yesterday I had the first slice of your lovely cake. I was so afraid it might disagree with me, but it has not, so I shall look forward to a bit each day.

I have been on barley water and chicken broth, then chicken and dry toast, and boiled fish and dry toast for a month on Monday! But so thankful I'm better.

They are building another much bigger boat under the mango tree now. It's wonderful to see them make it; a great deal – nearly all – the work is done on a barrel turned upside down. In the top branches of the tree the palm birds are most busy, weaving their nests; they ruin the palm and banana trees tearing strips off about ¼ yard long and ¼ inch wide.

After lunch

I think this letter will be very disconnected when you read it, because I sit down now and again and jot down what comes to my mind. I have now tried a new pen, the others are awful and the ink soupy.

We have not had rain or a tornado for more than a week which is a great blessing for the people. Now is the time they burn their land for sowing rice. They burn all the bush that grows . Every I forget how many years they let it lie fallow, and if they don't have a proper dry season they can't burn their farms. So now away on the mainland we can see columns of smoke going up, the different farms being burnt. It reminds me of the fires in the mountains we used to see at Crûg when they were burning their gorse.

One of P. & B's (Pidgeon's) men is very ill up the river, and Charlie has had to go out and see Mr Pidgeon about him. On Monday he is afraid he will have to go to Victoria and will be away two nights, horrid! Sam will sleep in the house.

Sunday

Yesterday was not such a very hot day, but today promises to be another scorcher. Charlie starts out at 12 o'clock. I expect there will be a nice breeze on the water, I wish I had been well enough to go with him. Did I tell you Mr Dubois offered the steam launch to tow me? I little thought then [that] Charlie would be going so soon.

2 p.m.

Charlie started at 12 o'clock. I think he was looking forward to going in a way; and now I have just seen through the bedroom window the overland mail arrive. The letters come in two tin boxes; it will take at least an hour to sort them. I do so look forward to them.

I have just finished *Monte Cristo*, too exciting to be really enjoyable, and I have been looking out for another book on the shelf and have found *Arethusa* by Marion Crawford, so I shall read that today and tomorrow.

The temperature is now 89° in the drawing room and there is no breeze although I think one is going to rise. I am writing with an awfully scratchy stylo so please forgive the handwriting.

Monday 18th

I am much better, temperature normal. Posting day, and the letters never arrived till this morning; there is shocking management at the Post Office at Freetown. The traders are complaining they don't get time to answer their letters.

After tea last night Mr Townsend came in, and Mrs Wiggs came too, and he asked me if there was anything he could do for me, and would I like him to leave Mrs Wiggs? I was delighted, she is the dearest little dog, a small white wire-haired little thing and extremely old-fashioned, as Miss Griffiths would say. I had a great business to keep her at first, and we had to have the front door closed. At dinner time Pooz came in and when he saw Mrs Wiggs on my knee he was furious. I never saw a cat like him. He came and put his paws on my knee and seemed almost as if he would jump up too, then he jumped on the table by my side and was most [illegible – loving?]. When dinner was announced Mrs Wiggs had to jump down, and then Pooz set at her on three legs, the other front paw held up to strike her. Poor little thing, she was terrified. He is the most extraordinary cat. I like him but don't love him! He is so weird. If the fowls are asleep under a tree in the heat of the day he will steal up and jump into the middle of them.

Well, after dinner, chicken soup and boiled chicken and dry toast, I am so afraid of eating anything the least bit rich, especially with my medical man away. Then I told Sam all my windows were to be closed (in case anyone climbed up – Charlie's orders) and he shut all the drawing room ones and every window in the house, I could hardly breathe; then he retired out to chop his rice and came in at 9.00 p.m. and I retired to bed, Mrs Wiggs on a chair near. At 9.30 p.m. [there] commenced a tornado, which continued till midnight. I was not too terrified.

I must write to dear Father now, so will end for this week. Tell dear Elsie how much I thank her for her long newsy letter of this week and such a cheery bit from Rob. If I can I will write her a line but I have to write to Wynne of Alderly to thank for the [illegible].
Your ever loving Twisty

22 April 1909

My darling Belle,
A month today was your birthday, and I was so bad that day I remember, and today I am glad to say I got up to breakfast and had it with Charlie, and I feel very much better. I am only going to begin this letter today as I have to write to Mrs Hodding. It appears Charlie had written to Captain Hodding to ask if they would put me up if I had to go to England. I did not know he had written. She wrote back to say she was afraid they would be full, but Mrs Renshaw would put me up – very kind of her because I have never seen her. Charlie says she is like Mrs Maltby, but like her very kind. So I may go in a fortnight to Freetown for a week or so if Charlie thinks I need it, but of course I would much rather not, it would be such a bother packing etc.

I was delighted to see my Charlie home. He said he would be back on Tuesday forenoon, so I got up directly after breakfast, and tidied up the pigeon holes, and got the house looking nice, and from 11 o'clock I began to look out. He never came till after 3 o'clock, wretched oars to the boat, but Sam, Jomendi and I were all watching the corner of the island to see the boat turn round. Soon Sam called 'He come', but it was a trading boat, then immediately after his came. When he got out he was carrying a lovely white bird he had shot for me; it was an egret, the most lovely white, far whiter than the one he brought before, do you remember? And lovely egret feathers, about four long ones. I was glad to have him back, and he thought me so much better. Mrs Wiggs had tea with us, and disappeared after and has never come back. Isn't she a killing little dog?

Sunday

The reason I have not added any more to your letter, dear Rope, is that I have been trying to write off a few notes that had to be done, to Auntie Kate, Katie of Bryn Teg, and my sister-in-law in answer to a short note I got from her in February sending a message from Mrs Coventry.

I feel ever so much better, and am so thankful although the heat continues just the same, and I have had no return of fever for about 12 or 14 days, but I had the laziest life, just tidy the house and sew. I am plodding on with the camisoles. I have to have a wee bag of bath brick by my side, and after every about 12 stitches I have to polish my needle.

I got such a nice budget of letters, yours and Father's and Kate's, Elsie's with postscripts from Roderic and Rob which I greatly enjoy, May, Miss Smith and Margaret Southport, all very nice letters, a big bundle of papers from Wynne, your nice *Gentlewoman*, and *Ladys* from Elsie. Dearest, don't send me any more *Ladies' Fields* or *Gentlewoman* as Charlie has ordered the Club to send *Country Life* instead of the *19th Century*, so we get that every week now. The first came yesterday.

I forgot to tell dear Father in my letter that we posted him by the *Biafra* a box of native coffee, the small berry, in one of the Treasury bags. It is what they call 'Mountain berry', and was given me by Mr Reaney, and is supposed to be very excellent. The other is the ordinary Liberian coffee they grow here. Now the *modus operandi* is as follows: get an iron frying pan, heat it, and put about a teaspoonful of butter on to it, just sufficient to grease it, then put the berries in (they say pick them as near as you can the same size, those in the bag are done that way I think) and have the frying pan over not too hot a fire, and turn them about all the time till they are as brown as what you buy. That's all they do to them here, but Mrs Johnson said Dr Burrows put them off the frying pan into a cloth wrung out of cold water till they were cool, that it was most important to keep in the flavour, then after put them on a plate rack, I should think just to dry.

Now, my young Belle, I am simply delighted to think that your screen is getting on so well, and I do hope it will be thought good enough for a prize, but, darling, I *absolutely refuse* to take it, you must keep it for yourself. It's silly, darling, and I should not feel justified in taking another. It will give me far more pleasure to see

One of Maida's pictures of Bonthe, from the family album

it in that nice frame in your possession. You know you spoil me, and it's not good for me. Thank you for sending my 'bairdie' to be reframed.[68]

I walked as far as the French Company twice this week, so I am getting on. The Judge has his lodgings in a house at the French Company. He came in to dinner last night and we had a very pleasant evening. The two Sisters came to see me last night, and stayed quite a long time. They were much obliged for the books on drawn thread. If you go to Ireland in May, I wonder if you would get me enough

---

68 This must be the embroidered Bird of Paradise now in my possession, which was I think copied from one done by my great-grandmother now owned by Aunt Trixie's family. M.B.M.B.

linen lawn, or whatever they use to make dainty drawn thread handkerchiefs, and I will give them to them to do. It will please them I think if they can do them.

Thank you so much for the white skirt, it looks awfully nice but I have not tried it on yet. I'm thankful to have it. The old native women were simply *delighted* with their photo, it was the first walk I took. I had put it into one of those brown mounts, and put a bow of that blue ribbon you gave me and a bit to hang it by the bows in each corner. I did not think they would be a bit interested, but when we got near the house I saw one of the women near the little window and showed it her. She came running out and about half a dozen women and heaps of piccins arrived from I don't know where. Then the big fat woman was recognised, and [there were] shouts and shrieks of laughter. Charlie and I were doubled up. 'Dat Jumbo, dat Tommie' we could distinguish. It was a great success; I will try and take some more.

Mrs Darbishire is quite right, this writing table is much too high.

Give my love to Kate and thank her so much for her letter which I hope to answer next week. I am shocked to hear she is working for the YMCA, I expect it's the YWCA she meant! I am so thankful she found those plants of Statice, fancy their getting covered up in the digging. They evidently haven't grown much, they don't suit the soil I suppose. If I thought we might be taking a wee cottage I would have asked Kate to get me a packet of each of the following: aubretia (Potter's variety I see by *The Times* is a good one), a good strain of polyanthus and a nice orange alyssum, and sow in good strong boxes.

Monday

Posting day. You will forgive such a short letter, won't you dearest? I certainly look very much better, and feel nearly all right now except that wretched tooth is giving me pain. Charlie has stuffed the cavity with carbolic and it's a little better, it comes and goes like your toothache last winter.

We had a big tornado last night, and this morning it was quite cold. I fancy May will see us through the hot weather. I shall be so glad if I can stay out the whole year and come home with Charlie, it would be so flat arriving alone.

The Sisters on Saturday said the first fevers are always the 'strongest' and they call my illness 'getting acclimatised'!

I an so delighted that you are going to stay with Paddy. I have two such nice letters from her which I have never answered, but they are going to be, all being well, at once. Give them and Molly my dearest love, they are often in my thoughts, and I feel so dreadful to think I have never written to Mary after her little boy's birth. My letter that I did write was returned wrongly addressed.

Goodbye for this week, sweet Belle, all my love to you, and I hope you will have a nice time. These are the stamps, keep what you want and send the rest to the boys. I also send the picture of a hat that I think would suit you.

Keep the picture, as it shows so well where bones in the neck ought to be put, also the blouse.

Ever your Twisty

I walked as far as the Hospital last night.

> I don't remember what day I started this, I think
> 29 April 1909

My darling Belle,

I fancy this will in all probability find you in Ireland,[69] and I am sure you will have a lovely time there. I shall be looking forward to your letters with such pleasure. I am ever so much better, all right in fact, only for that wretched tooth that the filling dropped out of. I get toothache every night for an hour or so at midnight, isn't it sickening? It was not quite so bad last night, so it may be wearing off. In the day Charlie stuffs it with carbolic which takes the pain completely away.

The *great* heat has, I think, passed. Since the last tornado we have had cooler winds, and the temperature in the room has not gone up to 90° since. It keeps to 88 and 87° in the afternoon.

I have been taking walks every evening too. Generally Mr Townsend joins us. The Court will be finished this week, I am sorry to say. It's nice having him here, not that he is in the least interesting, only just someone to drop in. Mr Page is really no good.

On Tuesday morning I cut up three oranges and two limes for marmalade and it had its final boil yesterday, and produced 6 lbs of delicious marmalade. I'm so glad it's made. This morning I (Pooz just galloped in with a lizard) am making some London buns for tea. We shall just have one piece each of your lovely cake left, never have I enjoyed a cake more, perhaps because at first it was my only luxury during the day, as I was keeping such a strict diet. Now I eat more or less everything. I take my bath every day at 3 o'clock now, and I find it much better than when I come in tired after my walk.

Charlie had such a nice letter from Dr Forde, the Principal Medical Officer, last night. He may he coming here in a week or two and will put up with us. That will be very nice.

My darling childie, I was re-reading your sweet letter over again last night. The maple-wood frame sounds charming; have you come to the end of the 30/- yet? Be sure to tell me. I am now going to begin a letter to Edith.

> Sunday

I wrote a long letter to Edith and I shall have to try and write to Mrs Finchett

---

69 This letter and the previous one were forwarded by Kate to an address in Belfast where Trixie was evidently having a holiday with friends. M.B.M.B.

Maddock this week. I am ever so much better. If only [I did not have] this wretched toothache, which comes at 12 o'clock each night. Otherwise I feel very fit and enjoy my food, and very much hope I shall be able to finish the tour. Dr Forde will be here this week, and if I am still bothered with toothache I may go back with him to Freetown for a week or so.

Your dear letters all came on Thursday, and I am so sorry to have given you all so much anxiety, and I wish I could let you know at once how much better I am. I was very ill just for the time, but now I feel a different creature. Dear Father wrote me such a kind letter, he is a dear, and I am looking forward so much to seeing you all again. On Thursday we shall have completed seven months, and now the weather is decidedly cooler.

I invited the Judge and Mr Page to dinner last night, and at 4 o'clock I got a note from Mr Page to say Lieutenant Addison had arrived by the German boat and was putting up with him, so he was afraid he could not come. I wrote back and told them both to come, and we had a very jolly evening.

For dinner I had pumpkin soup (our own punkie!), boiled groupa fish, salmé of duck with puree of peas in the middle, fillet of beef made into cutlets as you have them, and whole onions the size of pigeons' eggs in the middle; Cabinet pudding and wine sauce; and for savoury fingers of fried bread with sardines on and a hard boiled egg, white chopped, yellow put through the sifter decorating it. Dessert – prunes and bananas and ground nuts which were most popular; and a very nice dinner it was. Mormoh is an excellent cook and so willing. Sam waited well last night too, but he is always inclined to get sulky when we have company!

Mr Addison had spent two months of his leave in Florence, so we had a great Florentine talk. He goes up to Shenge (where Mr Paling died). Did I tell you? In confidence, Mr Paling practically drank himself to death quietly at night. It's very nice when men come back from leave who left after we arrived. It really makes one feel that the time is going on. They all departed soon after 10, and this morning before I was up came such a lovely little country basket from Mr Page to me. Nice of him, wasn't it?

After tea yesterday and after I had arranged the flowers for dinner with Charlie's help, we both went for a walk up to the Hospital, and on the way back he bought me such a jolly calabash. That is a sort of gourd, a round one split into two making two very jolly bowls, and they are decorated with a kind of black dye. They come from Lagos. We came round by the market, and then I dressed – my silk dress Charlie bought me last time. I wonder what you would think of me with my hair parted in the middle like Ann used to have hers, and Irene. You must tell me all about them, and Molly and her wean, and give my best love to Mrs Workman and Mr Workman. How often I think of the lovely cool breezes on the *Hotspur*.

I have read nearly every book in the house now. Never say again I can't read novels. And now I have found a book called *Life and Letters of Endymion Porter, sometime Gentleman of the Bedchamber to Charles 1st* – not half bad. I found two books here too of James Lane Allen. Have you read any of his? I liked them very much, only they are sad.

Monday 3 May

I have just written to dear Father and I must write to Kate and Elsie so this will have to be curtailed.

We had an awfully hot night, but thank goodness I did not get the neuralgia. I went to bed with a vest tied over my head, and my cheek well rubbed with menthol, and it really did me good, although Charlie says at 12 o'clock I tried to awaken myself and to get the toothache to come. I turned and scratched my foot and growled, so *he* says. He says I am not a good one for 'tholing pain'!

I fancy we shall have a tornado tonight, they cool the air very much.

I am sending half-blinds and the muslin cushion covers to the wash this week in anticipation of Dr Forde's visit. Mr Page is also hard at work getting ready for the Governor. The wharf is being mended at last, and the big boat being painted. Mrs Wiggs came last evening and stayed to dinner. Pooz was furious! She also arrived this morning when we were at breakfast and has gone off with Charlie to the Hospital. The Judge leaves this week for Shenge, or rather Victoria first, I believe.

Fancy Gertie with five daughters! Terrible isn't it? And I hear confidentially from Elsie that Captain Nicholas is in financial difficulties. Poor things, I am sorry for them. I fancy he is very extravagant. I don't see by *The Times* that he has had any ship yet.

When the men had all left on Saturday night I had a cigarette! Mr Page is always wanting me to join them and have a cigarette, but no thank you, it's very different with Charlie alone. I have had wretched luck at piquet lately. We began to play again a week ago; the other night Charlie beat me by 400!

I have some balsams, petunias (very few seeds in each packet) and coreopsis, and they are all coming up, also the three melon seeds came up, but the hens chopped one! Garden egg seeds very slow coming up, and I have this minute bought six garden eggs for 1 d! It's hardly worth the fag. We shall put in seeds of beans tonight or tomorrow; they are very nice.

Again with best love to all the dear ones at Belfast if you are there, and best to you from us both,
Ever, darling Belle, your own Twisty

The German lady swallowed a piece of ice when she was unwell and has never ceased [illegible] since! A month. She is better after a filthy compound of Charlie's.

You will growl that I have written such a short letter. I am going to try to write to Mrs Bodvel Roberts after lunch.

[*The next letter, dated 3 May 1909, is addressed to Mrs Richard Williams, her sister*

Elsie. Most of it is an almost exact repetition of the previous letters to Trixie, but the two following paragraphs are different.]

Tell the boys it's impossible to find birds' nests here. A great many of them nest in the tops of the palm trees. When Charlie and I returned from a walk one evening, we found Johnnie, the garden boy, at the top of our palm tree, which is much higher than the house, climbing up with his feet and hands, gone up for coconuts and didn't expect us back so soon …

The butterfly catching goes on very slowly, they are no bigger or more brightly coloured than English ones as far as I can see.

Our best love to you all. Trixie says your house is kept in lovely order! I quite long to see it. Ever your loving Maida

8 May 1909

My darling Belle Rope,
This will find you at home again safe and well, I hope, and that you found Father and Kate well.

I really am better, and the toothache is better so long as I keep the hole stuffed with carbolic acid. Toothache seems the fashion here now, poor Father Noirjant[70] had a bad swelled face. I really think I can do my tour. The cool is coming, at least the great heat has passed.

I have at last written to Mrs Finchett Maddock and Wynne, that's why your letter was not begun until today, and one morning this week I set to and made a chocolate cake with three eggs and ¼ [lb] of butter, an utter failure! Cruel wasn't it, and I was exhausted after beating it. The fact is, I fancy, it's difficult baking them in a baking pot. He burnt it on the top, and not done inside. I told him to leave it in one hour, and he came with it finished in a quarter of an hour.

We have been expecting Dr Forde but I expect he will not be here till the end of next week. The Governor was to have come, and great tidying had been going on in anticipation, but he has never turned up.

A week tonight I had a great dinner party, I told you of it, and on Monday afternoon Mr Addison came in to tea, and walked out with us afterwards. He told us at tea he was very anxious to bring his wife out next year when he was married, but that her father did not care for the idea, and I don't wonder. Shenge is three days away by boat and [there is] no doctor there. He said she would never find it lonely: she could shoot, paint and ride. She had been brought up in British Columbia. He asked me to write to her, and tell her all about the Coast but not to frighten her, not an easy task. During conversation I told him I had been at the Canary Islands, and bit by bit it came round I had met 'his girl'! Do you remember the man and his

---

70 As spelled earlier; here Maida spelled it Noirgeant.

daughter and a friend who arrived at Las Palmas while we were there, and then we met them again at Teneriffe and the man tried to persuade Father to go to his son's hotel and [illegible]? The father, if you remember, had been tomahawked by Red Indians! Well, he is engaged to Miss Worthington, his daughter, is it not strange? And if you remember the friend's mother or sister had married Dr Wheeler's son or daughter, who we met at Algiers? It is strange how small the world is, isn't it?

I walked with Charlie as far as the French Company last night and got weighed. I turned the scale at 7 stone 6 lbs, I used to be 8 stone 8 lbs! So I have lost a stone, this will make Elsie envious I'm afraid.

I very nearly made myself ill again yesterday by eating a mango. Charlie had told me they were nasty and indigestible, but an irresistible craving came over me yesterday seeing a piccin pass with a basketful on his head. They look like big apricots, most tempting. I called out 'You sell am?' and he said 'Yes, five for one copper.' I said 'Come inside', and Charlie and I partook of one. They were not half bad, in fact I think stewed they would be excellent, but they have a large amount of turpentine in them which makes them deadly. So no more mangoes. Mr Townsend says he can't eat them and has to be very careful with avocado pears. Mr Addison has to be careful of his diet too. I had rather Miss Worthington married him than I did!

I have just been to the medicine room window to see if the fishing boats are coming in, and I found the tide full and a lovely sea breeze coming in. We have had tornadoes for three nights, the first wind and rain, the second rain and thunder and lightning, and last night heavy rain, and everything looks delightfully fresh. Nearly everyone I have met likes the rainy season best.

Sunday 5 p.m.

The mail has never come yet, it is a disgrace, and the post goes out tomorrow. The traders are going to complain to the Governor. We met Mr Page last night who told us he had had a wire from His Excellency saying he would be here next Wednesday. While we were talking to him Charlie had a note put into his hand asking him to go over to York Island, [because] the manager of the Post Office [is] ill. So I went with him, starting at 6.30 and getting back at 8.40. I did so enjoy it, I had not been anywhere for two months. There was a thick hank of clouds over on the mainland in which the most lovely lightnings were playing in three different places, and in each lightning the fork like living snakes of fire. It was most lovely, and the coxswain said we should get it at midnight, but we didn't. We had dinner when we got back. The Judge left this morning for Victoria, and I miss little Mrs Wiggs very much. At the end she was continually with us. She had a terrible trick of chasing little bullfish in the black mud on the shore and would come in with the awful filth like black ink. The native name for mud is 'putta putta'. So when she was covered with putta putta she was not allowed in, and would go and roll in the garden. She used to show her teeth when she was pleased, like old Perro.

On Friday night Charlie was called in to see the German lady who is ill, not fever, and I followed him along the front past the French Company. All along there women and children do what they call trading. They pass here (some of them) every morning, a woman and generally two weans, the woman carrying on her head a bundle of lengths of print, and one wean carrying her mat and the other a large calabash full of little oddments, sugar, peppers, tin spoons etc., and when they get to their destination they spread the mat and on it they put an empty crate which they cover with the prints, and the oddments are laid in little heaps on the ground on the mat. These are the better ones, there are about five or six stalls of them, and on the other side of the road little girls sit with calabashes with the most frantic-looking fritters, and a tin bowl by the side with palm oil which is doled out on each fritter. Some of these little traders are not more than four or five years old, selling ha'penny worths. On Saturday nights they all take their goods on to the Victoria Road, and sit in an open drain, their feet at the bottom and their wares on the road; they do so amuse me. Last night Charlie and Mr Townsend and I walked up and one tiny girl of six had about nine heaps of rice in front of her, and one onion on each little pile of rice, ½d each.

I was so amused though on Friday when I went up to meet Charlie near the French Company. I could hear as I came along 'Dis na Doctor's wife.' Then 'Missis, good evening, how you do, how Master?' I can't make out what the word 'na' is a corruption of. If I ask Sam who did such and such a thing he says 'Na me, Mar', and Mr Townsend said it was the same in Gambia.

Monday 10 May

The mail was here when we got down this morning, dear Father's, yours and dear May's.[71] Isn't it sweet of May to write so often!

I am so sorry to hear you were so tired after the work. It is too much for you, dear Belle, to put such a strain on yourself. So sorry to hear of Kate's bird's escape, what a pity. I have to write to dear Father. Charlie has closed his, so I will enclose it in yours. I am quite well now, only for a wretched toothache.
Best, best love, Your own loving Twisty

Tuesday

My darling Belle,
I must begin my letter to you today, although I only posted the other yesterday; but I had had hardly time to read your letter before I had to set to answering and getting off my letters. To begin with, again my deepest sympathy with Kate in

---

71 Presumably May Bradford, later my godmother. M.B.M.B.

the loss – sad loss – of Robert.[72] It was really most annoying, and to be so near catching it too. I have just put a new pen in, because I must write smaller, as our paper is running short.

Second, condolences to you on what you consider a bad selection of tweed, also the rudeness of McDonald, and the supposed bad cut; but I hope with the [illegible] petticoat and hat it will not look so bad 'in the bush and your eyeglasses on'!

Third, no, I have no idea who Dr Edwards is who figures in the tennis club, another spark?

Little Belle, I do hope you will have had a jolly visit to Ireland, and plenty of good tennis. I am so cross with myself that I did not tell you to take that hat of mine I got from Miss McDonnel; please wear it in fine weather. The [illegible] you know is all I want; also I have been forgetting to tell you to wear my riding habit; the only thing is I might be worrying that you got a fall, but as far as the habit and hat go, please use them. It was so stupid of me not to beg you to wear them before, but I had told you to wear them so perhaps you have not felt inclined.

I am so sorry Aunt Annie has been so seedy and the Troscanols; what a lot of illness there has been.

I went to bed last night without the carbolic in my tooth and had a bout of toothache.

My pigeon holes look so nice this morning. At the end a 1 lb jam pot poised on a roll of toilet paper! (veiled in white paper) filled with red lilies, and a pretty white kind of periwinkle with a pink star in the middle; at the other end a big magnesia bottle full of the same lilies and some pretty grasses, then a small magnesia bottle with a very pretty shrub, clusters of this flower, and then another small magnesia or pickle bottle with lovely yellow cannas. What a mixture of colours you will say, but I'm getting like the niggers, I like them all jumbled together. Anyhow it looks very nice.

Dearest, I don't think it ever pays to go and work at such high pressure as you did with that work of yours, it's killing.

The day before yesterday I finished my first camisole, done at a snail's pace. It all looks a bit clumsy in the bush, but measured by my old ones it's no bigger. I've got so thin, I can't sit on a hard chair! Charlie and I were talking last night of what we would 'swill' on the ship coming home, all being well, and we both came to the conclusion, porter! He is to have a bottle for lunch and dinner, and I to split one for the two meals.

There is a good deal of illness about in a mild way. The Sisters say there always is in May; earache, toothache and joys of that sort.

Now I am going to do a little sewing. Charlie is at the Hospital. I went the old walk to the cassada farm with him last night, he carrying his gun. He left me sitting on a log under the tree and told the old man to 'look after Missis' and he brought me a sack to sit on. Did I tell you he sent me three pineapples when I was

---

72 Presumably the bird: see the previous day's letter. M.B.M.B.

ill? Charlie never saw a pigeon but shot me what he calls a 'fou' bird, it's a brown bird with small cinnamon-coloured wings, buff breast and big tail. I thought the wings would be pretty, but they are curious, they seem to have no quill feathers in them, but a nice colour.

I was looking at my butterflies this morning and disgusted to find mould starting on them, so I shall send them home. They are a disappointing lot, though; I have a few done up in cocked hats.

We have just had lunch, and I must tell you what we had. We began with cutlets off a very nice 'Spanish' fried, then haricots blanc, then savoury omelette, then a delicious paw-paw off our own tree; but I must tell you about the haricots blanc because I made the recipe out of my own fertile brain. Put the beans to soak overnight, then boil them and put them through a wire sieve, and if too dry mix with a little milk. Boil two or three small onions in water and when soft add flour and milk to thicken, and pour over the beans – delicious.

Saturday 15 May 1909

Since I wrote to you my toothache got beyond everything, nag, nag, nag and pretty bad for an hour and a half or so every night till Thursday. When I could endure it no longer, it was knocking all the stuffing out of me, I begged Charlie to pull it out. He sent Sam to the Hospital for the 'tooth irons'! and I thought he would never come back. At last he came, and the irons had to be boiled, then cooled, then a chair carried into the medicine room, and *then* Charlie took it out beautifully slowly in case it should break as it had two fillings in as well as the cavity. It's well I had it out, the hole went right through to the other side; and I've had no more pain I'm thankful to say.

Charlie had to go that afternoon to York Island as he did not get the boat in the morning; and today they sent their boat for him, another man down with blackwater fever. He went at 12 o'clock and will not be back till 6. This will mean a lot of worry because the man has not been taking care of himself, and Charlie recommended some time ago that he should go home.

The Sisters turned in this morning and stayed quite a long time. Mr Page left this morning for Victoria. The Governor is going there overland and will return with Mr Page Thursday, or so I fancy. We have heard no more from Dr Forde, perhaps he is coming with the Governor. Since Tuesday it has been awfully hot again, but last night we had a tornado, and today is cooler. Next month the rains begin in earnest.

I see by *The Times* of April 17th 'An Exhibition of Needlework' got up by Mrs Fitzwilliam at Peterborough; Miss Clemenger would be there I expect. It says Lady Exeter sent an unfinished panel representing the Golden Gates of Burghley House. I wonder if Miss Symonds helped her. Could my poor birdie go to no exhibition, wee Auntie?

Oh, I must tell you when the Sisters were here this morning I heard poor Pooz give a yell. I looked out and saw three big dogs attacking him. Fortunately Johnnie was near, and Pooz gave one leap through the hedge, I did not see what became of him after they had gone, I looked for him and could see him nowhere till I went upstairs. He had flown to our bedroom and he has not budged outside the house since!

A man came to sell a tiny deer, they call them 'tambo', it was not nearly so big as Pooz, but I would not have it, some dog would have killed it. But I told the man if he could catch a canary I would buy it.

Sunday 16 May 1909

We had breakfast in our bedroom and at 10 o'clock P. & A.'s boat came for us to take us to York Island, and Mr Patchinini (a nephew of Mr Zochoni's) asked us to lunch. It was most lovely on the water and I did so enjoy it. Mr Williams, the man who has blackwater, is very, very ill, it's to be hoped he will pull through. We stayed there till 1.30, Charlie going in and out of the sick room. He will have to go tomorrow too. The mail came in from Shange today bringing back *Diana Mallory* I had lent to Mr Addison, and *The Life of Benvenuto Cellini* who was born in Florence in 1500. I look forward to reading it after all the trash I've been reduced to.

Another good night without my old tooth, a great blessing. I've thought so much of all you suffered last year, darling. Do you ever get it now?

I quite thought the mails would have arrived by the time we got back, but they have not come yet, 4.30, too bad, all the traders are disgusted.

You will say I've written a short letter when you see this but I'm sure you will understand. (My paper is coming to an end.)

Mr Patchinini (Greek, my dear) went to see Dr Keenan before he left Freetown, and on his writing table was a Calendar [showing] October 7th. So he said 'Look at your calendar, that's not the date.' 'Yes,' said Dr Keenan, 'it's the date I leave here.'

After dinner last night the washerwoman came to sell me two carved gourds, 2/- for the two.

Monday No. 2

I did not see this space; I haven't half thanked you, sweet young Rope, for the cake, it's too good of you, but I have to finish my letters in such a frantic hurry.

Monday

We have just had lunch, and a note has just come for Charlie from York Island saying the man is much better. His temperature is down this morning to 100½°

and yesterday when we were there it was 105°. It's a feather in Charlie's cap if he gets over it.

How I did enjoy your letter, darling. You are a very great pet to send me another cake, it's very good of you. You have no idea how we enjoy them, young Rope. And, darling, thanks about the combies; but, pet, why send me yours? You *ought* not to have given them up so soon. The holes were in those combies, my dear, when I got them!

Now about myself. I am very much hoping I can stay till the end of the tour with Huz! (my new name for him). I am feeling ever so much better, and have not had fever as far as I know for more than a month. But I get breathless (it's the low-lying island air I fancy) so I have stopped my quinine for a bit; and of course when the rains come it will be much cooler. We have just four and a half more months more to do if I stay till the end. I am sure I shall have many regrets when I leave, and yet I long sometimes very much to see you all.

I had intended writing to Kate today, and now all this bustle hearing that the Governor and Dr Forde are expected here tomorrow, and Charlie off to York I've no time. I am so very sorry to hear of poor Aunt Mary, and that Aunt Annie has been so seedy. Give them all my love, and also the dear Aunties at Bryn Morfa. With our dearest love, ever your own Twisty

Fancy Kate getting a machine. I like treadle ones better than hand.

19 May 1909

My darling Belle,

Behold the great event come and gone, the arrival and departure of His Excellency the Governor. Mr Page had promised the black District Commissioner to send a canoe down from Victoria with timely warning but he didn't, and Charlie happened to see a boat arrive with a Court Messenger, and in less than half an hour the big boat turned the corner at 3 p.m. Charlie had just time to get into his grey flannels and get down on to the wharf, and I fortunately had everything ready in the house for Dr Forde, including, my little pet, your lovely parkin that had arrived at 2 o'clock. It was a great disappointment to hear they were going to stay such a short time. Charlie and Dr Forde came straight into the house, and the Governor and his aide de camp went to the District Commissioner's house. We were all three invited to dinner with the Governor, so the *great occasion* for which I had brought that little evening frock had at last arrived.

Dinner was at 7.15 p.m. The Governor was exceedingly nice, he could not have been nicer, and in going away he said 'I am very glad to have seen you again, Mrs Hunter, and looking so well.' Dr Forde's first words were 'Well, you do look well, Mrs Hunter' – rather a trial isn't it, Belle, after losing 15 lb in weight and nearly all my hair. It's this ridiculous colour I have, I tell Charlie, but I am very thankful I feel so much better.

Here and opposite, pictures from the family album presumably of the Governor's visit

It's a great sell for the poor traders that they have not seen the Governor. He left at 7 o'clock this morning. Mr Lukach, the aide de camp, is exceedingly nice, and has such a delightful way with the Governor, who reminds me greatly of Mr Darbishire and a little of Uncle William. You never can be quite sure how he will be; but with all his eccentricities I like him. He looked tired and fagged and is going home in August. It is supposed his health will not stand the 12 months. Dr Forde had intended coming with Mr Copeland of the Public Works Department, and I expect he will come back in a fortnight or so. I hope he will, he is so nice, and it is so pleasant having people here. My old man looked so nice last night in his evening kit, and he said I did, let's hope he was speaking true words. I wonder what you would think of me with my hair parted in the middle and all fringe gone, including the net!

We had a downpour of rain last night, and our windows open, and I suppose we were sleeping so heavily after our champagne dinner that we never awoke till we found the floor flooded.

Now I must thank you so much for all your trouble getting me the combies. I fancy I shall need them during the rains, but anyway on the voyage home, because I believe a day or two after you get out of Sierra Leone the trade winds are very cold, and one has to be most careful; and the two blouses you sent me will be very useful, dear Belle. The cake is lovely, so light, I was surprised when I cut it to find it perfectly light. Walters is very good making us such nice cakes, and your sweet thought ordering them.

I wonder how your work will get on at Wimbledon. I am quite longing for a bit of nice work to do when I get home. I wonder what I can do.

Mrs Forde is not coming out till October after the rains. He and Charlie are almost exactly the same height, but he has the biggest hands I ever saw. Dr Lloyd Roberts' are tiny compared to them.

We got up at 5.45 this morning so at 8.30 I had a delicious little cup of cocoa. Charlie goes to York Island today at 12.30.

9.30 p.m.

We had both just got comfortably to bed when knock, knock, came at the door, and the French Company watchman came with a note to ask Charlie to go and see a Mrs Soloman, who is the wife of a black trader from Freetown, who has strong fever and [is] delirious. Much groaning from Charlie. This Mr Soloman was at York Island last Sunday expecting his wife by a steamer which never came, and they evidently have gone into the French Company house that the Judge had. So I got up too, and have the wee kettle going to try and make myself a cup of cocoa before Charlie returns.

In my letters from dear Father and Elsie today I hear of the death of poor Aunt Mary. I am so very, very sorry to think of their sorrow, especially Uncle John. Elsie told me that he slept with her the night she died with her hand in his. It's very pathetic, I think, and she so bright to the last. I am very sorry to think I shall not see her again.

Monday 25 May 1909

My darling Belle, I had intended to go on with your letter yesterday, but at 11.30 a.m. the Captain of the *Batanga* and a friend came to ask Charlie and me to lunch on board, and then Mr Sharman, the manager of the Coaling Company at York

Island, who has just come back from England, was going to take us for tea to Bendu on his launch; and we were asked back to the ship for dinner, but we said we could not do that. So they brought us back here, and they (the Pidgeons and the Captain and two or three other men) went back to the ship. It was a very hot day and if it had not been for Mrs Pidgeon whom I very much dislike, she is so exceedingly impertinent, I enjoyed it very much. The men, between you and I, are very common but very kind, and it was such a nice change. The skipper of the *Batanga* is quite a young man, and kindness itself.

Charlie came back with a splitting headache, the result of too long a fast. We had breakfast of simply tea and dry toast at 7.30 and nothing till 1.30 p.m., so he went straight to bed, and Pooz and I had dinner together, but he was very sick, poor cat.

In coming back from Bendu in the launch it came on a terrific tornado of rain. We (Charlie and I) were the only ones who had brought coats from the ship, but it had an awning.

You must forgive these half sheets, my darling, we are getting so short of paper. Is it a bit of your tweed you sent me with the cake? The colour is lovely, but it feels heavy. I do hope, my young wean, that you had a nice time in Ireland. I have to write to Miss Worthington today. Fancy, Mr Page said on Friday night, [when] we turned in to see him, that he really did not sometimes think Mr Addison 'all there'!

I have written to Uncle John and Katie too so I have written quite a lot, but there is my poor Kate left again. I know she is a dear and takes these letters as her own. I am trying to get her a canary.

On Saturday I went over to York Island with Charlie. They sent a wee steam launch for us, and no sooner did it reach here coming back than it broke down. The man is much better and they hope to pack him home this week.

I have finished another camisole; I have put sleeves in them. I'm rather sorry in a way as my combies have sleeves to them. Now I am beginning to make drawers. Oh, I also wrote to May and Mrs Pugh, my dear! So I have done my duty, haven't I? It's very nice for these traders having the ships coming in because the captains and officers are all friends of theirs, but I find it rather a mixed joy, only anything for a little change.

Now, sweet little Rope, adieu for this week.
With best love from us both, Twisty

Please forgive this frantic smudge, our blotting paper is done.

12.30

Just had lunch, peals of thunder coming from York Island! I am so sorry to have given you all the trouble sending my things, my wee-est of Aunties, and if I were not afraid of being whipped when I get home I would ask you to go to the top shelf of [the] red wardrobe, and look for that flounce of black net Miss Fox gave me, but I fear there is not enough of the white thread! How amusing Berta Ruck must be. Who is it Miss [illegible] has married? Awful having a sister in law thrown in! Did Louie Darbishire that was know her husband before she went out?

The canary [has] just come! Please tell Kate it is a very small bird, not very yellow, rather like a greenfinch, only more yellow on it.

Saturday 29 May 1909

My darling Belle,

I am quite ashamed of beginning my letter this week so late, from pure laziness. I have been wasting time every morning with the bird, and also I've had to read long articles on the Budget to be ready to argue with Charlie, and yesterday morning I spent my time wasting, I fear, one roll of films. I was anxious to get the children of my next door neighbour and her little servants as I have spent hours watching them, and I also took one of Charlie coming back from the Hospital. I took two of each in case they were failures. The first I took the gate by mistake, I forgot the camera was loaded and exposed it! Second, Charlie; third, Charlie; fourth, Josephine McCauley and her little nurse; five, ditto; six, the three little slave boys; seven, ditto; eight, Edna McCauley on our door-step; nine, Josephine McCauley, her little nurse and Edna under our frangipani tree and Pooz in the branches. Oh before this I tried two interiors, but I fear did two on one film. The last two are the house from the other side and the frangipani tree, and Charlie in one of the windows.

We had such fun Tuesday evening. Charlie had to go to the Fever Hospital and all the Government boats were away, so we had a huge dugout that has been bought by Mr Page for carrying the prisoners on to the island opposite, so Charlie said we would go in this. The black District Commissioner was very nice getting it cleaned for us, and we had tea at 3.30 and off we started. It was a joke and very nice going in the canoe, much nicer motion than the boat; we took Jomendi with us and two other men to row. When we got there Charlie saw about a large tank for water they are having put up there, and I got a basket full of limes, and we prowled about, then we got into the canoe again and went round by some sandbanks and got two curlew. It was lovely coming home, so cool and nice.

On Wednesday we did not do anything particular, but made up for it at night by a most terrible tornado. (I had been dreaming just before that I had seen Mrs Finchett Maddock drive past, her hat off and her hair flying in the wind.) [I woke] to feel a most terrible wind; then Charlie awoke, it was awful, the house was rocking, and as black as ink all round outside and continual lightning. It raged for nearly an hour. We came downstairs, the noise was so deafening upstairs; and next morning found our landers blown down and a great many roofs off. When Charlie went to York Island they said it had been terrible there, some of the boats all broken up.

Bonthe today. Photo by Redmond Shannon.

On Thursday evening I went to thank the Roman ladies for a bunch of the most glorious lilies (white) they had sent me from the Fathers' garden, and they said they had made me six little doilies for putting under cakes, wasn't it kind of them? I am expecting the stuff for making handkerchiefs by this mail; the *Bonny* is at York now. It came in at 12 o'clock. I told them I had sent for it and they seemed very pleased to get the order.

Yesterday and Thursday Charlie did not feel quite the thing, I think he must have got a chill shutting the windows the night of the tornado, but he is quite well again I am glad to say. He is so uncomplaining when he isn't well, the dear old boy. On Thursday evening after going to the Romans I came back here and he didn't feel equal to a walk, so I took Pooz for his favourite walk up the road opposite, past the big tree and round past Mr Page's house and home by the wharf and the police office. It takes a quarter of an hour. He loves it and sits down sometimes and lets me get a good way off, then gallops after me and pants with his mouth wide open for quite a long time. He is killing, all the policemen and post office boys know him, and little boys say 'Look na Pooz.' I took him last night too. He follows us out of the gate always and if he sees we are going his way comes on; we never have to call him. Last night first Charlie and I went for a walk past the French Company.

I must tell you this canoe (Government canoe) is a new fad of the Governor. He found if we cut down the trees on the island opposite that we should be able to see the ships at anchor at York Island, so the prisoners have to go over accompanied by one warder. When Charlie passed them on his way to York on Thursday they had lit a fire and were all sitting round it! Mr Metzer, the black District Commissioner, says when they have cut it all the first part they have cut will have grown up! The Governor is full of luminous ideas of this sort.

My dear, the silver fruit knife I won on the *Karina* coming out has disappeared. I always have it, a small pair of scissors and a big pair, and my little silver nail file on the writing table, and I lent Mormoh the silver knife, to cut bananas to stew with pineapple for a summer pudding. Sam says he cleaned it and put it back and I saw it, and then Wednesday or Thursday it disappeared. Charlie has told them if it is not produced before next Tuesday 1 June, they none of them shall get any wages! Time will prove whether I get it back or not. I rather suspect Jomendi, he looks miserable.

This evening after tea Charlie and I will go for a walk and end up with the market; and also round by a house where we saw custard apples growing to see how they are progressing. I got a lovely ripe paw-paw for 1d from Sarah Peters, the washerwoman, the other day. I am having the Roman Sisters to tea on Monday, and I have the parkin, and I made a little cake, weight of two eggs, flour, cornflour etc. etc. and am going to chop it up, put butter and sugar over them and dip them into chopped burnt ground nuts; I think they ought to be rather nice.

Did I tell you Mr Addison lent me *The Life of Benvenuto Cellini* written in 1500? At first I did not think I could get through it, but now am enjoying it immensely. It's rather after the style of Bozzy's *Life of Johnson*.

I am so sorry to hear from Charlie, who saw it in the Reuters at York Island, the death of Mr Meredith.[73] What a lot of literary men have died this year. A week today I heard of the death of poor Aunt Mary too.

Sunday 30 May 1909

My darling little Belle,
Your nice long letter came yesterday afternoon, also a nice one from dear Father, Elsie and Kate, all most interesting and containing good news of you all, which is a great pleasure to me. I do hope we shall all keep well till we meet D.V.[74] in October or November. The time is going on now and the weather lovely, rain and sunshine and cool breezes. By the time this reaches you we shall be most likely more or less in the rainy season.

Darling young Belle, you didn't send me the linen lawn for hankies. Perhaps it will come next week, if not I know you will want to cut off my head. Will you get me enough from Robinson and Cleaver to make six hankies, and also cotton and thread to embroider them. The Romans will be so disappointed if it does not come.

Charlie has just read me that the Duke of Norfolk is selling his Holbein's

---

73 Clearly George Meredith, the novelist, who died in May 1909.
74 i.e. God willing.

'Duchess of Milan' owing to the precarious state of landowners! Just fancy it coming to that in the Duke's case.

Monday 31 May

I must wind this up now. I am so sorry I can't send the butterflies home this week as there is no steamer, so I will also keep the films. I am going to try and make scones like the Bryn Morfa ones if I can today, and shall use the baking powder I got from Mr Reaney; the Seidlitz powder I used last time was not an unqualified success. The following is a pudding I have invented and called 'Bonthe pudding': half a cup breadcrumbs, half cup flour, half cup sugar, one dessertspoonful marmalade, two handfuls of currants, one tablespoonful of lard and butter mixed and one teaspoonful baking powder. Mix with one egg, and steam in a 1 lb marmalade jar (that has been well buttered) for two hours. It just makes enough for four, and is extremely good.

We had a very nice walk yesterday evening up past the Hospital and on into the bush. The old man of the cassada farm has taken to coming here with pineapples for me. He knows he will get a 3 d bit. I am very glad of the pines, Charlie likes them stewed, and the oranges are out of season.

Fancy, Whit Monday. The only difference it makes to me is that Charlie does not go to Hospital this morning, but he has now gone out to the jail and to the Postmaster who has a cold. It was very stuffy in the night, Charlie could not sleep, but I thank goodness did.

With our best love, darling little Belle, for this week
Ever your own Twisty

I am so sorry I shall not see Llewelyn.[75] Please tell me all his news and give him my best love. Don't forget to let me know if my grey coat and skirt wants new grey braid, and how it looks. I'll have it sent to Marcus to press, I think.

Thursday 3 June 1909

My darling little Belle,
I am going to begin my letter this morning as I believe the mails will be in today. There are two German and one English boats expected. It's a little too early in the week for them to come, as I dare say we shall have to wait ten days for the next batch.

Charlie has just gone off to York Island. I had half intended going with him, only I heard Mr Williams, the man who had blackwater, has not gone yet, so I should have had him sitting on the verandah.

We had a nice walk last night, passed the French Company and called in to see Mr Larout who is back from his holiday. He is a much more entertaining man

---

75 Her brother, always called by me Uncle David. M.B.M.B.

than Mr Dubois. He weighed me and in three weeks I have put on 3½ lbs! He said he would not have known I had been ill if Charlie had not told him. I know you will be glad to hear all this, that's why I put it in.

When I got back from my walk I found the overland mail had come in from Freetown with such a kind letter from Mrs Renshaw begging me to go to the Hill Station for a week, awfully kind of her, and saying if I came at once I should be in time for the weekly 'At homes' of the West Africans, but I am not going as I feel so much better. It would be such a bother, and I would not like to leave my old man, but I can go any time I want to so that's nice.

It's come on a downpouring shower so it's as well I did not go to York; we are nearly into the rains now.

My little chicks are very fine; they had some of our baked cassada after breakfast today, and Pooz had kedgeree. I have begun to take coffee again every other day; Charlie thought tea would be good for him now and again, so we take it like that alternately. I much prefer coffee. We are now using what grew in the Hospital garden and it's quite good too.

I had Mrs Pidgeon to tea on Tuesday. She really is too impertinent and common for anything. She has been evidently made a good deal of by the sea captains, and I should think never having been accustomed to having servants it's quite turned her head; but she is unknowingly so rude. She said 'I have great faith in Hone's pills, do you know them, Doctor? Your medicine does me good for the time but the pain comes back, but these pills have quite cured it.' It's too silly of me to quote her, she is so common.

I have made myself one pair of drawers but am waiting for the embroidery from M.M. Co. to put on them.[76] I shall begin a second pair today.

I want so badly to write to Paddy and Muriel Robinson, I must try and do it. Did I ever tell you or Father that I cut Charlie's hair? I've done so ever since I have been here; I had no idea how to begin the first time, but suddenly dropped into it, and really without boasting I don't think there is a better barbered head on the Coast. I roared over it at first, and Charlie was so nervous, putting both hands over his ears; but now he has more faith in me and sits with one hand holding a looking-glass! and now and again says 'Take care now', or if the scissors pull his hair out without cutting it I hear muttered swear words. I did it yesterday and excelled myself! Will Father let me do his? Charlie says we might set up a barbering shop, he would sell the washes etc.

The day the servants' wages were to be paid I went into my box of papers with 'H' on it, and lo and behold the silver fruit knife! Charlie now suspects me. Anyway he said to the servants 'The knife come back, now no humbug any more.' I think one of them put it in there.

---

76 I can remember pattern books coming from the Manchester Manufacturing Co. when I was a small child. They contained strips of lace edgings etc. mounted on shiny darkish blue calico and the choice always seemed quite exciting. M.B.M.B.

They killed a cow on Wednesday and we bought the tongue and are having it cold for lunch, with fish and spinach and eggs. I am going to have a cup of cocoa at 9.00 a.m.

10.15 a.m. Delicious cocoa and a lovely fresh petit beurre biscuit. The whole time I have been here Sam has never once made me tea with the water not boiling; that's one of his great virtues. Another is that both he and Mormoh are most awfully punctual: as the clock strikes 12 lunch comes in. But sometimes Sam is so lazy that I hardly know what to do with him. Then Charlie smooths me down; or if he sees it too he will go at them hammer and tongs. 'If they humbug Missis he cut their copper!', that is, reduce their wages. Jomendi has been sent off to the facki near the Smallpox Hospital to buy a good fowl for 1/6. If they are not good he will have to take them back. So we go on from day to day.

How nice that Lizzie said your hair was so nice and that your blouses were neat. I hope you have plenty of them for the summer. I also hope, dearest, that you will not overdo yourself playing tennis. I really sometimes think you overtax your strength. I hope you will have a very nice and happy summer, and dear Father and Kate, not to mention Mormoh and Sam[77] and the bird Susan and of course poor Perro.

We have had the big mango tree pruned 'within an inch', all one side facing us cut off, the District Council did it after first asking our permission. It is not an improvement as far as appearances go, but we get ever so much more air through the house.

Saturday 5 June 1909

The lovely bundle of letters came while Charlie and I were at tea yesterday. We have it round the dining room table now as at the end of the dry season the sitting room got so awfully hot. It was a drenching afternoon, and I had been watching the Customs boat arrive with the letters in a perfect downpour as I was having my bath (I have it at 3 o'clock now) so did not expect the letters so soon. And when Sam walked in carrying a sack which he dumped down on the rug I thought, someone had sent us a present of a young pig!

I am so very, very sorry I shall miss seeing dear old Llewelyn, but I am very glad to hear he is looking so well and in such good spirits. It will be a lovely time of the year in Switzerland. Tell me all about him; does he still lie in wait behind doors and then leap out and scalp you, or terrify you with 'Your money or your life'? I am awfully sorry to hear of George's troubles, but really it was a case of 'I told you so'. It was most injudicious for him to marry, I shall always maintain that, but I do hope poor Winnie will get better.

It is a nice cool morning, and just at 9.15 a.m. I walked up to the Hospital with Charlie and then came home another way and bought ½d of red peppers, the little bird loves them. We are dining with Mr Page tonight; we had asked Mr

---

77 The Bronceris cats. M.B.M.B.

Harrendorf (the manager of the new German Company) to dinner tonight and were going to have the Padré too, but Mr Harrendorf can't come, so we can go to the Hon. G. W. Page's!

For lunch today (you will think I am extremely fond of my little Mary) we are having stewed beef and pumpkin and rice, oh, first fish, then beef, then macaroni cheese and fruit.

Charlie has threatened to lock me out of the medicine room as I had mislaid a knife of his, and helped myself to ammonia and things and used his scales, but I tell him he would be the loser as I do so many odd jobs for him.

I don't know whether to be glad or sorry that you are in the match set of tennis; you will be wearing yourself out, but I must say it's awfully plucky of you to have stuck at it and got to play so well. I am very proud.

Will that grey coat and skirt of mine look very antediluvian when I come home? Of course I am not in mourning for poor Aunt Mary, I have no black with me; and I fancy I should not need to get it in October, would I?

I am now going to pack up the butterflies, they are beginning to mould. They are very disappointing and I see very few now.

Please thank Llewelyn so much for the book, I shall enjoy reading it, and shall pass it on to Mr Addison.

I will try and get Willie Workman a skin or two but they take two hours at least to do and I have not tried it yet.

Be sure you send me some fine linen lawn for my hankies, sweet pet. I find I have to declare the value on this parcel, I have put 6/-, now for goodness sake take it out of my money if there is any left, or if not put down against me and I'll pay the 'dem. total' when we meet, D.V. young Seal.

Monday

I have just written to Father and Elsie, and must end yours up and begin my work; I have to mend Charlie's trousers, alter the band at the back, he says he has got so thin! And I have to arrange flowers, and make some cakes for tea. The lovely parkin is finished.

It's pouring with rain now and very dark, and big claps of thunder beginning. I think I shall like the rains, but I shall so soon finish the drawers, don't forget the flounce, young wean; and also in your next letter put in a few invisible hairpins; I find I have come to an end, and I can't understand it unless the servants take them for their women to do their wool up with! They never touch my big hairpins, and young wean, I must tell you my hairpins never leave me now! I have still one of those bronze ones we bought 18 months ago, and all my hairpins the enamel has worn off with use!

We had a very pleasant evening at Mr Page's on Saturday, We had left Jomendi in the house, and Pooz who had had no dinner and had been prowling amongst the saucepans and is black, he can't wash it off.

I went to the French Company and bought Charlie an umbrella the other day. Today Sam brings me money and asks me to write him a chit for one, and he has come back with one exactly like Charlie's! I think he has the greatest admiration for Charlie!

My best love, my darling, take every care of yourself.

Your loving Maida

P.S. I had closed my letter up but must open it to say we are having such a thunderstorm. I went into the medicine room now and a flash of lightning greeted me with the thunder, crack, crack!! Floods of rain, but I hope my poor boy has not started from the Hospital, it's light over our heads. The garden, roads and everywhere one pond.

Sunday 13 June 1909

My darling Belle,

Here is Sunday and I have not written a line of my letters, just pure laziness.

It has been an uneventful week, some days pouring but then a fine one, but every day it has cleared some part of the day and we have had a walk. Last Monday when I wrote we were in the middle of a tornado, and it poured all day till evening when I put on my serge skirt and Charlie and I went out. We called first on Mr Page; we found him outside so he joined us in a walk. Next day he left on patrol.

I made some scones and a small cake, not bad, and on Thursday I asked the little German woman to tea, and said I was having the German Sister to meet her. Her husband wrote back to say she was ill with fever, and I met the Sisters coming that evening from her house. The firm they belong to is a new one and they have no agreement with Charlie, so I did not like to go there.

The Sisters said they had suggested sending for Charlie and they did so; she was pretty bad, and Charlie had to go twice the next day, but she is getting better. Sister Stanislaus went there all day yesterday, and she told Charlie in the evening she had such a business to get her to take her quinine. Aren't some women fools? She said it left a nasty taste in her mouth.

I had Kate's complaint the beginning of the week, bad eyes, in fact conjunctivitis like Auntie Kate last year, and my head all hot, however it's better. Thursday was a very hot day, and we had a tornado and heavy rain all night.

It's very hot again today, 85° in the sitting room now at 11 o'clock.

Our little chickens are getting on splendidly. I caught Pooz stalking them this morning. Kate's little bird is so funny, he eats seeds from my hand, and loves hemp. He also is very fond of red pepper and groundsel. The groundsel here has a little purple flower.

Last night after tea we saw the big Government boat return full of people but not Mr Page, fifteen cannibals, my dear, from not 20 miles away! the chief of the place among them. Afterwards when Charlie, Pooz and I were returning from our walk round Mr Page's we met a woman trying to cry. We said 'What's the matter?' and she said 'They done lock up my famble.' She was the chief's wife! So there are two chiefs in jail now to be tried for leopard murder. One of these was in before for four months awaiting trial and afterwards got off, which of course does more harm than good, but this time Mr Page thinks he has plenty of evidence; but I believe Mr Townsend is too lenient.

Today we finish another week, that's three months three weeks left to do! I don't know *what* to do about Pooz, he is such a dear, and yet I'm afraid of his being such a nuisance on board ship. He would cry the place down. One day Mr Harrendorf called and he has a wire-haired terrier who is death on cats, so Pooz had to be closed in the medicine room. Well, you never heard such a noise, he rattled the door, and then he thought if he knocked some bottles over that might alarm Charlie which it did, and I had to go and get him out!

To our surprise after lunch we saw two masts over at York, and now we hear the *Ilaro* is in, and she has brought the papers if not the mails, and also she has brought a Captain Vaudry who is going to relieve Captain Bailly at Victoria. We shall have to ask him to dinner, as I fancy he will put up at Mr Page's house, the under part.

I have so very much enjoyed the book Llewelyn sent me, *The Ladder of Swords*,[78] the only thing is it's too short.

Monday

We did get such a lovely budget of letters last night, they arrived as we came down for dinner; they came by the overland mail. Charlie, Pooz and I were at the wharf when the boat arrived. The men had practically no clothes on, they had the wind and tide against them the whole way. Their skin looks like very lovely polished old black oak when they are hot, and all their muscles stand out. What strength they have!

The *Ilaro* brought the papers, so many thanks to dear Kate for *Punch* and the book by Vachell; I am so thankful to have it. I did so enjoy *The Ladder of Swords*. Thank you darling *so* much for the linen lawn, the Sisters will be so pleased to get it I think. The German one goes now every day to sit with Mrs Rugi. She had fever, 105.2° last night again and very depressed, poor little thing. You see, he is not a manager, and they get very little pay, the assistants, and have to be out three years the first trip. He has done one year and she will have to do two years, and now Mrs Harrendorf is coming out in August so it will be very awkward for her. Mrs Pidgeon said 'I don't think she will have much to do with her, as Mrs Harrendorf is related to a baron.' I said at once, 'West Africa is not the place to think of those things even if she were a baroness herself !' This pen is so awful, I must go and search for a new one, Charlie ruins all pens.

---

78 Presumably *A Ladder of Swords* by Gilbert Parker, published in 1904.

I've told Father in my letter about the cannibalism. I must tell you though a funny conversation I had with that Mammy who in joke offered me her 'lillie piccin'. I was coming back from a stroll with Pooz the other night and she came to meet me, and this is the sort of talk we had. She roars with laughter, I must tell you. 'Missis how do?' I say, 'I well; how you do and how the little piccin?' 'He well the little piccin, he sleep.'(He was on her back.) 'That a nice pooz you get, you ge' me a lillie one?' Me: 'I no get.' She: 'Oh, he no born piccin.' Me: 'No, he man cat.' She: 'Ohhh! Missis, good evening Yees', and off she goes shaking with laughter. They are always laughing, some of them; but that's the pigeon English they talk.

Little Belle, would you put in an envelope a skein of fine cotton for embroidery like we used to use for hankies.

I was telling Father Charlie may leave me at Bronceris for a week or two. It will be lovely seeing you all again. His sister enclosed him such a jolly letter from Hugh.[79] He will he home in the autumn too, that will be nice for Charlie, and I should like to meet Barbara too. I have had our bedroom scoured today as it's fine, but I'm a poor housekeeper I think, and I'm getting easy going, goodness me, goodness me!

I am sure you and Kate swear when I ask you to do things for me, but tell Kate I have a deal of trouble with her little bird, so will she see about the embroidery cotton! And also a few yards of that blue ribbon, 1 d a yard, for running through underlinen, the *very* narrow. Lees were such idiots, they sent me entre deux without holes. I also want a dark blue petersham belt for coming home with, but there's no hurry for that. You poor weans.

Best of best loves, my young barnacle, from Twisty

Wednesday 16 June 1909

My darling Beatrice!

I am beginning my letter today so as not to have a frantic rush again on Monday. By lunch time last Monday I was fairly done up: writing all my letters, getting the washing off and seeing that Sam and Jo turned my room out well, which they did, Jomendi being in a most industrious humour as I had given him two old shirts of Charlie's on Sunday, and it was a lovely breezy sunny day, so it dried beautifully. Yesterday morning I made a cake, and after lunch did a little to my drawers. I've as usual ordered ¼ yard too little of the entre deux, so have had to alter the legs of one pair. The M.M. Co. had no more of that lace I put on my wearing drawers three years ago, so sent the nearest, 6d a yard, not bad for good wearing pants.

At 2 o'clock I took Vachell's book upstairs and had a lie down. Just as I was dropping off to sleep Charlie came up to say he had to go off to Bendu (the white speck in my academy picture!) and would I like to come? I did not answer but jumped into the middle of the floor and started dressing. We were to have tea

---

79 Charlie's brother. M.B.M.B.

'A strolling snake charmer', old postcard sourced from http://www.sierra-leone.org/Postcards/NEW-CARD7386.jpg

and start *at once*, not a servant on the place! Charlie had to go and put the kettle on the fire, and then Jo turned up; he with many Ds!![80] was sent flying to the Hospital. Well, we got started, wind and tide against us, and after we had gone a short way the Sergeant found out the body (it was an inquest) was an hour's walk beyond Bendu, and parts of the road up to his waist in water! The black District Commissioner had said it was a few minutes from Bendu! Charlie saw it would be dark before we reached Bendu so useless to go, so back we came and the big canoe was sent for the body, which never arrived back till 3 o'clock this morning. What luck it was we came back as at 8 o'clock last night it began to rain, and never could I have believed rain could make such noise. At about 11 o'clock it seemed as if the heavens were opening.

This morning Charlie is having the post mortem. It was a snake charmer, and one of the performing snakes bit a boy who died six hours after. Charlie had a preliminary enquiry on the doorsteps this morning at which I was an eager listener. If you could have seen the bottles the snake man had his medicine in! They were covered with snake skin. I begged Charlie to try and get me them, but he said they would never part with them. As I looked at them I could almost hear the witches murmur 'Bubble, bubble, toil and trouble!'

The sub-chief of Bendu was there with his dog, a small edition of old Perro and a darling!

---

80 Presumably damns.

Kate's little bird is really quite a dear although he is not much yellower than a green finch, and has a little grey head, but he is so tame, eats anything out of my hand. I always make the same noise whenever I go near the cage, you know that noise one makes when one is told one's favourite vase is broken! And he now knows it quite well.

It's awfully wet today. I took the linen to the Sisters yesterday. The little French one was ill with neuralgia; I made Charlie come back and see her. (They don't like sending for him as he does not charge them anything.) I asked him if she wore that white arrangement over her head in bed, and he said no, he had been wondering if he would find her head shaved, but she had nice fair hair. I like her and the German one far the best, the Reverend Mother is rather a 'corker' I think.

I see Mrs Pritchard's wean announced in *The Times*. What relation is she to the noble Minister of the Admiralty? Talking of the Navy, what billet has Captain Nicholas now? Do you know, and did you see Gertie?

I'm awfully afraid you are overdoing yourself with tennis. I'm getting old I fancy, and am taking things softly softly; 'dolce far niente' for me in future, and when I come to Bronceris you will find me most stick-in-the-mud, I know! Charlie may bring me down and leave me and come back for me, but this is only talk, it's only June now!

10.20 a.m. Friday 18 June 1909

The *Bakana* has just passed on her way to York Island. That means mails today!! Goodness me, goodness me, goodness *me!* Also fresh butter, we had come to scraping the pot at breakfast today.

Yesterday was a pouring wet day from morn till after tea when I was able to walk with Charlie up to the Hospital and back with only a spot or two of rain. It was cold all day too, and I decided to begin combies today, but as it is fine and warmer I have postponed the agony.

At the gate on our way back we met Mrs Pidgeon. 'Could I have a few words with you privately, Doctor?' I nearly smiled thinking of Hone's pills that never failed! After all her cockiness, the firm has written out to say they cannot leave till the beginning of August and must return end September! only giving them a month in England. They have both been much too 'cocky', please excuse the expression, and one of their old hands resigned the other day, so I think she has not been finding everything *color de rose*.

Did I tell you we had three fowls stolen the other night by the yardman of the Coaling Company? Charlie wrote to Mr Rowland, the white manager, and he had the impertinence never to answer till next day, so Charlie sent the police there. Nothing could be proved, and the 'fowl palaver is very strong here'. That means very difficult; it appears cooks are very fond of stealing fowls and selling them to their masters, so there is no saying Mormoh may have been up to some tricks and this was his reward. The sergeant told me he had had six fowls stolen 'at one blow', as he said, the other night.

The snake palaver is over. Charlie found the boy had unmistakeably died of the snake bite, a very poisonous one, so Mr Metzer ordered all the heads of the snakes to be cut off! And he gave me the charm bottle; it's certainly a curiosity but decidedly dirty.

Saturday 5.30 p.m.

Did I tell you that poor Charlie let us in for a dinner at the Swiss Company tonight, where the German lady has been ill. He tried to get out of it by saying would Mrs Rugi be well enough, but Mr Harrendorf the manager said 'Oh, but it's my birthday, and I must have a party.' He is a big edition of Arthur Bodvel in look and manner; and now it looks as we are going to have a big tornado, so how we shall get there I don't know.

I finished off my last roll of films today, they are not so good for twelve for out here you can never take them quick enough. I'm afraid the last twelve are spoilt by being in the camera too long. I'm sending them straight to Rose to save you the bother.

Mr Page arrived back yesterday. I'm going to ask him to tea tomorrow to get what poor Aunt Mary used to call the [illegible]. He has sent another boat load of cannibals, so there are now 37 of them in the jail, and 70 prisoners in all. Charlie fears they will get suffocated; but the black District Commissioner told Charlie today that they actually did a leopard murder, or tried to, while Mr Page was there. They were round his house all night, he never slept. I'll give the account to dear Father, all being well, on Monday. Now, about the bird for Kate: will she care to have it now her little Robert has come back?
Ever, my darling, your loving Twisty

23 July 1909[81]

My darling Belle,
It really must only be two sheets this week. I have come to the end of the last box of paper. I think I told you that some time ago, but I found another box, thank goodness!

Wednesday and yesterday and up to now today have been perfect, a lovely breeze and beautiful blue sky with big white bulgy clouds. We have had no rain since Tuesday night when Charlie and I got a soaking. We had gone to the French Company, I in the white linen (yours), all nice and clean and my best low shoes as the skirt is so short! But as we got to the French Company it began to rain, and poured and poured. Jomendi arrived with our raincoats but we had to walk home through rivers of wet, and my feet were in a glow after it.

---

81 There is a long gap between this letter and the previous one; probably some have not been retained.

Yesterday Charlie and I went to call upon Mr Page after tea, and he came with us for a walk to the cassada farm, but the last remaining planks of the pond we have to cross just before getting there have now fallen, so we can't cross. He is going to have it repaired. The pond now instead of being a filthy stagnant pool has a lovely white sandy bottom, and there were what looked like small trout in it; I am going to try and catch one and bring it home in pickle. They have five or six black spots on their sides, whether that is natural to them or a disease I can't say.

Yesterday afternoon while Charlie was at York I cut up oranges for marmalade, and Mormoh has just come back from the Hospital with a borrowed pan to boil it in, ours wasn't big enough, 5½ lbs fruit. 5½ lbs sugar. The last was good in the extreme. I evolved a new punny again which I have called Sherbro Punny. I'll write it on a loose slip of paper to save you the bother of writing it out and you can paste it in the new cookery books. My darling, I never thanked you for making me a new one. You are a dear wean, what lots we shall have to talk of when we meet, all being well, in October. It appears Dr Jackson Moore is doing all in his power to get back here, and the dresser told Charlie yesterday that if he comes the 'old people' of the town are going to make a petition to have him removed, and Mr Page said 'It will be a misfortune for Bonthe if *he* comes'!

Saturday

The latest news is that Mr Page leaves on 7 August and Mr Reaney is to come and act for him, to the utter disgust of Mr Vergette,[82] who said to Charlie 'You see Mr Reaney and Mr Addison will never get anything now as I've been put over them'! Charlie put a spoke in for Mr Reaney by saying to Mr Page, 'Well, I must say it looks funny your having two assistants and neither of them acting for you when you go on leave.'

We are having brilliant days. Today promises to be if anything too hot; it's a practically cloudless sky. The little canary is a dear little thing. He took a bath the first two days but now he is awfully afraid of the tin. Pooz is utterly demoralised, won't come in for chop or anything, like poor Pop.

We can't get bananas these days for love or money; tonight we may get some in the market.

We had a nice walk last night, and I found two mushrooms in a disused little hut on the street. They are real mushrooms, but Mormoh says they are not the good kind, that if natives eat them they have to boil them in two waters first and then cook them in palm oil. Charlie asked Sam at dinner if they were good. 'No, Sir, they no kill you but they humbug your be-l-y'! I did laugh.

The marmalade is not the huge success the last was; the rain has washed out the flavour of the oranges, and Mormoh has boiled it a little too much. Still it's quite good.

---

82 Mr E. D. Vergette was the Crown Prosecutor, appointed in 1908.

Mushrooms, from Maida's sketchbook c. 1897

Mr and Mrs Pidgeon left on Thursday without saying goodbye to anyone. Funny people one meets in this world.

Oh, my little Belle, would you send me a *Lady*, the newspaper; they have houses advertised sometimes, and we greatly enjoy looking out for cottages. The ones advertised in *Country Life* are all 'Mansions, D__ it!' Father will understand the quotation.

I see Trixie Davison had a wean who died; I am sorry.

Sunday

Yesterday after Charlie came home he skinned a wee bird he had shot for me the night before. It is a little honey bird. They come, heaps of them, on the hedge round the garden; but this is a male one, and we don't very often see them although there must be heaps of them. The hedge is alive with the little olive green and yellow hens. It took nearly two hours to do and the body was only the size of my thimble; it's very well done, I think. I saw a lovely little bird today, all the back and head jet black and the underparts pure white, and a tiny bit of white round the bill; it was the size of a tom tit. Last night we saw a lovely bird, the size of a blackbird, black and a purply black and bright red in the wing. Charlie is going to try and get it.

In the photo No. 1 you see our bit of garden with the white spider lilies all round; the red ones come up among them, and when they are both in flower they are very pretty. Would you care for a few bulbs of the white spider lily? The orange tree is at the end, and the few big leaves in the right-hand corner are a cocoa tree. In No. 2 you see me with my hair parted. Something has gone wrong with it; Mr P. is going to try and get a better one. I'm in that white island dress with box pleats, not pleated. That's why I look such a figure. No. 3, Charlie feeding his chicks, the two mammies eating out of his hand, and one of the chickens is sitting on his hand. The figure behind him is old Greybones, our cock. Don't I look like Wynne in this one?

Monday

My darling, your dear letter never came till this morning overland; but the papers came yesterday afternoon, so we had the full enjoyment of them, and found the *Tatler* most interesting, but what an ugly photo of Princess Patricia.

I have a horrid headache this morning. Whether it was beer I took last night or the pill I also took and cocoa (Charlie's idea!) for breakfast I don't know. Anyhow I've just summoned Sam and ordered a cup of tea, and I heard him through the window, 'Mormoh kettle tea!' Sam takes first place as a tea maker.

I am so glad you did not have Hob for the spring-cleaning, it really would have been too rough on the servants, poor things, otherwise it was a pity as I know you would have enjoyed his racy society. I hear from Elsie she left him copiously crying, but that she had heard from him 'He was very happy, wishing that they would stay away longer'!

Fancy Kate's birds flying away into the garden. I was afraid the young ones had hatched too late to do well. She will have better luck next time I hope. Which of the Vicarage are going to have the saddle? Is the umbrella going to ride?

It was so funny: your letters arrived at breakfast time, and we were looking at the photos, and as soon as we had finished we found Mrs McCauley and her two weans at the door, whooping cough, and the baby a huge gathering on her cheek.

Pooz came in this morning thin and dirty. He is utterly demoralised. If you could have heard Sam on the subject at dinner last night, I could hardly keep grave.

I am so very glad Elsie and Richard have had a change to Bray.

I can hear the tea coming, oh goodness me! If only you were here. I am beginning to feel I've been here over nine months and look a guy.[83] My hair has got so thin and my face so peaky; and yet I'm really wonderful considering. Charlie is very well and very kind to me, but not so kind to Pooz these days!

Ever, my little Ropey, your own Twisty-toe

Please give my kind remembrances to Walters.

---

83 Guy meaning scarecrow-like, not like a man.

Friday, 30 July 1909

My darling Belle,

I am beginning my letter today after tea. When I was lying down Charlie came up to say he had to go again to York Island, Mr Patchinini [is] ill again. Mr Cortie and his wife are supposed to have sailed yesterday to relieve him, and it's high time he went, he looks bad, heavy and fat.

Mr Copeland called yesterday to say goodbye. The steamer left this morning. He reminded me of Mr Izzard Davies and Mr Morgan Lloyd. He would not come in to any meal, but a jolly kind of man; he said he had a room at his house to offer us when we went on leave, very kindly.

It's awfully amusing, the people are so concerned as to who is going to relieve Charlie. They dread Dr Jackson Moore. Mrs McCauley was in from next door this morning getting more medicine for her little girl, and she said she would be so sorry when we left, and 'after you go back to England, you come back here'. Father will say all truth a ha'penny a thousand![84]

Yesterday morning when Charlie was at York I skinned my first bird myself with Jomendi helping me. It's a queer bird, I forget the native name; then in the afternoon Charlie did the yellow kind of lark he had also shot the night before; and today my poor back is so stiff from sitting in the same 'poz' for so long, three and a half hours at least! The yellow bird has the most extraordinary claws.

The night before that (Tuesday night) Charlie and I accompanied by Jomendi went the long walk past a pond with waterlilies where on Sunday night we had seen a curious black bird with cardinal colours in the wing; and as we were walking along we heard Jomendi (he had no idea what bird we were looking for) [say] 'Look am' and there, sure enough, it was. Charlie fired and hit it, but the shot is too small in the little gun to carry so far. We were so disappointed. We have had some lovely days again, but today and all last night [were] soaking; today it's a fine drizzle, that's what you get all August.

Sister Felix and Sister Stephen called last night and brought ten handkerchiefs they have made out of the stuff. I like them so much. Five have broderie anglaise in the corners. They have taken them back to initial them. I awfully afraid they are not going to charge me for them.

When I came down to tea, I found a big bunch of bananas on the writing table, and leaning against the wall a huge bunch of sugar cane! Neither Sam or Jo know who brought them. I don't care for sugar cane, it's so awfully sweet.

Last Saturday though I fell on luck. Two piccins came to the door selling sticks of white peppermint rock. Charlie would not let me buy it when I had seen it in the market, but I pointed out that in any case it must be cleaner than bread which they knead with their hands. I asked how they sold it. 'Copper copper' – that means a ha'penny a stick. It proves delicious. I am sure I'm getting greedy,

---

84 This sentence does not seem to mean anything, but the writing is quite clear. M.B.M.B.

I write [about] nothing but what I eat! And I eat well, my appetite is simply en-or-mous.

Saturday

As we were at breakfast we heard the boatmen 'hollering' as Sam says, which meant a steamer in sight, and sure enough, it was the *Prah*. She was expected yesterday, but must have grounded on a sandbank and come off at high tide this morning; so we shall get our letters today. That's very nice.

I've just been buying ground nuts; I get the sugar bowl Aunt G. of Rhyl gave me full for 1d, quite hot but their skins on.

Charlie came back before 6 last night. It was raining and he had let it fall on his face the whole way, so he came in with a fine colour, had a hot bath and came down like a lion refreshed; but this morning we both awoke with headaches, not serious. Pooz is quite a good cat again and very sweet. What drivel I'm writing!

The other morning one of the District Commissioner's clerks came with a country cloth and a leopard skin to sell. Chiefs give them to Mr Page and he is not allowed to accept them, so sells them and the money is supposed to go to the Treasury. He wanted £2 for the country cloth and 10/- for the skin. The clerk said when he found I was going to buy it, not Charlie, 'I will find out from a woman what its worth is', and he came back to say 27/- or 30/-. So I said 'Well, go back and tell Mr Page.' He came in an hour and said Mr Page said no less than £2. I sent a cheque and he has never acknowledged it. That's the sort of bounder he is. It's only blue and white, but I thought would make me dining room curtains, and it's got designs on it that make it much more valuable, but it's a huge price to pay. Charlie bought the skin.

5.40 p.m.

Disgusting, the *Prah* brought no mails, I'll have to wait till tomorrow or Monday for letters, and Charlie has finished all his newspapers and the last *Spectator* so he will be very miserable. He was sent for again at 3 o'clock to York Island, Mr Page's temperature has gone up again, and has not got back yet, but I hope he is not in a bad way; he is a bad subject, fat and liverish.

Pooz is sitting in his favourite place on the window sill, and a little naked nigger boy of 8 or so has just passed with a tiny little fish he has caught holding it by the tail. He is innocent of clothes but for a battered sailor hat. When he saw Pooz I could hear him call 'Pooz, Pooz' and I went to look and there he was dancing a little war dance and showing Pooz the fish! Killing little things they are and most taking, I think.

Talking of the *Spectator* I saw a book called *The Veil* very well reviewed a week or two ago, by a man called Stephens I think.[85] The scene was in Algeria, have you read it?

---

85 She must mean *The Veil: A romance of Tunisia* by Ethel Stefana Drower, formerly Stevens.

Monday 2 August

The overland mail to our astonishment arrived yesterday morning, so we had the pleasure of getting them when we came downstairs. A nice one from dear Father, you and Elsie, and Charlie got a budget including one from Captain Bond, who expects to be stationed at Exeter when we pass through, funny isn't it? He seems such a nice man and evidently a splendid athlete, having won now no end of cups etc.

I am so glad, my darling, you are enjoying your tennis so much. I'm sure it's good for you so long as you don't go and overdo it; and I'm so glad the piqué dress is such a success, a great blessing indeed to look decent.

I am so sorry to hear of Mr Clemenger's death, it will be a great blow to Mrs Clemenger. Charlie can't believe that his pension was so much; you say Maude C. is quite overcome and not at all 'went'. 'Well' I expect you mean, my poor wean. I do love your letters.

I'm enclosing a picture of me taken with an ear to ear grin on; and my hands looking twice their size. I had had such a business to get Pooz to be taken and all the boys watching and catching him to bring him back, and Charlie's patience ebbing, and Pooz dreadful cross. I've other killing snapshots of some weans crying which I will bring with me.

Fancy my poor sketches being framed in mahogany! Goodness me, goodness me, it makes me blush.

I had breakfast in bed today, kind Charlie brought it up to me: toast buttered and cut into snippets, delicious tea and an egg which I did not eat, a 'bilious fever' being the cause, but without fever, only bilious. I had taken calomel on Saturday night and took a long walk with Mr Page and Charlie last night. I'm better now. Mr Page leaves today or tomorrow. I had him to tea yesterday, but not Mr Reaney, he can wait a little.

I had asked E. Pattullo to get me a little present for the Corties, and she has sent such a very nice photograph frame; I have to write and thank her.

So now, little love, goodbye for this week; but oh thank you so much for the old clo' money, I shall be quite thankful to get it. Be sure to tell me how my coat and skirt looks. I would like to go to Miss Beuly but fear I could not go to Mrs Page simply to get the black velvet altered, what do you think?
Ever your own loving Twisty

Charlie has asked me if you could find out from Mrs Ruck or Berta if flats are difficult to get at Hampstead, and if you can get any clue as to rents. We sometimes think a tiny flat would be useful as headquarters, as our leave falls in the winter. Could you do this, wee Rope?

7 August 1909

My darling Belle,

We have not had the letters this week yet and there is no boat expected now till the *Olinda* on Thursday, so the overland mail will bring the letters tomorrow I hope, and will bring good news of you all.

Last Monday, Tuesday and Wednesday I was quite bad with indigestion and a feeling of languor and depression, but was better yesterday; today I've a headache again. I expect I shall be like this off and on now till we leave, it's just a change I want, and I am beginning to long to get away. Two months today we are due for leave, it's lovely. I feel I shall like to stay a week in London and get a few clothes, and then race home and have a nice rest. It will be lovely to see you all again and you have been so good writing me such nice letters. I mean you and dear Father and Kate, every week, and the papers. I really am a very spoilt individual.

Sam has been taken ill too with strong fever and a little dysentery, and went home on Thursday or Wednesday, and will not be able to come back till tomorrow. Charlie is seedy today too. We had a downpour at dawn this morning, which flooded the room, and we both awoke cold; and it's given me a sick headache, goodness me! We are a couple of crocks. On Thursday night I went to call on the Sisters, and found Sister Stephen had been in bed since Monday with a bad 'go' of fever. There is a great deal of sickness about, it's the wet and cold.

Sunday

Charlie got up to tea last night but did not go out, feeling rather a weed; he is decidedly better today. But the rain, my dear: this morning when we were just getting up it was raining a drop or two when all of a sudden, with a blast like thunder, came deluges of rain. The noise! You can hardly hear yourself talking. Now after lunch it has cleared a little, and I'm trying to get my cushions dry. The rain came straight into the sitting room, and although I heard Jo fly to them when he heard the rain still they got wet. There is also a leakage in one of the landers, and the rain pours into the house near the front door. Sam has never turned up; he was to have come back today, 'too plenty' rain I suppose. I feel much better, thank goodness.

I see no sign of the boat so I don't fancy we will get our letters till tomorrow. The Governor and Mr Page left for England yesterday, the wretches after only doing nine and ten months. To Charlie's great relief, the five condemned prisoners have been taken to Freetown for their latter end, so [that] will save Charlie an unpleasant journey this weather to Victoria. Mr Reaney is away on patrol, or I would have had him in to dinner last night. We had roast duck, and Charlie loves it cold, and I don't like it so I'm always glad when there is someone to help us finish it up.

On Thursday afternoon, just as we were expecting tea, in Jomendi rushed. 'Massa, look the bird.' 'Where?' says Charlie 'Look am, look am' – and there on the beach were about nine pigeons. Charlie crept down accompanied by Jomendi, crack! – and there lay three nice fat pigeons. There were a lot of sailors under the shed, and they evidently had not seen Charlie and got such a fright, you should have heard the yells of laughter. We had them stewed and sent up in the Gambia pot. They were excellent, Charlie said he had never tasted better; and last night one of the Frenchmen sent us two more, so we are having them tonight.

I am going to write to Miss Clemenger. I feel sorry for her. Do tell me where they are going to live, now or never for Mr Stokes to lead Miss Clemenger to the altar, say I.

Mrs Cortie is due to arrive by the *Olinda* on Thursday. Today we begin to 'dig in', as you say Walters says, into our last two months. Don't forget to let me know about my clothes, how they look etc., and please try and find out from Bessie without letting her know whether brown or black boots and slippers are being worn. I have re-beaded my best black ones with beads off my old ones, an awful job, last week, but they look as new, so it's only wearing slippers I shall want. Charlie says if I go with him to Rabbits he will give me a pair of boots. Which shall I get, brown or black? Rabbits is the wholesale bootshop he swears by.

                                                                    Monday

Rain, rain, we are getting a thorough good dose of it; but it cleared up yesterday at about 11 o'clock and we were able to have all the windows open at tea time. I saw Mr Reaney coming, he had just returned from Victoria bringing two letters for Charlie, one from the Court summoning him to Victoria and one from Mr Vergette asking Charlie and me to chop with him and Mr ?, the officer in charge of the WAFF while at Victoria, and I'm going, rain or no rain. I've not been two miles from this place since Christmas! All being well, we shall leave at about 8 o'clock tomorrow morning.

After tea we all walked up to the Hospital and then back with Mr Reaney to his house, picking up the mail at the Post Office. Lovely it was, such nice cheery home letters, I do love getting them. I had a nice long letter from May too, she sounds very tired.

My childie, I feel too ashamed to think of your framing those little daubs of mine, they are not worth framing at all. It's a great grief to me that I can't sketch though, because I love 'mussing with paints and water' and each time I put a stroke it makes things worse because I suppose I don't know how. If I had any sort of coloured picture to look at to see how it's done it would be a help, but the only coloured thing I have is the Oakhurst Christmas card.

I am surprised Wynne of Alderley and not young John of Ashfield is

A framed 'daub' of Maida's, perhaps of the Bonthe house, from the family's collection

made trustee for Mrs Ffoulkes. I suppose Aunt Pattie had worked that oracle!

May tells me James and Emily are going to Bryn in September. I hope they will have good weather.

Charlie is better but still looks a little washed out. I feel much better, I really looked a crock a week today.

Only two months now – exclamations of joy! With our best love, ever Childie, your own Twisty

Please excuse [me for not sending] a longer letter. Many thanks for blue ribbon, you young wean. I enjoyed your gossip about Irene Duke. What talks we'll have, young Ropey.

If a doctor comes here with a wife, Dr Burrows or Dr Ward, I would leave Pooz. Charlie won't hear of poisoning him, he is so sweet these days, but has got those tiny lice the kittens used to get at Crûg. Sam hasn't come back yet.

23 August 1909

My own darling little Belle,

This will be a very short letter, as I've not felt able to write a line all last week. I've given an account of it to Father and Elsie; but things are all brightening up again, the weather better and the patients are all doing well. We were both desperately tired Friday and Saturday, and could hardly crawl upstairs, but otherwise well. But I'm longing to get away now, although it has been such a happy year. I've thoroughly enjoyed the life out here with Charlie. With the exception of a few squalls, occasioned by our both having very strong wills, we do get on so well together, and he has done well too, and kept so far such good health; so I do feel very thankful for all our mercies. The only thing is I've only been to church twice, my wee Belle, and last night Charlie shot four pigeons on the beach below the house. Somehow I could not feel it was wicked, although I'm sure it was, as we do so enjoy them done in the Gambia pot, they are such a nice change.

Little Belle, I am so glad you are going to Bryn to stay with dear May. You will enjoy the lovely walks and prowls by the dear old river, but above all you will enjoy being with May. There's no one I enjoy myself with so much as May, dear Mother was so fond of her, and I look forward so much to giving her a good hug; she and Lydia and E.P.[86] are very dear to me. Somehow out here those we love at home seem to stand out like pillars in our memory.

After tea, and after Charlie had shot his pigeons, we all three went to call on Mr Reaney. It's really very jolly having him here. He has Twopence now, the Judge gave him to him. We passed Twopence at the Post Office, and he turned and followed

---

86 Her cousins Lydia Roberts and Emily Pattullo, daughters of Hugh Roberts of Alderley Edge, Cheshire. M.B.M.B.

us, so Pooz finished the journey with his tail five times its size and walked sideways. He walked 'hisself' up to the door, and I carried him upstairs and after one or two wails [he] sat on the window ledge of the verandah. Charlie and Mr Reaney had great talks about travelling allowances, new ordinances, etc., and I was given a stick almond toffy to keep me quiet! We left at 6.30 and he came with us as far as the wharf and Twopence. The whole way Pooz was flying at the dog with his head up and his tail like this [upright], and such spits. Mr Copeland says that Mary's kittens are all like that, they chase dogs. I'm going to write to Mrs Renshaw to ask her if any one at Hill Station would like him. Mr Reaney calls him Smuts. I've given the canary at last, he's to go when I do, to Mr Rupli of the Swiss Company.

At this point a large silver tray covered with a Teneriffe tablecloth made its appearance poised on the head of a black boy, and accompanied by a black school-master. On the tray a huge bunch of bananas from Mrs Williams, the parson's wife. Charlie had seen him about his ear, and doesn't charge parsons although he says such naughty things about them! We had a letter from Mr Williams on Thursday saying the Bishop was coming this week, and I had gone to call to tell them that I might be up the river, but Charlie would be very glad to see him and could we do anything? Mr Williams came to the door 'hisself' with a large plaid hand-kerchief over his head. Now I don't think the Corties are going, such a nuisance as with infinite trouble I had copied a map the size of a drawing board to mark the places as I went along. It took me three days to do, not working very long each day.

I do *so* enjoy your letters, no one knows, wee Belle, how much. I had gone to lie down yesterday after lunch, and Charlie had been sent for again to the German boat. When I got to tea there were the letters. You have been a darling and a brick, all you have done for me. I have been so sorry to give you those awful journeys to the attic, my poor wean. Now you will be glad to hear that you need not post any letters after 17 September, goodness me, goodness me, goodness me! I only hope we shall get away to time.

Charlie brought the third officer of the *Jeanette Woerman* in to tea yesterday, such a nice young German man. He had run away to sea when he was a boy. He and Charlie told me the Captain had ten lovely Pollies on board, and Charlie, my dear, to my great astonishment said to him 'So you think the Captain would sell me one?' Charlie will get about 10 or 12 guineas for this, and as the money comes from a firm and that firm *German* I feel quite content. He (Charlie) has now promised me a blouse, also boots and a petticoat! I am so glad the grey coat and skirt does not look too bad. Will you, darling, send a wee note to [illegible] to ask them first what they charge for pressing, as you know what Jews they are.

I am going to try to write a line to dear May. I may be able to post letters by this German boat tomorrow.

I am glad to hear of Miss Menzies' engagement to Mr Ernest Jones although surprised. Fancy poor old Kate falling off a chair. Does she remember getting on to a table at Crûg and it closing with her on board? I laugh now when I think of it.

With our best love, little Belle,
Ever your own Twisty Toe

Saturday 28 August 1909

My darling young Belle,
The *Bakana* is due today, I do hope she comes. She has been expected since Thursday; she is bringing *my* cake! Very very many thanks my darling, it is so good of you, you have no idea how I shall enjoy it. I have not the energy these days to make anything, but just enough energy to be able to enjoy yours.

For the last few days we have both been feeling exhausted, since Thursday. We went to lunch to York Island, and much as I enjoyed the day still I came home looking a wreck, and awoke next morning with Kate's complaint, a bad eye, and felt chippy all day. But today we both feel much better; so now I must tell you our news, which is absolutely nil. All the white people if not downright ill have been feeling out of sorts. Mr Reaney has been quite bad, Charlie going there twice a day, temperature 104, bilious fever. The German man off the ship was very ill one day, [and] Charlie [was] there (at the French Company) three times. However Charlie has managed to get him to take quinine (he had declared he could not take it, it gave him blackwater), so as he was having fever alternate days Charlie plugged him with 15 gms on his good day, and he is now nearly all right to his great relief, as he was afraid he would not be able to come back to West Africa.

The man next door who has taken Mr Rowlands' place has bad fever every other day; and two deaths last week at Freetown of blackwater, so it's been a bad time. I hope things will get better now; the man at the French Company who was so ill is back at work, and Mr Reaney up and about. One more invalid though who I nearly forgot to mention: poor Pooz was out all Thursday, never came in for his food, arrived yesterday morning limping and very sad, one toe nearly off! He cries about it 'drefful', but I can't quite understand whether it's another pooz or barbed wire that has done it. I must tell you Bonthe bristles with barbed wire.

Charlie has heard he has to go to Victoria again, two witnesses sick, and if they don't get better they may have to adjourn the Court. We are only hoping they will come down and get these two cases here, the two Sierra Leonians who are to be tried for the Leopard palaver, and the snake charmer, as Charlie is witness in both. If Victoria Sessions are not over quickly it may mean we are kept here after our time, but I don't think it likely. If all goes well, and we get off to time and sail on 9 October. We shall be coming by the *Landana*. She is the old *Leopoldville* and good, Charlie says, due at Plymouth 20 October. Goodness me!

On Thursday evening Sister Felix called and brought me the dozen hankies made out of the linen. I think they are lovely. Poor little things, they won't take a penny for making them. 'Dr Hunter is so kind to us,' she said. I shall have them to tea when your cake arrives, wee Belle, they do enjoy coming. They have all been seedy too.

6 p.m.

A soaking night. Charlie has just gone next door to see how the man is. He got £15 today from the French Company for the German ship palaver, they are the agents. Long live the *Jeanette Woerman*, with her sickly crew! The *Bakana* has never come. They were expecting the Bishop (Anglican) of Sierra Leone on her. I'm rather glad she has not come for that reason, it would have meant going to church at 8.30 tomorrow and I really don't feel up to it. I heard from Mrs Cortie she will be delighted to come and spend Monday night here. I had written to ask her; she is a down right jolly sort.

My darling, very many thanks for your dear letter, and also for dear old Kate's. I have so much to do this morning. I've made a small batch of cakes, some for Charlie to take with him, and have one more to make as there is no sign of a steamer from Freetown with yours. Shame, shame, on the Post Office at Freetown.

Charlie and I had a lovely walk last night round by the Hospital and Swiss Company. I had a letter from Mrs Pidgeon this morning, so sorry she had not time to call before leaving! Most condescending, I'm sure. She hopes to be back before we leave! Although Charlie said she should not come after so short a holiday.

1.15 p.m.

Charlie has just gone off, waiting in the boat for the boatmen. I think they are all slack with Mr Reaney; so I've been on the jump till now, and feel dog tired. I've had to make another cake too, and Sam is half asleep. He really is past work. With best of loves, my own wee Belle, Your own loving Twisty

No steamer in yet!

6 September 1909

My darling Belle,
Monday morning and I've not written a line to you, but now the time is so short that it does not so much matter, and I have very little news. Last Monday I was busy all morning getting (oh, no, it was Tuesday) Charlie off to Victoria, and making cakes as I was expecting Mrs Cortie in the afternoon. Charlie went off at 2 o'clock and I went to lie down and got up at 3 o'clock, had my bath and waited for Mrs Cortie who never arrived till 5 o'clock! I was so glad to see her, she is such a very nice woman. We had tea, then went for a short walk, and had a nice little dinner, and never went to bed, my dear, till 12 o'clock; and then we slept together as we were both a bit nervous and had only one mosquito net, and talked in bed

till nearly 2 o'clock. I then tried to sleep but the bed was so uncomfy I simply couldn't. Sam brought us a lovely cup of tea at 6.30.

We sat and talked all morning and after lunch we lay down. Charlie and Mr Cortie arrived at 5 o'clock. I was delighted to see my old man back. And then Mr and Mrs Cortie went off after tea, and Charlie, Mr Reaney and I went off to the Swiss Company; it was a lovely evening. On Thursday I went with Charlie to York but came back before lunch. We saw the *Warri* come in which brought the lovely cakes. Little Belle, you are a darling, it is so so good of you to make such *lovely* cakes for me. You have no idea how we enjoy them, and I feel now disinclined to make cakes. Although I feel quite well, still I've not much energy in a way. The steamer also brought all our letters and three lots of papers and the dear little books which I look forward to reading so much. I shall bring them home with me, they are such [illegible]. The mail arrived at 5 o'clock and I had just begun Father's when the Bishop arrived. I didn't bless him, and quite forgot to offer him tea, so at last Charlie said, 'Won't the Bishop have some tea?' Charlie told me afterwards 'You are no use, you know.'

We asked him and Mr and Mrs Williams to dinner on Saturday night, and Mr Reaney. I made a little tiny cake for a trifle, and Mormoh cooked a beautiful dinner, really it was good. I'll tell you what we had: soup (a bit greasy), a piece of boiled Spanish decorated with limes and red pepper; chicken stewed in the Gambia pot and green peas; beef cutlets and petits carottes for the middle of the dish and potatoes, trifle, and cheese savoury; dessert: prunes and [illegible] cherries; and Sam waited very well. I had stormed at them on Friday night and fined Sam 2/- so I was thankful they hadn't sulked. Oh, but it was a ghastly evening. I don't care for the Bishop *at all*, I 'll tell you about him when we meet. We had a small tornado too at dinner. Mr and Mrs Williams are heavier than lead! Mr Reaney had promised me he would entertain her and he failed miserably. I told him last night I'd never depend on him again!

Yesterday morning my poor Charles was dragged to church. They spoil every-thing by yelling. I looked at Charlie once or twice and nearly laughed, he looked as if he had swallowed a poker, and no sooner had we got out then he gasped 'Oh, you do let me in for things,' and this was repeated the whole way home! A consolation awaited him in the shape of a red-headed German sailor off another German boat, £1.1.0!

After tea yesterday we just walked to the Hospital and back and then went with Pooz and sat on the wharf, and Mr Reaney came and joined us. I'm bothering the life out of them both to take me to Yonné, a place beyond Mokolo. We are both dining with Mr Reaney on Wednesday night.

I forgot to tell you the Sisters Felix and Stephen came to tea on Friday. I had the Trefarthen cake, biscuits, bread and butter and Guava cheese that I've made, I'm bringing a pot for dear Father.

The latest idea is to take a flat in London when we get home. I am so glad to hear Eileen Clemenger is to be married this month. I fancy after all the tennis you'll be a perfect wreck when I get home. Won't it be funny seeing the train swirling in and seeing my little peaky face pushed out looking for you? Mrs Cortie says I'm 'nut brown coloured'! I wonder what the Atlantic will do for me.

The enclosed letter[87] came from Mr Addison last night. I think he is mad, don't you? So does Mr Page, and Mr Reaney is sick of him and wants me to have 'a quiet talk with him, he wouldn't listen to Hunter or me'!

Now I must end because I've Elsie's to write, and I know you'll forgive such a short note, Seal, won't you. With our best love,
Ever your own Twisty-toe

20 September 1909

My darling Trixie,
Every letter I begin now is full of apologies for not having begun my letter sooner, and alas saying that I can't write much, but today it's 'true words I'm saying', as the 'paper palaver is strong'. I've only about six sheets of the blue left and Charlie wants those to send off receipts at the end of the month. So I will write very small so that I can get as much in as possible.

First and foremost I'm ever so much better, we both are, and the two picnics on Saturday and yesterday have bucked me tremendously. Yesterday afternoon really was a spree, my wee childie, you will think me degenerate.

But first of all business. Charlie thinks I had better send all directions in this letter, but I'll send them on a separate sheet of paper so as not to confuse you, and return to my accounts of my doings. I felt dreadfully seedy all last week, and really felt utterly done on Friday and nearly fainted at lunch, quite exciting, but we went for a picnic on Saturday afternoon and it did me no end of good, and I did enjoy it. Mr Vergette took Charlie and me. He is so kind, and then yesterday morning before we were up he wrote to say he and Mr Van der Meulen[88] were going for lunch and tea to Mokolo and would we join them. Charlie wrote back to say it would be too long a day for me; and he came round himself to say would we come in the afternoon in hammocks overland and join them for tea, and so it was arranged. We had lunch and then started. Charlie borrowed a hammock from the District Commissioner's office and we went with eight hammock boys. There was a slight shower just before we started but after that [it was] lovely.

The Victoria Road along which we go till we reach the creek is cut out of a mangrove swamp, and in places the mud was so awful all the hammock boys were over their knees in this thick slimy mud. Jomendi was with us carrying (my poor Belle, Sunday too) the gun, and he came and took the front of my hammock or I

87 Sadly not surviving.
88 An Acting Circuit Judge.

should have been touching the mud. We arrived however safe and sound at the creek and let the hammocks go back. There was a boat to take us over this time with two oars which Jo and Charlie had to cope with, while the boatman had a paddle to steer with, killing it was, but you know how I love anything like that, and to hear Charlie saying 'Take caare, take caare'! We then started that lovely walk, it is the prettiest bit of walk I've ever been on. On the way I found a new white orchid, and Charlie had a shot at one of those lovely tree pheasants that I had the wings of last year; it was too far off so only got wounded I fear. On we went and soon met Mr Vergette and his doggies. He returned with us and he shot one grey pigeon and Charlie a green one, they were feeding in a patch of ground nuts; and on we went to Mokolo where we found tea all spread out waiting for us and Mr Van der Meulen.

While we were at tea the Swiss, or rather Germans, arrived also for a picnic. Mrs Harrendorf is a nice woman. They just had a cup of tea with us and went on. Charlie went back to the ground nuts as Mr Van der Meulen is dangerous with his gun! Mr Vergette and Mr Van der Meulen went after guinea fowl. The Germans walked back the way we had come, and little Twisty went to pick seeds on the beach, it's quite interesting the different ones there are. I got six different kinds, I'll show you them. Three are big ones and Charlie says you can make matchboxes of them.

It had been arranged to meet and start back at 6 o'clock, but it was a quarter past and getting dark when we started, and we found Mr Vergette was going to steer. All the boatmen were novices, one did not know how to hold an oar! Well, my dear, I soon saw Mr Vergette could neither see nor steer, and when we got into the maze of mangrove islands Charlie said 'Now we go through this narrow cutting,' but Mr Vergette said he thought it was further on, and as we got on a sandbank Charlie let them have their way. On we went down a wider cutting, dark by this time. When we had got a good way down we got on to sandbanks, and the boys said we had gone wrong. Charlie's way was right. So we had to turn. In turning, we jammed the bank and I thought we were all going over and should be chopped by crocodiles, and we got off, thank goodness, and I was dying to ask for Charlie to steer.

We got back to the narrow cutting at last after getting on to sandbank after sandbank, and at the narrow cutting Charlie said 'Let me take the rudder, Vergette, I'll stand up behind and can see over the awning.' We went through this narrow place, catching oars in the trees, and the most awful sound of crackings, I thought the oars were broken, but at last we got into open water and could see the friendly lights of Bonthe. There's no doubt Charlie has the bump of locality and is dependable.

It was killingly exciting, we had no lights except a few lightnings every now and again, and these mangrove swamps are rather awesome in the day but after the shades of night have fallen they are fearsome. We arrived back at 7.30 and Charlie asked Mr Vergette to dinner, which we took just as we were. He left at 10 o'clock. We were all yawning one after the other and were very glad to get to [illegible] after a most lovely picnic. Every time I've been to Mokolo I've enjoyed it. Mr Van der Meulen got one guinea fowl. The shooting here is disappointing, it's so difficult to get a shot at the birds and to find them when they fall.

Charlie will have to go to Victoria on Thursday for a hanging. I don't quite know what I will do. Mrs Cortie has asked me to York Island but I don't very much want to go. I'm afraid she won't come here again if I don't go there.

I must call on Mrs Harrendorf this evening. I've asked Mr Reaney in to tea; he is a great tea man, the others are not, and I know he will enjoy Walters' parkin. He never comes these picnics, I don't know why, whether they don't ask him or what. He is a very queer fish and yet we both feel sorry for him.

I had such jolly letters from May and Emily last mail, and all the letters including Elsie's brought good news. Mr Bryn Roberts seems such a good friend to Richard, I'm so glad. I hope Harrogate will do him good. Your letter was awfully jolly all about Ann and Hilda: it made me long to be with you. Ann owes me a letter, I think.

Pooz is a great pet these days, he talks so much when he comes up in the mornings: he talks all about the room, 'Why aren't you up?' and things like that! I've written to Mrs Renshaw at Hill Station to ask her if she knows of anyone who would take him. If not, I really think I'll bring him home. I'll see how he behaves from here to Freetown. The bird is very tame too; I hold a little tin in my hand and he bathes in it till I'm drenched. But I don't think he is worth bringing home.

Now, my darling, goodbye for this week. I'll send the instructions when Huz comes back from the Hospital.
Ever your very loving Maida

Getting civilised again!

No date

My darling little Belle,
You will see by Father's letter what a busy week it has been, and besides that Charlie [is]so busy, [with] so many people ill. Really considering I suppose we are wonderfully well, but we both feel and look exhausted now. And the rain last week was awful, I never in August even saw places so flooded.

The letters arrived on Thursday evening. Mrs Cortie was here so I had to retire upstairs to read mine. I am so glad you got second prize at the Preeces. It is really a comfort to get a prize after all the slogging. By the now the tennis season will be nearly over, and I think not too soon for you my young Belle, as you had a bilious attack in this letter. I've also had a genuine one. Charlie started on Monday, and looked so pulled down after it, and then on Friday after Mrs Cortie left I retired to bed with a splitting headache. Mr Reaney was most interested, what did I take etc. It had been a jolly week too. Mr Collins was here for two days and Mrs Cortie, but it was the dinner at Mr Reaney's that did for me, the cooking was *awful,* and it was his birthday and he had champagne, poor thing, which I took, and port! I've just had a letter from Mrs Cortie. She was ill on Saturday too, it was the damp I suppose.

Mr Reaney asked me to go shares in a leg of mutton from the ship, but he only managed to get a half, so asked if he might send it here and dine off it himself. We had such a jolly little dinner. Mormoh is cooking so well. I had bucked by then and ate rather too much, so was not feeling too fit yesterday, and I cut Charlie's hair in the morning before I dressed which quite exhausted me; and then these men (the Circuit Court) all arrived at tea time, and after tea when I was going for a little stroll who came but Mr and Mrs Harrendorf. She arrived on Wednesday, a very fat fair pretty woman, *very* like Katie of Aber. She makes no bones of thinking this an awful place, so does Mrs Cortie, and tell their husbands so. I tell Charlie it would do him good to live with them for a bit!

Well, after they left and after making a pudding I was dog tired. We had an excellent dinner beautifully cooked really, but I had a bad night, never slept after 3 o'clock with a bad pain between my shoulders. I fancy I ought not to have taken so many potatoes. However I feel better this morning, and we shall soon be off now. I've lost all my colour, and look real West Coast-ish.

Our plans at present are to take a small flat in London as headquarters. Charlie wants to get it and furnish a bedroom and kitchen before we come to Bronceris, and in some ways it would be better, but at present I feel too done up to think of flats or furniture or anything else but getting clothes and coming down to Bronceris. I really want a holiday. I think my liver is out of order because I'm doing nothing but grousing!

The Circuit Court has just sat and been adjourned till tomorrow. I hear Mr Cortie coming (he came just for a wee chat) up the step. If only you were here to see all the people coming and going. It's too amusing, the grand young niggers on the jury dressed up in their best.

My darling childie, I do thank you for all the trouble you have taken over my clothes, you have been very, very good to me. I fancy we shall put up the first night in London at the Great Central, so *be sure* and tell me if you advise me to get a coat and skirt.

I've been forgetting to tell Kate that the wood has been packed up the last fortnight lying at York Island waiting for a boat to Liverpool. The homeward bound ship never came in, she was full up. There is a little of the wood, not kak, which I'm keeping for myself, I'll show Kate which. Beg of the dear girl to forgive my not writing to her; I know she will share yours and dear Father's letters. I feel so lazy and good for nothing.

At last we have been able to secure a little official paper, it's the black clerks that get it all; but Mr Reaney has taken it all and locked it up, and sent some by Mr Collins. I enjoyed his stay so much, he was quite a nice young fellow. His father is a parson in Hampshire. He knew the Cornwallis Wests very well. How they all hate this little Van der Meulen, the acting Circuit Judge, he is a horrid little man and despicable I think. Charlie loathes him too.

It's a nice day today, and the moon changes on Wednesday so we might have better weather. They say Mr and Mrs Pidgeon are arriving this week! She won't like Mrs Harrendorf, she was dressed like a fashion plate, and really looked awfully nice. Her husband is a jolly man too.

Now, little Belle, I know you will be good and forgive such a short note. My pen is a beast too.

With heaps and heaps of love, Ever your own Twisty

Postscript

By Maida Bulman, 1991[1]

My parents returned home from Sierra Leone in the autumn of 1909. Both were by then feeling exhausted: not for nothing was West Africa known as 'the White Man's Grave'. However they much enjoyed their leave. Part of the time they spent in furnished rooms in Half Moon Street, Piccadilly, the rest at Bronceris or visiting friends and relations. They went north to my father's old haunts in Glasgow, and spent a few days with Lord and Lady Newlands at Mauldslie Castle, Carluke, at the time of the General Election of early 1910. It was a very grand house-party, and in spite of suffering from pregnancy sickness Mamma was thrilled by the experience. The election results were marked as they came in with little flags on a chart showing a Liberal victory, not what was wanted in that household.

I was born at Bronceris on 22 September 1910. My father, who had by then returned to Africa, sent a cable saying that I was to be called Maida. They had taken a flat, 70 Yale Court, Arkwright Road, Hampstead, and furnished it with much of the furniture I have always known, mostly old oak bought partly in Wales and partly from antique shops or in London. It was unfashionable in that mahogany-dominated period, but my mother liked it and it was comparatively cheap. The only pieces which reflect Edwardian taste are the couch-bed and the brass tray on legs in typical Liberty style of the time.

When I was five months old Mamma engaged Adda as my Nanny. I remember being told how she came to be interviewed at the Bradfords' house in Manchester Square, so that my godmother could give advice and moral support. Agnes (as she would be known until my pet name had been adopted by the family) arrived accompanied by both her parents. Mr Buggey was tall, red-bearded and confident (he was for many years head carter to the Rothschild family at Halton, and had charge of forty men and horses in spite of being unable to read or write); Mrs Buggey, who worked as a laundress, was small and timid. They had one son and eight daughters, two of whom were already in service in North London. I have a wonderful photograph of them all at the parents' golden wedding. Luckily there was mutual approval, and Adda settled in. She was 25 and it could hardly have been anticipated that she would stay with us (apart from two short unsuccessful periods of retirement) until she was nearly 80.

She had the unenviable task of pushing me in my large high-sided pram up and down Arkwright Road, which was then, as it still is, almost perpendicular. Sometimes she would take me out to tea, presumably to the houses where her

---

1 This account has been edited from the original to separate out reminiscences related to Maida's childhood and other events after her parents' return from Sierra Leone from the material she provided on their earlier lives, which was incorporated into the Introduction.

Maida and her daughter Maida, early 1911, from the family album

sisters worked, and two treasured books survive from those days, gifts, I imagine, from the ladies who employed them. I can hardly have been old enough to appreciate them at the time; they were *The Animals' Trip to Sea*, still enjoyed by my grandchildren, and, rather less suitable, *Misadventures at Margate*, which I knew by heart from an early age. When I was about 8, and a very junior pupil at Oswestry Girls' High School, I can remember being seated on the knee of one of the sixth formers to recite it.

When my father returned on leave in 1911 the family all lived at the flat, certainly until after May when his will was drafted by a London solicitor, but we must have been at Bronceris in the summer as it seems to have been then that my parents rented a house in Anglesey and moved up there to be near my grandfather. The address is usually given as Maen Hir, Llanfair P.G., the P.G. standing for Pwllgwyngyll. There was even more to the name of the small village, said to have been the longest name in Wales. It often featured on local comic postcards, but unfortunately I do not have an example in my two postcard albums which have been preserved. The cards have however been extremely useful in enabling me to date, usually by the postmarks, our various addresses from 1912 to 1919. The origin of the house's name is 'menhir', which my dictionary defines as a 'tall upright monumental stone found in Europe, Africa and Asia (*f.* Breton: menhir long stone)'. The gateposts looked like menhirs though they were not as tall as others I have seen in Wales and Brittany. I don't know how old the house was; it stood by itself surrounded by fields. My husband John and I looked at it from the end of the drive in 1993 when we were on a birding holiday in Anglesey, but stupidly did not go any nearer. It looked a nice house, and a few photographs survive. It is difficult to be sure when we moved in, but I think my mother and I with Adda were probably there through the winter of 1911–12, and my father must have spent at least part of his leave there in 1912. There is a postcard to me from Tricka dated 2 November 1912 which ends, 'Best love to Mamma, Daddy and Ickle Babba'.

My father was now working in the Gold Coast (now Ghana), where he is listed as promoted to the grade of Senior Medical Officer in the Government of the Gold Coast Medical and Sanitary Report of 1912. When my mother joined him there at Seccondee (now spelled Sekondi) from April to September 1912, Adda and I were transferred to Bronceris and the welcoming arras of Bamps (my grandfather), Tricka (Belle) and Nonin (Aunt Kate), where I was probably horribly spoilt.

I have only four letters [of my mother's] from this tour. They show how her heart was torn between her 18-month-old daughter and her husband; but the wonderful welcome he gave her must have made her feel how right she had been to come back to West Africa. They returned together in September and we all went back to Maen Hir, so I consider it my first home, though I cannot remember it at all. Adda used to talk about it as I grew up, and some of her stories have remained in my memory;

for example, if I heard anyone shooting round the fields I would say 'That's Daddy shooting bungas (bunnies) in Accra.' There is also a half-remembered tale of a pet lamb at the neighbouring farm which created a sensation by following its owners to Chapel one Sunday and walking unaccompanied up the aisle to look for them.

My father must have been a strict master of the house in the manner of his generation, and I remember Mamma telling me that he gave instructions to Adda that if I did not eat my rice pudding it was to be served up again at the next meal. Adda was evidently much in awe of him but apparently on one matter she won the battle of wills, as he expected her to wait at table when the parlour maid was off duty, which, being very shy, she flatly refused to do.

Looking at an old map of Anglesey to see exactly where our home was, I find a steam ferry marked from a tiny hamlet called Foel, only about two miles from Maen Hir, across the Menai Straits to Caernarvon. This has stirred a very faint memory of indeed crossing the water by this convenient boat. We would have shared it with farmers and their livestock: cows and calves, sheep and lambs, all standing, I recall, in a casual manner on the deck – a very enjoyable experience. I wish I could remember it better. We would have been met at Caernarvon's little port below the castle by Ganga with the wagonette. I believe by mother had her own pony and trap for going about in Anglesey, but I have no memory of this nor any photograph.

It was at Maen Hir that the nicest photographs were taken, presumably early in 1913, one of my father holding me by the hand, a similar one of me with Mamma, and one of myself alone with a restraining hand visible at one side; this, I have always understood, shows me forcibly being prevented from strangling a chicken. At the time I was in gingham smocks, usually pink (in the day) over lace-edged drawers (as knickers were then called), and I would have been based in my nursery until tea-time when Adda would change me into a clean white muslin dress and bring me down to the dining-room to join my parents until it was time for me to go to bed. Adda at the same period would wear her uniform of rather dark grey gingham with white cap and apron. The grey was an unusual choice of colour by my mother, but it looked very nice with her wonderful long auburn hair piled on top of her head. Though never pretty, she must always have looked striking, especially among the dark-haired inhabitants of Wales, and I have often wondered if she ever had a 'young man'; but alas, she was one of the generation of surplus women left after the slaughter of the First World War, with not enough young men to go round. I can just remember the feeling of total comfort and security I felt when sitting on her knee with my head leaning against her stiffly starched apron. Even at that early age I must have sensed that though she was a strict disciplinarian her steadfast loyalty and affection would never fail – and it never did.

I have some picture postcards from this time, two from Mamma, written on the voyage out to the Gold Coast, one on board SS *Elmina* and one from

From back: Agnes Buggy (Adda), Maida jr's nanny; 'Aunt Ah' (Elsie, Mrs Richard Williams), Maida jr and Maida, c. 1914

Las Palmas to 'darling little Pip'. In her letters to Tricka I was usually called 'Noll' or 'Piccin', the African term for a small child. The others are from my father:

10 May 1912 ('Warehouse at Sekondi'). There is a ship in the background. 'Love from Daddy and Mammy. Look at the ship that brought Mammy out.'

27.7.12. 'Daddy sends his best love and this is to tell you that he will soon be coming home now with Mummy.

After his leave he must have returned to the Gold Coast in the spring of 1913. There is one card sent to Mrs C. B. Hunter, Hotel Great Central, London, written by what is evidently my hand guided by Tricka, saying 'Darling Mummie, X.X.X.X.X. from Baba.' It is postmarked 13 May 1913, which is probably when Mamma was seeing him off for his last tour before retiring from the Colonial Service.
    He sent me three postcards addressed to Maen Hir:

31 October 1913 (European Houses, Accra, Gold Coast. W.A.)
'From Daddy with love.' and several kisses drawn not in a row but one on top of another to form a star; and

14 November 1913 (Surf boat on the Gold Coast, Accra, showing how a traveller gets ashore there)
'With love from Daddy. Isn't this a funny picture?'

Then came his last letter to Mamma from the Coast, which, although it is with the rest of the African letters, I must include in this record as it is so much part of the story of the three of us.

Victoriaborg, Accra
Friday 26 December 1913

My own darling,
This will be a surprise for you. I am coming home soon. The day after my last letter went off to you I felt a bit out of sorts. Next day, Sunday, more chippy, and on Monday after I did my morning's work I retired to bed and a pretty bad go of fever came on. It came down a bit in the afternoon and I came over to hospital to lay up there, as it's more comfortable in a way than in my quarters. That bronchial affair came on again, but thank goodness no pains. I had no fever yesterday nor all night nor today and my cough is nearly gone and I'm feeling much better but they think I better go away from the coast and I am leaving by the *Elmina* on the

Postcards to Maida junior, 1912–1914. (See overleaf for the messages.)

9th, two weeks today, and should be at Plymouth on 24 January. It's lovely to feel that I am getting quit of the coast. I've got sick and tired of this place, and begin to loathe it, oh how glad I'll be to be back to you my darling.

I won't make any suggestions about our plans for when I come. It's better to wait till we meet and discuss things. I know you will be just as glad as I am to think I'm coming for good this time. Can you come up to town and meet me at the Great Central Hotel? If you come up on the Saturday, 24th, it will be in time enough as it would be the evening before I would reach there, or it might be Sunday, being winter the steamer night be a little late.

Your dear letter reached me yesterday afternoon Xmas Day which was very nice for me to read yesterday, and I am so sorry darling you have had all the trouble

Postcards to Maida junior, 1912–1914.

about my Xmas box. I think I'll just bring it back as it comes and we can chop the lot together! With a small bottle of the brandy! Won't that be nice?

You think out what we should do, but for my old kidneys I think it would be best for me to stop down south for a couple of months or so before going to Maen Hir till it gets warmer.

What a trouble you have had with [illegible]. I am so sorry, Maida dear. When you come up will you bring my Burberry suit (not knickers), and black morning coat and vest, and that knitted silk vest, and a pair of thick trousers and my dark overcoat, oh and thick underclothes and top hat and bowler, I think that's all. Oh and my black tie.

They are having a regular Xmas week here, the Races, a cricket tea from Lagos, the band from Coomasssie down, a fancy dress dance tonight at Government House etc. etc. I'm not a bit sorry to be out of it all.

The Governor and Lady Clifford came in to see me yesterday evening, very nice of them.

That piccin of ours has her head screwed on the right way! It was splendid of her to want to know if there was money in the pudding. I am glad to know they are all well at Bronceris. I had a very nice letter from Trixie yesterday too, and am going to send her a wee note in answer.

I'm writing a line to Jess to tell her I'm coming home soon, but not telling her the date. I don't feel I want to be bothered with her coming messing around; if she writes to you say you are to have a wire from Plymouth from me when I arrive, and don't say you are coming up or that we shall be at the Great Central.

Now don't be worrying my childie, I expect when you see me you will think me a fraud coming home so soon. It will be lovely to see your bonny wee face again and feel you close to me.

All my love darling and kisses to Piccin.
Your own loving old Cokey

I never saw my father again, and he never returned to Maen Hir. He came back to England in January 1914 as planned, and I have a card from the Hotel Great Central 'From Daddy with love' (26 January 1914), and one from Mamma on 28 January with a picture of a small child with a teddy bear like my own Bickie. They were still in London on 4 February when another postcard came showing a black cat bowling a hoop: 'Mummy thought of you when she saw this. Can you run along quickly with your hoop now? Best love from Daddy and Mummy.'

By 19 February the next postcard shows that they were at Teignmouth (Devon) where they had gone as suggested in my father's letter for the warmer climate. They had friends there, a Dr and Mrs Patterson, but they did not stay with them but in 'rooms' (what would now be called a guest house) at 9 Powderham Terrace. Two cheerful postcards arrived, the second of 3 April saying 'Please thank A. Tricka so much for her long letter. Daddy and Mummy thank you so much for your sweet letter. How nice that Adda found a diggledy's nest [my word for a bird]. Daddy laughed very much that you want sand. I think he is quite certain to get it for you. Tell A. Tricka Mummy will write to her tomorrow. How do you like the diggledy?' Ironically, the picture shows a red cock digging up worms with the caption 'I am picking up wonderfully at Teignmouth.'

Five days later on 10 April, Good Friday, my father suddenly had what I think must have been a severe heart attack. Mamma looked after him with the help of nurses until he died on 14 April. l can remember her telling me how distressing it was that he could not speak, but I am ashamed to record that although I think she would have liked to talk more about those last days I could never bear to hear of them.

No one from the family came to Devon to be with her, and she would have been short of money if she had not received a cheque for £50, a large amount in those days, from Lord and Lady Newlands, sent off immediately when they saw the announcement in *The Times*. This enabled her to pay for the funeral, and she often told me how touched she had been by this prompt and practical help, and how grateful for the extreme kindness of complete strangers at Teignmouth.

My father was buried in a beautiful graveyard above Teignmouth with a wonderful view over the Channel. My husband John and I took my mother to lie with him when she died on 1 October 1949. On the stone cross she had had inscribed:

Sacred to the memory of Charles Buchanan Hunter
of Maen Hir, Anglesey,
born Dec. 22nd 1859, died Easter Tuesday, April 14th 1914.
'Till the last bright Easter Day be born.'

I made a little sketch of the stone in my diary. There was still room for her name to be added, and I feel almost sure, but have no record, that when I had this done I also had her favourite verse, 'In quietness and in confidence shall be your strength' (Isaiah 30.15), which she often quoted to me, telling me it had been a special favourite of her much loved mother, who knew her Bible from end to end.

She came back to Bronceris wearing 'widow's weeds', the deep mourning customary at the time, closed down Maen Hir, and settled once more in her father's house with me and Adda. It turned out that my father had died six months before his pension was due, so there was no money at all for her from the Colonial Office, and there were of course no state pensions at that date. It is only now that I realise the full sadness of it all.

Meanwhile dear Nonin, the plainest of the four sisters, had found an admirer, Mr Llewelyn Phillips, a solicitor from Llanidloes, Montgomeryshire. I do not know how they met, but she brought him home and, alas, he fell in love with pretty Aunt Trixie. They became engaged and the wedding was fixed for the summer of 1914. I have never been able to understand why the sisters had remained unmarried for so long. Was it lack of money, or did their parents chase all the young men away? Nonin and the eldest sister Elsie trained as nurses, suggesting a need to earn their living, and Elsie was the only sister to marry relatively young.

One of my first memories is of standing on a table by an upstairs window and pins are sticking into me. The atmosphere is charged with impatience and rage. I must have been having my bridesmaid's dress fitted; it was made of white muslin and lace, and was to have a blue sash of a shade then known as Nattier blue, and a lace-edged mob cap to perch on my dark curls. In that summer of 1914 I was three and a half.

I have always had this memory in my mind but have only lately in old age had time to think about it and realise the situation in which I was an unconscious participant. The pinpricks were the least of my troubles.

Tricka and Uncle Louis were married on 25 June, and I was the sole bridesmaid, as reported in press cuttings preserved with other treasures of family reportage in 'Nonin's scrapbook', an invaluable source of information for this record. I can just remember walking down the aisle, but when I saw Mamma I rushed to her, buried my face in her lap and there remained. I can also just remember the reception at Bronceris, and my indignation at being removed by Adda to my nursery where a tea of rock buns was provided instead of the delicious food downstairs.

A note on the Hunter family

As far as I know, Mamma never saw her step-daughter Ena, and I certainly never did. I got the impression that my father's first marriage had brought him so much unhappiness that he wanted to put it all behind him, and I never remember questioning this attitude, which now seems unkind and uncharacteristic, particularly as by the terms of my father's will made in 1911 after my birth, Ena inherited a third share of his estate, Mamma and I getting the other two-thirds.

In the will she is described as living with a Miss Lewis at Findhorn Place, Edinburgh. Was this perhaps a school? What is certain is that she was married at Aden on 14 July 1914 to Lieutenant James Walter Foley, 1st Royal Irish Rifles, by Harold Frote, Chaplain at Aden. She was 19 and her residence is given as Aden. This would have been three months after my father's death, and less than a month before the outbreak of the First World War, in which the young couple must surely have been involved. On her marriage she would have inherited her share of my father's estate, which was left to her in trust 'until she reaches the age of 24 or marries'. Mine was similarly in trust, but I had to wait, somewhat impatiently, until 1934! As the whole estate only amounted to the rather pathetic sum of £3,986.18.4d it is easy to see how straitened were my mother's means.

Years later in 1945 John and I met Ena's daughter Joan, then the wife of Major (I think) Davis, and others of their family at Aunt Billy's funeral. We liked them very much and made vague plans to meet again, but in the hectic post-war years these never materialised, and as far as I am concerned that is the end of this particular story. But, writing now in 1991, I feel, and certainly hope, that contact would have been maintained had my father lived, for though, judging from the African letters, he sometimes found his sister irritating, he had made her home his base when in England before his marriage to my mother, who remained on cordial terms with her sister-in-law although she did not altogether like her.

I must describe Aunt Billy a little further. She was the wife of John (Jack) Herbert-Williams, a barrister who enlisted in the First World War and served as Captain and Judge Advocate. He died of illness contracted on active service in 1917. His name is on the Roll of Honour in Trinity College, Cambridge. They had no children. They lived in Harrow-on-the-Hill quite near the school in a pretty road running down at that time to open fields. I remember my mother taking me to stay with her there in, I suppose, about 1920. She was a lively and attractive woman, clever and sophisticated, and I am sorry now that I did not see more of her, but I suppose I was too busy with my own affairs. She took a kindly if distant interest in me as I grew up, and introduced me to various Hunter relations and old friends who always turned out to be pleasant and interesting people. She must have been somewhat irresponsible, as I recall Mamma telling me that she had cut out from the Hunter family Bible the page recording generations of births, deaths and marriages to prevent people finding out her age!

Then the door of memory closes once more.

Acknowledgements and references

The editors owe a considerable debt to Peter C. Andersen, who administers the sierra-leone.org website (www.sierra-leone.org) which is a treasure trove of photos, postcards, maps and other resources. He kindly gave us permission to use all the out of copyright material on this site, and we have done so extensively.

Grateful thanks are due too to Redmond Shannon, whose modern photos of Sierra Leone appear on the cover and on pages 97 and 164, and to the staff of the Rhodes House Library division of the Bodleian Library, Oxford, who provided the scan of Maida's letter reproduced on page viii. Maida's original correspondence is all in the hands of the Rhodes House Library. Family members provided Maida's sketchbooks, photographs and other material.

Some other out-of-copyright and freely licensed material was sourced from the Web; details are given with the illustrations.

Books consulted, or that may be of interest as further reading, are listed below.

On Sierra Leone and West Africa

Beatty, K. J. *Human leopards: an account of the trial of human leopards before the Special Commission Court; with a note on Sierra Leone, past and present.* London: Hugh Rees, 1915. 140pp. Hardback.

Macintosh, Donald. *Travels in the white men's grave: memoirs from West and Central Africa.* London: Abacus, 2001. 256pp. Paperback. (Though of a later period, it covers experiences in this area in a very entertaining way.)

Moore, Decima and Guggisberg, F. G. *We two in West Africa.* London: William Heinemann, 1909. 368pp. Hardback. (A book owned by Charles Hunter. Sir Frederick became governor of Gold Coast in 1919 and of British Guiana in 1928.)

Newland, H. Osman. *Sierra Leone: its people, products, and secret societies.* London: John Bale, Sons, and Danielsson, 1916. 308pp. Hardback.

By or about members of Maida and Charles Hunter's families

Bradford, May. *A hospital letter-writer in France.* London: Methuen, 1920. 108pp. Hardback. (May was a cousin to Mary Adelaide Hunter and godmother to Maida Bulman. Her husband Sir John Rose Bradford was President of the Royal College of Physicians. Maida and Charlie were married from their house in Manchester Square, London.)

Fox, R Hingston. *William Hunter: anatomist, physician, obstetrician.* London: H. K. Lewis, 1901. 75pp. Hardback. (Biography of one of Charlie's great-uncles.)

Gloyne, S. Roodhouse. *John Hunter*. Edinburgh: E & S Livingstone, 1950. 103pp. Hardback. (Biography of another of Charlie's great-uncles.)

Roberts, Robert. *Mynydd-y-Gof: The history of a Welsh Calvinistic Methodist family. By A 'Lax' one of themselve*s. London: Swan, Sonnenschein & Co, 1905. 443pp. Hardback. (Autobiography of the author, Maida sr's father Robert Roberts, 1828–1916, with his seven brothers.)

Index

Also from the Lasse Press

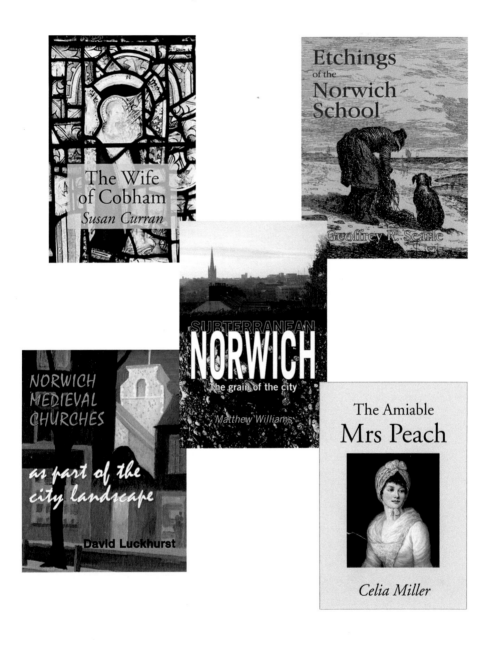

Details of all our titles are available on

www.lassepress.com